THE
HORSE*less*
RIDER

THE
HORSE*less*
RIDER

**A Complete Guide
to the Art of Riding,
Showing and Enjoying
Other People's Horses**

Revised Edition

BARBARA BURN

Drawings by Werner Rentsch

HOWELL BOOK HOUSE
NEW YORK

Also by Barbara Burn

A Practical Guide to Impractical Pets

Howell Book House
A Simon & Schuster Macmillan Company
1633 Broadway
New York, NY 10019

MACMILLAN is a registered trademark of Macmillan, Inc.

Library of Congress Cataloging-in-Publication Data

Burn, Barbara.
    The horseless rider : a complete guide to the art of riding,
  showing and enjoying other people's horses / Barbara Burn ;
  drawings by Werner Rentsch. — Rev. ed.
        p.   cm.
    Includes index.
    ISBN 0-87605-745-8
    1. Horsemanship.   2. Horses.   I. Title.
  SF309.B92   1997
  798.2—dc21   97-4490
                                                                  CIP

Manufactured in the United States of America

10 9 8 7 6 5 4 3 2 1

DESIGN BY HEATHER KERN

Dedicated with love to my parents,
without whom this book would
never have been possible.

CONTENTS

FOREWORD

ALTHOUGH IT MAY not seem so at first, professional show riders are not very different from occasional riders who don't (and may never) own horses. For example, I've been a "horseless rider" for much of my life. As a teenager serving as Whipper-in of the Rapidan Hunt, I often rode members' mounts that needed a little education in the hunt field. Also as a teenager I showed ponies and horses that belonged to other people. My first professional job was working for a dealer in Florida, schooling his horses and showing them off to customers. Later on, as a professional rider, I earned a living "catching" rides before I started to buy and sell, train, and exhibit horses, a few of which I have even a part ownership interest.

And I'm not alone. Look at U.S. Equestrian Team show jumping riders and others who compete in the Open division. They ride animals that are lent or donated to the Team or else they have some sort of ongoing arrangement with owners. Many exhibitors in Saddle Horse, driving, and Western divisions, to name a few other fields, do much the same thing. So do jockeys, rodeo riders, and professional polo players.

Not owning your own horse is a real advantage in one particular respect. "He (or she) has ridden a lot of horses" is one of the highest compliments a rider can be paid. That's because of the many experiences these people have had. Every horse you climb aboard, whether it's a public stable hack, a neighbor's backyard horse, or something fancier trained for a specialized sport, will teach you something. I've learned that fact firsthand from the hundreds of horses that pass through my barn every year and the hundreds more I show. I can honestly say that without this exposure to such a wide variety, my education would have suffered.

Barbara Burn understands this positive approach, and she uses it throughout this book. She shares her many years of experience, as well as the experiences of grooms, stable managers, and riders and trainers involved in many areas of horsemanship (and in that regard, few books give such a good overall view of riding as a sport and as a business). There's lots of imaginative and realistic information in *The Horseless Rider*, and I recommend the book to anyone who, like the author, won't let not owning a horse stop him or her from being on and around horses.

RODNEY JENKINS

PREFACE

When I was about ten years old and quite seriously infected with horse fever, I mounted a strenuous campaign to convince my parents to buy me a horse. One of my friends had succeeded in getting herself an old cow pony by the name of Martini, and I thought that ordering a Martini of my own would be equally simple. For years I had entertained fantasies of waking up on my birthday to find a pony tied to a tree in the backyard (we didn't have a barn), but at ten I was mature enough to realize that adding a horse to the family was going to take more effort on my part than wishful thinking.

Since direct requests hadn't worked, I decided to start the campaign by using the art of suggestion. I learned to imitate my mother's handwriting, not for the purpose of forging checks made out to the local horse trader, but in order to work the word "horse" unobtrusively into her shopping list. (I don't know how I expected her to find a horse in the aisles of the supermarket let alone fit it into her shopping cart, but I was pretty desperate.) Then I set about quietly making our house suitable for a horse. When my friend's pony got a new halter, I asked for the old one, which I carefully mended and put away in my underwear drawer. When I mowed the lawn for extra cash, I'd collect all the mown grass in a heap beside the garage to use in bedding down the eventual equine. I scrounged old pails and scrubbing brushes and even designed a convincing floor plan showing how our garage could be adapted as a stable once the family car had been evicted.

Next, I proceeded to educate myself in horsekeeping. My father, in one of his routine responses to my constant request, pointed out that I wasn't strong enough even to cut the wire on a bale of hay, let alone handle a horse. So I spent hours practicing with wire cutters and soon developed the appropriate muscles, although I was still incapable of carrying a full bucket of water without spilling it. My horse-loving aunt explained that no one who hadn't fallen off a horse at least seven times could claim to be a true horseman, so I enlisted Martini's aid and spent some fruitful sessions in the apple orchard until I became a true horseman. (Although the experience didn't do much for my riding skills, I did lose my fear of falling and learned what it was like to have the wind knocked out of my chest—awful.)

And then I worked out the hardest part—the finances. I spent less of my allowance on candy and records and set aside a quarter a week in a shoebox. I figured out the cost of carrots, hay, and horseshoes and balanced the total against various family expenditures. Armed with this information, I presented my case to my parents: If they would give up drinking, they could afford to keep a horse for me. And of course, I offered to do all the work and help out as much as I could with my dollar a month.

Needless to say, it didn't work. Not only that, my mother threw out the halter when she found it in the washing machine along with my underwear, and she turned the grass heap into a compost pile. (I never found out what happened to the floor plan, but it may have been what gave my father the idea to turn the one-car garage into a two-car facility a year or so later.) As I grew older, my approach became somewhat more sophisticated, but they never budged. "We aren't zoned for horses," they would say. "We don't have room for a barn and a pasture." "Who's going to feed and exercise the horse when you're away visiting friends?"

Even though I had ready answers to these arguments, I could never get around the fact that they simply weren't enthusiastic about the idea. My mother had grown up in a horsy family as the one daughter in four who was afraid of horses, and the only time my father ever rode he was arrested for trespassing. They did allow me to take an occasional riding lesson and to hang around Martini's stall a lot (I think they liked his name), but for some reason they felt that straightening my teeth, buying me books, and putting clothes on my back were more important contributions to my upbringing than having a horse around.

Without a horse in the backyard, I had to work pretty hard at getting myself into the saddle as often as my horse fever demanded. Occasional riding lessons at the local hacking stable were not nearly enough to satisfy my needs, and yet daily lessons were far too much for my budget. I learned to muck out stalls and clean tack so that I could trade my work for rides on friends' horses. I offered my services as exercise rider to horse owners with broken legs (from skiing, I told my parents) and to people who were dumb enough to find a trip to Europe more attractive than staying home with their animals. I managed to get myself sent to camps that offered riding, and I ingratiated myself with counselors who could take time off while I worked in the camp stable. In college I found that riding counted as a physical education credit, and in New York City I eventually got myself a job as an editor so that I could work on books about horses. I found stables that gave lessons at night and on weekends, and I got friends with cars interested in riding so that we could get out of the city. In short, I learned to hack around.

Like malaria, the horse fever never truly subsided, and "horse" still appeared automatically at the top of my birthday and Christmas lists, but it wasn't until I married a veterinarian that the idea of getting a horse became more than just a fancy. At that point I was taking lessons twice a week and getting interested in horse shows. When my husband looked over my birthday list, he asked "Why *don't* we get a horse?" and I was stunned. It was possible. We could board it just outside the city and he could keep it sound and my life could be complete at last.

But then it hit me. I realized suddenly that after all these years it might just be possible that I didn't really *want* a horse. Boarding was expensive, my schedule was full with a house to renovate, a full-time job, four cats, two dogs, and two stepchildren, and besides that I was having a pretty good time doing what I was doing. Because I had ridden many different horses, I had managed to develop a flexible riding technique, and I enjoyed horses for different reasons—trail riding, jumping, dressage, and so on. I knew that if I tried to put all my eggs into a single equestrian basket, I'd be asking more of one animal than it could possibly deliver.

Through my work as a writer and editor, I have had the chance to meet many well-known riders and trainers and to read many books written by expert horsemen. In the course of asking questions and looking for answers, I have always been surprised to find how many people have advanced far in the profession without actually having horses of their own. In fact, many of them told me that using different horses could be good for one's riding and that a single horse could be limiting. I have also been dismayed to find that most horse books were written for horse owners and not for people like me—those of us who love to ride but, for one reason or another, must ride horses belonging to others. And so I thought I might set down some advice for horseless riders like myself, along with the comments, stories, and suggestions from professionals in the field. It isn't always possible to make a negative situation into a positive one, but I have come to believe that not owning a horse can be a rewarding experience. Like any activity, riding can be expensive, but riding other people's horses is a lot cheaper than paying for upkeep, tack, veterinarians, farriers, and equipment before you even get into the saddle. Horses, like all animals, require a responsible commitment of time, energy, affection, and care, but if one has a full schedule, one hour of commitment a day is a lot more sensible than twenty-four. It will take effort and ingenuity to appreciate the advantages of not having a horse in the backyard at your constant beck and call, but it doesn't take much imagination to see that if sickness or bad weather makes riding impossible, a horse that isn't there won't need to be exercised or fed or turned out or cleaned up after.

I can't in truth say that I will never want a horse of my own, but for the time being I am happy enough being a horseless rider to pass along my enthusiasm to others in the same situation. It's not a perfect life. Horses for hire are not fine specimens capable of competing in the Olympics; sometimes they aren't even capable of delivering a comfortable ride. But they can teach you a lot and, if you have a mind to do so, you can teach them something too, making a comfortable ride more likely the next time around. Renting or borrowing a horse doesn't require you to borrow all the problems of the owner, but you do have certain responsibilities and must be willing to take certain risks when you take the horse. Knowing what these responsibilities and risks are and how to deal with them is part of the education of *any* rider, however, and learning to become expert in handling other people's horses can be an important step toward the goal of everyone who takes horses seriously—that of being a true horseman. In spite of Martini's lessons in the apple orchard, I still haven't achieved that high level, but I have discovered that proof of ownership is not necessarily a proof of horsemanship.

The first six chapters in this book are dedicated to all riders who must look beyond the backyard for a mount, and though some of the advice will be aimed at the novice, riders at all levels of expertise and experience should be able to use the information about equestrian opportunities, methods of analyzing stables, instructors, and horses, and ways of adapting one's riding style to whatever animal comes along. Careful readers of the contents page will note that I have put the cart before the horse by discussing riding styles and instructors before exploring the local hacking stable and its noble inhabitant—the hack horse. This is a deliberate ploy on my part to convince the beginner (and even more advanced riders) that there is more to riding than just renting a horse. I have seen too many people take their first ride at public stables with no prior instruction and be so unsettled (if not actually unseated) by the experience that they determine never to ride again. This is an unfortunate situation if only because it can be so easily avoided. Since this book is not addressed to stable operators, I can only appeal to you, the horseless rider, to take that all-important step of educating yourself before you pick up the Yellow Pages. I don't mean that you should study the serious manuals or apply to Olympic coaches for instruction before you meet your first horse, but I do implore you to familiarize yourself with the styles of riding and the ways to learn them before you get into the saddle. You wouldn't dream of driving a car on the Santa Monica freeway or try to shush down Mont Tremblant without a lesson or two, and the same goes for horseback riding. You can rent cars, skis, and horses, but you'll be doing yourself (and your companions) a disservice if you don't know how to operate them!

The last part of the book is designed for riders who consider themselves more obsessed than occasional, those who are willing to spend more than an hour or two a week in the company of *Equus caballus.* For you I'll include ways of earning money around horses, improving your riding chances, and participating in sports usually considered the exclusive domain of the horse owner. And for the hopelessly incurable, I'll describe the various professions in the field and, last but not least, that ultimate alternative to horselessness—getting a horse of your own.

ACKNOWLEDGMENTS

IF I WERE to thank in print all of the instructors—human and equine—who have helped me through years of horselessness, the list would be longer than any reader could bear, but the following individuals deserve special mention for assistance beyond the call of friendship:

Allegro

Bedford

Bigfoot and Billygoat

Bill Brayton

Dennis Byrnes

Harry Case

Chief

Michael Cody

Helene Conway

Jim Conway

Copperhead

Martina D'Alton

Anthony D'Ambrosio, Jr.

Bill Decker

Norman dello Joio

Tracy Doolittle

Eugene Edwinn

Carol Epstein

Carlos Estol

Doina Fischer

Susan Goode

Susan Heath

Hoffman

Chris Howells

Geoffrey Hughes

Rodney Jenkins

Larry Joyner

Charlie and Sandra Kauffman

King

Danny and Karen Lutz

Alexander and Marilyn Mackay-Smith

Wingate Mackay-Smith

Sue Maher

Carlos Marban

Rebecca Martin

Martini

Catherine McWilliams

Kay Meredith

Joanne Michaels

Darryl Montoya

Jill Murphy

Bertalan de Nemethy

Amy Pershing

Evelyn Pervier

Elric Pinckney

Gail and Werner Rentsch

Rex

Lt. Richard Risoli

Malley San Marcos

Sam and Bette Savitt

Gretchen Singleton

David Spector

Bill Steinkraus

Jerry and Rita Trapani

Amanda Vaill

In addition to these horseless riders, horses, and horsemen, I would like to give very special thanks to my late husband, Emil Dolensek, who was never able to find in his veterinary bag a cure for the disease known as horse fever, and to Steve Price, who got me back on a horse after a lapse of ten years and gave me the idea for this book. In spite of the passage of years, Steve Price more than ever epitomizes the horseless rider: he rides regularly on other people's horses, takes horseback vacations, and in spite of occasional forays into books on fly fishing and the like, manages to keep his authorial presence firmly in the horse world. He assisted me in revising this book, and I continue to be grateful for his help.

THE HORSE*less* RIDER

1

THE RIDER

ALL HORSELESS RIDERS have at least two things in common—
an interest in riding and a lack of the animal on which to
ride—but there are a lot of differences too, in ability, ambi-
tion, and available time and money, to name only a few.
Before you start bemoaning the fact that there isn't a horse in
your backyard, try to figure out what your own problems are,
work out some solutions, and then start thinking like a
horseless rider. I'll be willing to wager that for every problem
there is not only a solution, but also a distinct advantage over
the horse owner.

HORSELESSNESS EXPLAINED

First question: Why don't you have a horse? Is it a lack of
money, time, or expertise? Is it an unsympathetic family? A
backyardless house or apartment? Or is it just that your
interest in riding is relatively recent and you aren't yet sure
just how committed you want to become?

The best way to deal with those negative reasons is to take
a positive attitude. Since it does take a minimum of money
and time even to ride other people's horses, figure out how
much room there is in your budget and schedule and set aside
the surplus for riding. One of my solutions was to sign up for
a course of ten Wednesday night lessons, for which I paid in
advance but for which I got a substantial series discount. That
way my riding budget was safe from special sales on clothing
I didn't need and my Wednesday evenings became sacred. (A
couple of my non-riding friends were hurt when I turned down

dinner invitations because I "had to go riding," but they soon learned to try me on Thursdays instead.) If you find as I did that a weekly lesson isn't enough, there are several ways to earn extra money and time to ride, which I will elaborate on in Chapter 7.

Lack of expertise may be a good reason not to own a horse, but if you plan to ride, it's a good idea to overcome that lack by learning as much as possible about horses—not just how to ride them but how they are put together, cared for, and trained. Even if you are at the stage where you feel you know nothing at all, there are plenty of good ways to find out. The best way to start is to ride under expert instruction, which will mean lessons at first, but you can continue or supplement that education on your own by practicing on hourly hacks, by reading books and applying what you read to what you do, or by hanging around horses and horse people a lot. This is one area in which the horseless rider has the edge on the horse owner, who must ride the same animal all the time. Kathy Kusner, a former member of the U.S. Equestrian Team, worked as a dealer's rider early in her career, showing off hundreds of animals to prospective buyers. "This was marvelous experience," she reports, "and so many horses did a lot to make riding become almost as natural as breathing. . . . Maybe it wasn't very classical or conservative, but it was a very practical education."

And William C. Steinkraus, Olympic gold-medal winner and a leading American rider for years, points out that "spoiled horses, difficult horses, and even rogues can teach us much that is important; the rider who is too well mounted may never really learn to ride."

If your main problem is that your family thinks you are crazy for wanting to ride, take heart. Even if they won't let you add a horse to the household, you should be able to convince them that you are serious enough to deserve some support—whether that means giving you money or time off or simply keeping their mouths shut when you put on your riding clothes. Bill Steinkraus recalls:

> Neither of my parents was a rider, and it always seemed to me as a child that my strange passion for horses was more tolerated than encouraged—in any case, I never seemed able to do as much riding as I would have liked . . . . But I am grateful to them for not having

permitted me to become too early saturated with riding, or to regard riding as more of an obligation than a treat. So many children of fine horsemen, who get every encouragement from their parents to follow in their footsteps, lose their enthusiasm for riding very early because the riding is so available, and too easily a matter of "If you don't exercise your pony today, you can't watch television before dinner."

So even if it infuriates you that your parents or your spouse or your children giggle uncontrollably every time you pull on your boots (or, worse, resent the fact that you have your own "thing"), don't despair. They'll be delighted when you come home with your first blue ribbon.

Perhaps you have time, money, expertise, and an encouraging family, but you don't have any place to keep a horse. Many suburban areas are not zoned for backyard horses, and most city apartments simply aren't large enough. Boarding a horse in the country or even in a city stable is often possible, but it is usually terribly expensive and very time consuming to commute on a daily basis when a job or school takes up most hours of your day. Don't feel that you must move to the country to do some riding. Most cities have reasonably good riding facilities within reach—by car if not by public transportation—and you need only find out where they are and how to get there. Here, too, is where not owning a horse is an advantage. When the weather is bad or you are ill, you needn't make the trip to the horse. If it belongs to someone else, it won't need you to look after it or to feel guilty that it isn't being exercised. If the public stable near you isn't very good (see Chapter 4 for some ways of analyzing stables), look elsewhere. For a couple of years, five of my colleagues in the publishing field joined me in a car-pool arrangement driving to a riding school outside the city once a week after work; in addition to expenses, we also shared friendly critical advice about our riding and lots of gossip about publishing.

If the primary reason you don't own a horse is that you're not exactly sure just how deeply into riding you want to get, consider yourself sensible. Many beginners jump into horsekeeping as soon as they learn which side of the horse to mount on, and too often they find themselves overburdened with responsibility. A number of the horse books written for beginners extol the joys of owning a backyard horse, but what the authors usually leave out is an accurate analysis of the money, time, and effort involved. It may cost as little as a thousand dollars a year to maintain a horse, as the books put it, but a horse that becomes injured or ill can cost a great deal more than that and you won't even be able to ride. It's a wonderful experience to get to know an animal intimately, but you will quickly find out that familiarity can also breed contempt, especially when it means mucking out a stall every freezing day in midwinter when riding is impossible. Dedicated horse people learn to accept this as one of the realities of horse owning, but novices will often find their interest becoming weaker as the buckets of water become heavier.

If you restrict yourself to a lesson or two a week, you will be able to determine the extent of your interest more accurately than you would if dobbin were a daily chore. If a small amount of riding doesn't seem to satisfy you, good. You'll probably make more of your occasional rides, learn more from them, and find yourself progressing more rapidly.

AMBITION AND ABILITY—AN EXERCISE IN SELF-ANALYSIS

Now that we have made a virtue of not owning a horse, what next? What kind of a horseless rider are you going to become? Many people ride for simple enjoyment—getting out into the countryside, communicating with an animal, or exercising in a pleasant way. Others ride because they love horses and want to be around them as much as possible. Several athletic people I know have gone into riding with the idea of mastering yet another sport—taking up the challenge of learning a new game with new rules (and new muscles) and experiencing the exhilaration that comes when one is capable of playing polo or making it around a hunt course. Excellence in riding for its own sake—because of its beauty and difficulty— appeals to many of us who thrill to watch an expert at work on a cutting horse, in the dressage ring, or over huge fences in open-jumping classes. And there is the competitive element as well—the pride involved in carrying home a silver trophy for equitation or in winning a barrel race.

Any and all of these ambitions are attainable for the horseless rider, even at the highest level, for many of our finest horsemen managed to make it to the top on the back of other people's horses. Although we may never get the chance to throw a leg over an Olympic jumper or to perform a levade aboard a Lipizzaner, it is entirely possible for us to learn to show successfully, to go fox hunting with the best packs in the country, to spend whole vacations on horseback or just a satisfying hour going around the ring at a fine stable, and to become horsemen in the process.

Learning to ride well enough to pursue our various goals is not, of course, a simple matter of checking the Yellow Pages for the closest stable and forking over a few bucks for an hour's worth of experience. On the other hand, you needn't go to the best instructor in the land and proclaim your intention to make the Equestrian Team or to win the Tevis Cup endurance ride. (In addition to requiring a commitment of a few thousand dollars a year, the instructor would also insist on selecting a horse for you to buy.) But you *should* make the effort to learn the basics on the back of the most appropriate horse you can find under the supervision of the most appropriate teacher. Even if you have already progressed beyond the novice stage, you should consider taking lessons occasionally rather than just going out on your own. For one thing, you'll learn something and for another, you're likely to get yourself a more interesting horse. Not long ago, when I was taking lessons at a stable that did not offer hacking to the general public, my mother remarked: "Haven't you learned how to ride *yet?*" I don't remember whether I explained that this was the only way I could ride at that stable or whether I pronounced loftily that even the best riders in the country never stop schooling themselves or their horses, but I do recall feeling rather pleased that I had reached the point where I knew I didn't know it all. Colonel Alois Podhajsky, former director of the Spanish Riding School in Vienna, wrote a book entitled *My Horses, My Teachers* about the animals that had taught him so much over the years. It seems that even after he graduated from the "high school" of dressage, he continued to learn something from every new horse he mounted. "Retrospectively," he says, "I realize that the constant endeavor to understand the creatures entrusted to my care became the reason why, though I was their trainer, I feel as their pupil today."

As you spend more time on horseback, you will undoubtedly find that your ambitions will change as your ability increases. Each new horse you ride should open a door onto some aspect of riding or horsemanship, and every experience will lead to another. I have known people who were convinced that trail riding was the ultimate pleasure on horseback but who started setting up fences for the fun of it, only to find that the new ultimate pleasure then became cross-country jumping. I have known dressage enthusiasts who fell in love with cutting horses and cowboys who became expert polo players. Many riders have traded in their saddles for harnesses, and dedicated stock-saddle equestrians have even been known to enjoy English saddles once they got over the idea that those little bits of leather were more than just "postage stamps."

ATTITUDE

As I guess I've been implying, becoming a horseless rider involves first and foremost a question of attitude. An open mind is as important as natural ability and far more crucial than a fancy set of riding clothes. Before we get to the practical matters of what to wear, how to ride, and where, let's consider for a moment that while you are analyzing the prospective stable and horse, they will also be analyzing *you*. So prepare yourself to make a good impression rather than one that will put you on the back of the least promising horse in the barn. How you ask your questions, how you act, and what you wear may or may not be noticed, but it's worth taking the trouble to do things properly, just in case. You'll find that a certain degree of proficiency in these areas will add a great deal to your self-confidence, no matter what your level of expertise.

Pay attention to your manner and your speech when you approach a new stable for the first time. Don't come on like gangbusters and tell the owner that you can ride anything in the place. Not even the jockey Julie Krone would make such a boast. Answer all questions honestly, including the one about the amount of experience you have had. If you rode once seventeen years ago, don't tell anyone that you have ridden for seventeen years; the jig will be up the moment you attempt to mount. On the other hand, if you have ridden every other day for the last year, don't be shy; tell the management that you are beyond the beginner stage and can handle the walk, trot, and canter with confidence. And if you are subjected to an evaluation test or told you must have a guide accompany you, don't be insulted. Welcome the chance to prove yourself. This initial conversation is where vocabulary will count. If you are at a stable where the horses are ridden in Western tack, speak of the jog and lope rather than the trot and canter. If you see the horses in English tack, don't ask where the saddle horn is or call that martingale a tie-down. But be careful using terms if you aren't really sure what you (or they) mean. Nothing sounds greener than a novice who demands a horse that can perform a rack or a piaffe just to show off; what shows is that you don't know much—yet.

If something puzzles you—or if you are anxious to learn, say for instance, what the stablehand is doing to get that bridle in place—by all means ask questions. Don't be a pest (stable-hands at busy stables don't often have a lot of spare time), but a good, thoughtful question and close attention to the answer will usually result in information. Whatever you do, please don't treat the stablehands or grooms like lowly servants. All too often, I have seen renting riders (and even owners) act superior to the people who muck out the stalls and clean the horses—this attitude is an unattractive one, to say the least. Keep in mind that the people who work around horses probably know more about horses than you do and certainly more about the charges in their care. Some stables and grooms have a policy not to allow amateurs to get involved in tacking up or down (for reasons of safety and efficiency), but if a stable seems shorthanded, it is never out of place to offer your help. You can learn a lot in the process, and your cooperative attitude will be rewarded in kind. A rude individual who insists that the "help" give him or her a leg up and adjust the stirrups without politely asking for assistance is invariably going to arouse resentment. Tipping is not necessary except for special services beyond the call of duty (if you ride regularly at a stable, perhaps a Christmas gift would be in order), but common human decency is. After all, many grooms are doing their work because they love it and not just because they need the money. I recall one occasion when an older female rider behaved rather haughtily to the younger female stablehand who tacked up her horse, only to find the girl at her own dinner table the following evening. It turned out that the "servant" and her daughter had been classmates at college!

APPAREL

Old clichés notwithstanding, clothes do not make the horseman, but they do help, not only in terms of making a good impression and giving the rider a sense of self-confidence but also in pure practical terms of comfort, safety, and proficiency. Although riding clothes are fashionable these days—jeans, boots, and hacking jackets are as common on Fifth Avenue as they are at the livery stable—they were not designed for good looks alone. Each piece of riding apparel has been developed over the years for rather specific purposes—to be comfortable and long-wearing and to assist the rider in maintaining a good, secure seat in the saddle. In the next chapter, I will briefly discuss the appropriate types of clothing for different styles of riding, and if you know that you are interested in one style and are committed enough to make the investment in proper apparel, go ahead and do so. But if you are unsure about what kind of riding you plan to do and don't know whether this will be the first of several rides or the last, your best bet is to wear simple, workaday clothes and to borrow some pieces of basic equipment for your first few times out.

Although you may end up investing in a pair of jodhpurs, breeches, hunt boots, or fancy Tony Lamas, you'll be perfectly well dressed at the beginning in a plain pair of well-fitting, broken-in jeans and some kind of shoe or boot with a leather heel. Pants should be snug at the knee and over the calf to prevent chafing (or "strawberries"), which can be painful later on, but you may want the extra insurance of some seamless underwear or thin cotton tights beneath them to avoid discomfort in places where it matters. Flared jeans are not appropriate, but if that's all you have, put a rubber band on each leg to keep them from flapping. If your boots are low rather than mid-calf or knee-high, wear long socks. Avoid sneakers or soft shoes without a heel; being stepped on is painful and having your foot caught in a stirrup aboard a runaway is downright dangerous. In warm weather, a T-shirt or a jersey with short sleeves is perfectly acceptable; low-cut shirts or blouses look out of place on horseback and may result in painful sunburns. Equally out of place is long hair (on males or females) that is not put into ponytails or otherwise collected and confined. It may look romantic in advertisements for cologne or whatever to have a lass with flowing locks matching those of her horse ride off into the sunset, but that sort of romance doesn't mix very well with serious riding. Jewelry and heavy makeup are also inappropriate; the former is all too likely to be damaged, and the latter will probably become covered with a noticeable layer of grime, but more important they indicate that the rider has something other than the horse in mind and should thus be treated as a dude. If you wear a jacket, make sure the sleeves are generous enough to allow flexibility at the shoulder and elbow. Down vests are practical in cold weather, since they give the arms great freedom; denim jackets that button at the waist are good so long as they are not too tight.

If you know that a stable uses English tack, you should wear jodhpurs and jodhpur boots or breeches and hunt boots if you have them. But if you are a beginner and have not already invested in these articles, don't race out to buy them. Wear the well-fitting jeans and the good shoes or boots with heels, and after a lesson or two, ask your instructor for advice about clothing. There's no point in wearing out your best fox-hunting outfit on a casual trail ride or a dusty session in the ring.

Many people feel they will make a poor impression by not dressing to the teeth. I have two conflicting stories on that subject—so take your pick. Once, while I was visiting some friends in Maine, we decided to go riding at the local stable where no one in the party had been. On the chance that they might have a horse broken to an English saddle, I wore my breeches and boots and ended up with a relatively unschooled but lively and interesting horse. (It turned out that no one had asked for an English saddle or this horse in several weeks, so my ride was eventful, to say the least.) The owners of the stable must have decided on the basis of my clothes that I knew what I was doing—or deserved to be embarrassed if I didn't. But on another occasion I tried the same approach at another stable, only to find that all their tack was Western, and I was treated to a few embarrassing moments by having to hoist my duded-up self into a down-to-earth stock saddle.

No matter what your basic gear is, however, you should have in your bag or car, or whatever it is you carry things in, a crop or a riding stick of some kind and a hard hat—the latter being especially important if you are a beginner and essential if you plan to do any jumping. Gloves are perfectly okay, though not necessary, and they should be made of a thin, supple material that will help (not hinder) your grip on the reins. Spurs, on the other hand, are to be avoided by the beginner or by riders mounting unfamiliar horses unless otherwise instructed. Spurs can be invaluable aids to the experienced rider, but they are too often instruments of torture on untrained heels. If you have a pair of beautiful, expensive Mexican spurs, leave them at home hanging on the living room wall as decoration until you know how to use them.

If you are fully grown and know that you will be riding regularly, a good investment is a pair of chaps (schooling or shotgun chaps are suitable for both Western and English styles).

If your family objects to your interest in riding, here are some arguments you can try.

Don't tell me that riding is exercise. The horse does all the work! Only a poor rider is a passenger on a horse. A good rider is constantly working to make the horse perform well. This is good mental exercise and is excellent physical discipline as well. Why do you think they give Olympic medals to the riders instead of to the horses?

Riding is dangerous and bad for your health. True, taking a fall can lead to injury, but skiing accidents are far more numerous and driving a car is even more dangerous. A good rider can learn how to prevent most accidents and to fall safely. Also, riding strengthens the lower back muscles and is good preventive medicine for lower back problems, which are common, but not in those who ride regularly.

Riding is cruel to animals. A bad, abusive rider can be cruel to a horse, pulling on its mouth and running it ragged. But a good rider who understands equine mentality is good for a horse. Remember that modern-day saddle horses are domestic animals and will be far healthier and happier when trained properly than when they are allowed to run wild. An unruly, undisciplined horse can be a joy to watch in a field but will never be handled or cared for very well. A good horse-and-rider team depends to a large extent on the willingness of the horse, not on the rider's ability to force it to go.

These will give you better contact with the saddle than jeans will, without wearing the material as happens with fine breeches and boots. Since chaps must fit properly, they should be purchased with care, but they will last a very long time. If you show up at a stable with a pair in hand, you'll undoubtedly be taken more seriously than someone in polyester slacks and sneakers.

As soon as you are sure enough of yourself to buy chaps, though, you should also get yourself some real riding apparel, since, as a horseless rider, you never know where your next horse will be taking you, whether it's to a fine private stable belonging to someone you met on the trail or into the show ring. Last-minute purchases or loans from friends for the sake of a special occasion may not be properly fitted or broken in,

You aren't strong enough to handle a horse. No human is stronger than a full-grown horse, so we have developed ways of handling them that take brains and technique, not brute strength. This is why children and women often make better riders than men who rely on muscle to do the job.

Horses aren't even as smart as pigs or dogs, so what's the challenge? It's unfair to measure horse intelligence by the standards we use for other species. Horses are just as smart as they have to be for what they are. Your average "dumb" hack horse knows a great deal more than most of its riders about how to get its own way—and that's a challenge right there. And when was the last time you tried to ride a pig anyway?

Horseback riding is expensive and snobby. True, it does take money to feed, equip, and care for a horse, but riding once or twice a week is far less expensive than skiing or other sports involving an investment in equipment and facilities. As for snob value, horses aren't snobs and couldn't care less about the social or financial status of their riders so long as they ride well.

Trail riding is nice, but hiking or jogging is better. Jogging through the countryside may be better exercise, but for seeing the sights, riding a horse is more rewarding. Shy animals are less frightened by a horse and rider than they are by a human on foot, and menacing dogs that can attack a runner will usually give up on a horse after barking a few times.

and you'll probably feel uncomfortable just when you want to be looking your best. If you are shopping on behalf of a child and worrying about the fact that the expensive clothes will be outgrown before the year is out, check with your tack shop for used items or think of the purchase as a potential hand-me-down for other kids in the family or at the barn. Stable bulletin boards are usually covered with ads for outgrown garments, so be sure to check there too.

One accessory that is never mentioned in the horse books but that I have always found important regardless of where or whom I'm riding is a carrot, which I invariably steal from the refrigerator whenever I head stableward. So while you are packing up your gear or getting yourself all gussied up to

RIDING EXERCISES

Becky Murrell, a physical therapist, contrived some simple exercises for the horseman/horsewoman to train the muscles used in riding, specially for those interested in jumping but useful for anyone who spends time in a saddle. Here are a few suggestions based on her techniques:

1. To help keep your head and back straight and your shoulders well back, lie face down with your hands clasped behind your neck and a pillow under your abdomen. Raise your head, shoulders, and elbows as high as possible and hold the position for a slow count of five.

2. To help you post at the trot and to keep your knees in position, get down on your hands and knees and look up. Slowly raise one leg straight backward. Lower, relax, and repeat with the other leg.

3. To help keep the inside of your knee and leg in contact with the saddle and to keep your toes pointing ahead rather than off to the side, sit in a firm chair with your feet flat on the floor. With your knees together and pointing straight ahead, lift your feet slightly off the floor and spread your ankles as far as they will go without separating your knees. Hold for a slow count of five and relax. Weights on each ankle will be useful if you wish to increase the strength of these muscles.

4. The hip abductors are the muscles that usually become sore in beginners, since they squeeze your knees together, but they are important for a strong seat in any rider. To strengthen them and help prevent soreness, sit in a chair with your knees apart and put a large beach ball between them. Squeeze your knees together as hard as you can for a slow count of ten.

5. For heel extension, you can use George Morris's exercise of standing on the balls of your feet on a step and pushing down on the heels. Or you can sit in a chair, raising your toes and feet toward the ceiling while your heels remain on the floor. You can make this exercise even more effective by adding a weight to the top of your feet.

meet the horse of your dreams (which for the horseless rider may be the next animal you ride), stick a carrot into your pocket or glove compartment and don't forget to use it after the ride is over. The stable management may not be impressed, but it will be appreciated by the recipient, even if he never lays eyes on you again.

PHYSICAL CONSIDERATIONS

One question that often arises when people set out to ride for the first time—in their lives or in the past few months—is "How can I avoid getting sore?" Unfortunately, soreness is one of the inevitable results of using muscles that have not been employed in some time. The degree of soreness depends, obviously, on the length of time you spend in the saddle and the type of riding you do, but some discomfort is probably in store, unless you take some precautions. I have already spoken about proper clothing that fits well in the interest of preventing chafing sores, but what about those painful strains in the leg muscles, particularly in the thigh region? A person in good physical condition who exercises regularly by swimming or jogging may be using these muscles already and may experience little or no pain at all the day after spending an hour in the saddle. But if you do not exercise at all and would like to help loosen up those muscles before riding, you might try the exercises described in the box on page 14. For those of us who don't tend to plan ahead, the best precaution may simply be to get some ibuprofen or to have some Epsom salts or baking soda on hand to add to a hot bath following your ride. You will probably have some pain anyway for a day or two after you ride, but there's nothing like another horseback ride to work out the muscle strain. If you continue to ride on a regular basis, you will find that the pain will gradually disappear altogether.

George Morris, the dean of American trainers in hunt-seat equitation, has only two exercises to recommend—standing on the balls of your feet on a step and pushing down on the heels to improve heel flexion and (perhaps more important) pushing away from the dinner table if you have a tendency to be overweight. Like many experts, Morris believes that a fat rider is at a distinct disadvantage, and not just in the show ring where appearance counts heavily, so to speak. A few pounds may not matter if you are able to develop a good seat in the saddle and can afford well-tailored riding clothes to hide your bulges, but no one, unless he or she is pretty weak or emaciated, can be too thin to ride. One look at the top horsemen in the country should be enough to curb the appetite! Remember, too, that riding is an athletic endeavor and that any athlete (equine as well as human) is better served by a trim physique, which will aid in achieving and maintaining balance, flexibility, and skill. Slender thighs are more capable of holding their proper position to establish contact with the horse's sides, for example. Extra pounds of flesh that cannot be considered muscular are of little assistance to the rider and will add an unnecessary burden to the horse below.

Perhaps as important as weight and fitness is the mental attitude toward physical discipline—mind over matter, if you will. One problem that many beginning riders have, especially adults, is the awkwardness and resulting self-consciousness that comes with learning something new. Mentally we want to learn, but we may not be prepared to undergo the physical demands that the education involves. When one reaches an advanced level, it seems almost automatic and natural for one's legs, heels, hands, seat, and head to move independently and yet in complete coordination, but for a beginner, many of these movements and positions will be totally unfamiliar. Keeping one's heels down, head up, eyes ahead, elbows at the side and hands both gentle and firm do not add up to the usual position that one maintains in an office or around the house. It is very difficult at first to remember each of these components of the good "seat" on a horse, especially if that animal is going at a gait faster than a walk. Simply keeping your balance and your wits about you is difficult enough.

I recall watching one lesson where an obvious beginner was having the usual problems learning to post at the trot, and I was surprised that the instructor kept harping on the rider's heels rather than his hands, which were flopping all over the place. Later, the instructor told me that there wasn't any point of getting the hands right until the legs (and the horse) were under control—so long as the horse's mouth wasn't being damaged.

Although it is embarrassing not to have your body under complete control and to look clumsy in the saddle, please keep in mind that everyone who rides has been through that awkward stage before you. Some people take to riding more quickly than others—you will often hear someone called a "natural rider"—but no one achieves perfection or even a good imitation of it without some good, hard work. It takes practice to get to the stage where riding is enjoyable, let alone expertly done. It also takes a teacher, a stable, and, last but not least, a horse—each of which will be discussed in the chapters that follow. Equally important, however, it takes a good attitude and a willingness to learn and to undergo the mental and physical discipline involved in learning.

I have asked several riding instructors and trainers how they evaluate new riders—on the basis of appearance, clothing, manners, vocabulary, or attitude—and without exception each one of them told me that the only important requirement in a student was the last one on that list. The first four can be improved, cultivated, or purchased, but the right attitude has to be there at the start and cannot be taught, no matter how good the teacher. With that in mind, let's look at some of the things that *can* be taught.

2

THE METHODS

ANYONE WHO HAS ever seen a Western movie knows that riding is a pretty simple business—all you do is leap into the saddle (making sure that you end up facing the horse's head), grab the reins, and kick like crazy with your spurs until the animal takes off, right? Wrong. Chances are that if you tried leaping into a saddle first time out, you'd end up on the ground on the other side of the horse. And that would only be the beginning of a fairly disastrous ride. Unlike cars, motorcycles, or skateboards, horses are big, strong, living creatures with varying personalities and physical capabilities. Learning to handle let alone master such an animal takes knowledge, experience, and skill on the part of the rider. Note that I didn't say strength. Horses will always be stronger than humans, but luckily we have a slight edge in the brain department, and through centuries of trial and error we have developed a number of effective ways of getting horses to do what we want. Since we have always wanted them to do different sorts of things—pull buggies, carry riders for long distances, chase cattle, and show off their beauty, speed, or jumping ability—the methods of training have varied considerably. Although most people in this country today use horses for pleasure riding, not all of those horses have been trained in the same way. Riders, too, are trained in different ways, or methods of equitation, depending on the horses they ride, the regions they live in, and the types of riding they do.

A great many people ride horses without ever taking a lesson and some of them turn into perfectly good riders if they are persistent and have a degree of natural talent. But learning to ride by the seat of your pants without any prior knowledge or instruction is done primarily at the school of hard knocks, and there are easier and far more effective ways for the beginner to learn the ABCs of riding than that. Before we head out on the road looking for the ideal stable and horse to ride, let's put the cart before the horse and discuss the importance of good instruction, the types of instruction that are available, and the ways to find them.

Actually, learning to ride is not quite as demanding as getting through medical school, so don't be discouraged before you start at the idea of taking lessons—even if you are well beyond normal school age. Once the basic techniques have been mastered, you will need to practice as often as possible to improve your skills, but, happily, practicing on horseback is one of the most pleasurable activities I know. You can always take a break from the work of concentrating on the placement of your heels or hands by taking a relaxing ride through the countryside, refreshing your horse and yourself and finding out what all those lessons have really been for.

Many people beyond the beginner stage stop right there at the basics and never consider the idea of taking another lesson, but I find that most of these riders fail to get as much out of their occasional hacks as they could by considering each ride a learning experience. When I started taking lessons as an adult after ten years of only occasional trail rides, I found that my interest quickly increased to the high pitch I had enjoyed at the age of fifteen. While I certainly advocate riding lessons for every beginner, I also recommend them for more experienced riders—not as a regular routine but as a useful way of increasing one's riding enjoyment. When you approach a new hacking stable, for instance, taking a lesson rather than just renting a horse will enable the powers-that-be at the stable to evaluate your expertise quickly so that you'll be trusted with a better horse the next time. Many good stables do not offer hacking at all, so that the only way to ride there is to take instruction. Once, when I was visiting my parents at a southern resort area, I dropped in to the local stable to inquire about riding. The trail rides involved only walking and trotting because the stable catered primarily to novices, but there was a lesson program as well. So I signed up for a class and within half an hour was cantering around the instructor picking up a few pointers about saddle-seat equitation in which I had never been schooled. The next morning, when I came back, the stable manager offered me a good horse and allowed me to ride by myself, since he knew I could handle the animal.

Because most stables don't offer a wide range of instruction, you will probably have to decide what kind of riding you wish to learn before you select a stable. Most people tend to divide riding into two distinct categories—Western and English—depending on the types of saddles that horses wear. But a quick look at any tack-shop catalogue will indicate that there are many more than just two types of saddles, and a quick study of equitation books and magazines will reveal that the dividing line between Western and English is fairly fuzzy. Many Western riders enjoy jumping their horses or teaching them the basic elements of dressage, and riders in English saddles are a familiar sight on competitive trail rides. Even jumper riders often use hackamores on their horses and wear shotgun chaps in the schooling ring. The two styles are closer than they look, and no one stands to benefit from this more than the horseless rider, who should be ready and willing to adapt to whatever horse or saddle presents itself. Nevertheless, there are real differences in riding styles and simply being adaptable isn't enough. A good basic "seat" is required as well as a sensitivity to unfamiliar horses, but it also helps to have some knowledge of the different aids, equipment, vocabulary, and apparel involved. What follows is a brief description of the basic types of riding now practiced in this country with some tips on how to adapt from one to the other.

First, however, let's clear up some confusion caused by the meaning of the word "pleasure." Riding for pleasure is what most horseless riders do, and yet asking for lessons in pleasure riding will often raise more questions than it will answer. To some horsemen, "pleasure horse" has a specific meaning, referring to an animal that has been specially trained for pleasure-horse classes in shows—as distinct from trail horse, jumper, hunter, reining horse, or what-have-you. In either Western or English tack, a pleasure horse is shown at the walk, trot, and canter (with occasional requests to back up), but the forms of equitation used in riding these horses can vary from stock-seat to saddle-seat to hunter-seat, depending on the show. Therefore, you won't find a "pleasure" style in the following descriptions, though you may very well find a pleasure horse at the next stable you visit.

Another verbal tip. When you are asked whether you want to ride Western or English, keep in mind that those terms are almost meaningless except for the presence (or not) of a saddle horn. "Western" saddles come in different styles—reining, cutting, bronc-riding, all-purpose—as do "English" saddles—jumping, dressage, saddle-seat, eventing—so spend a few minutes looking through a tack shop or a tack-shop catalogue and learn to distinguish between the types. A livery-stable owner may only be interested in which type of saddle to put on the horse you're about to rent, in which case "Western" or "English" will do fine. But an instructor needs to know more about what you want to learn, and it will help your advancement as a rider if you ask for instruction in one discipline or another. The four basic disciplines are stock-seat equitation (the most popular in the country), saddle-seat equitation (most common in the Midwest and South), hunter-seat (or forward-seat) equitation, and dressage. Three-day eventing (also known as combined training) is a combination of disciplines (cross-country jumping, stadium jumping, and dressage) and like dressage itself has increased greatly in popularity over the past few years. The last chapter in this book contains information about the competitive aspects of these types of riding, but before we enter a competition, we should start with the basics, and for the horseless rider, that is with the all-purpose balanced seat.

BALANCED-SEAT EQUITATION

Unlike dressage or stock-seat, saddle (or park) seat, and hunter-seat equitation, the balanced seat is not a formal style, although most good riders use it. It is closest to classical dressage in that it promotes perfect harmony between horse and rider and achieves the best results in the most effective and efficient way. Perhaps the easiest way to describe the balanced seat is for me to ask you to picture someone riding bareback, without the benefit of any special saddle to keep one's weight forward or back and without stirrups to regulate the extension of one's legs. As anyone who has ridden bareback knows, balance is what keeps you aboard—not the reassuring presence of a "horn" or a high cantle or a set of stirrups to help you post at the trot. On a malnourished or tiny horse, one can (maybe) stay in place by holding the animal in a death grip with one's legs, but on a normal horse, the legs must be in the right place (directly below one's shoulder-to-hip line); the seat

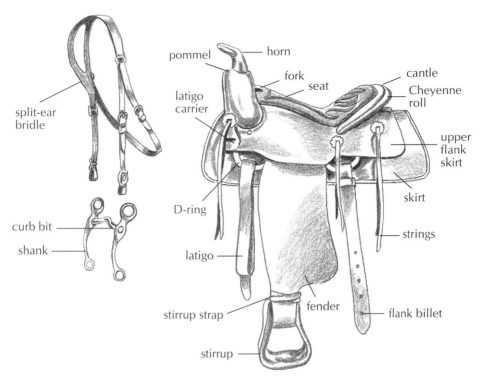

split-ear
bridle

curb bit

shank

pommel — horn

fork

latigo
carrier

seat

cantle

Cheyenne
roll

upper
flank
skirt

skirt

D-ring

strings

latigo

stirrup strap

fender

flank billet

stirrup

Horses at public stables offering Western riding will usually wear this kind of tack: an all-purpose stock saddle and a split-ear bridle with a curb bit.

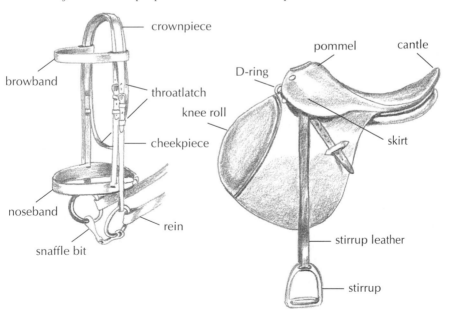

crownpiece

browband

throatlatch

cheekpiece

noseband

rein

snaffle bit

pommel

cantle

D-ring

knee roll

skirt

stirrup leather

stirrup

What the well-dressed hack will wear at stables offering hunter-seat equitation: a snaffle bridle and a forward-seat jumping saddle.

must be deep and over the horse's center of gravity; and the hands must work independently rather than being used to hang on, which will only jab the horse painfully in the mouth. At any gait faster than the walk, the rider must remain in perfect synchrony with the horse's rhythm—neither ahead nor behind—to remain on the horse's back, and the legs must be free not to grip but to regulate the horse's speed by giving and relieving pressure against its sides. (This involves keeping one's heels down, incidentally, as in a saddle so that the calves may be in constant contact with the horse for impulsion. Keeping one's toes pointed down may seem more natural or more secure, but the rider is actually in a poor position to maintain control.)

Because this book is addressed to the rider who is committed to riding but not to one particular animal trained to one particular method, I recommend the balanced seat as the most adaptable of styles and—for many experts—the most effective. Whether you are to become interested in dressage,

This is a form of balanced seat adapted to a Western saddle. It is not typical of stock-seat equitation (the legs are not straight in long stirrups and the reins are held in both hands), but it is perhaps the best all-purpose seat to learn as a beginner, since it can be applied to any horse no matter how it has been trained.

barrel racing, open jumping, or trail riding, the balanced seat is the most useful basic approach. One can learn it in a stock saddle, a jumping saddle, or a dressage saddle and on a school horse or a fine, privately owned purebred, even one that has been trained in a specific discipline.

For example, during one period when I was concentrating on hunter-seat equitation—with my weight forward, my legs strong, and my hands relatively low—I found myself one week-end on a friend's horse, a show Morgan that had been trained to a park or saddle seat. Although this was a horse I had been able to ride effectively on earlier occasions, I suddenly found that my constant leg pressure and forward seat were invitations to gallop, and I had to readapt pretty quickly to regain my composure, as well as my balance. If I had never had instruction in balanced-seat equitation, I might still be on that mad dash through the countryside.

Although many instructors may not even know what you mean by the expression "balanced seat," you will probably find that most of them—if they are not dead set on hunter-seat or saddle-seat equitation—are teaching at least some variation of what you want. As you can see in the drawing, the rider's seat is well into the saddle, the back is straight (at all gaits, except a gallop and over jumps), the legs are on a line with the back, and the hands are resting neither on the withers below the horse's head nor carried higher than the crest of the neck. This is the most secure seat available to the rider, and though it won't work in special equitation classes or in specific activities on highly trained horses, it is easily adapted to those, as we shall see.

Certainly your chances for a more pleasurable ride on an unfamiliar horse are much greater if you employ the balanced seat. Any horse will find it more comfortable and thus easier to carry a rider if the rider's weight is balanced over its own center of gravity. Think about what it would feel like if you had to carry a heavy package on one side of your back rather than in the middle, where the weight would be supported by your legs as well as your back. When a rider sits too far forward or back or leans too far to one side or the other, the horse is obliged to compensate for the off-balanced weight and may resist your efforts to move the way you want it to or, worse, suffer discomfort, which can result in a sour or unwilling attitude.

Most people who jump horses feel that the hunter, or forward, seat is the only way to make a horse jump effectively, by keeping one's weight forward and off the animal's back, freeing its hindquarters to do their stuff. This is all well and good for the well-schooled horse that needs little encouragement to take a fence. (The two-point forward seat—which involves saddle contact only with the legs, not the seat bones— is used even by balanced-seat riders at the gallop and during a jump after the horse takes off.) But when one is trying to jump an unwilling horse that is hard to control, most trainers will agree that a secure seat in the saddle with one's weight back rather than forward will give more impulsion, more control, and more safety for the rider. Just as it is effective to lean back rather than forward when a horse disobeys, so it is more effective when one is asking a horse to jump to make sure that one has control of the rear-end "engine." It is a rule of thumb on horseback to correct a horse by moving forward (not stopping), and it is only by keeping one's legs and seat in the position of control that one can keep the horse going. (Another useful rule to remember is that a rider has very little control when out of the saddle—either over the withers or on the ground!) Experienced riders can maintain strong control with their legs alone, but until you reach that stage, your seat is an essential adjunct to the legs.

At a horse show someday, watch the open-jumper classes, especially the horses that are obviously excited and difficult. The riders don't look at all like their colleagues in the hunter classes, for they are back in the saddle until the point of take-off, keeping as much control as possible. Steeplechase or cross-country riders also stay back, especially if the takeoff is anything less than perfect, for it is important that they remain in the saddle—not just to win but to stay in one piece. School horses are not comparable to the brilliant open jumper capable of leaping a six-foot fence or the steeplechaser who can clear five feet going thirty miles an hour, but the principle remains the same: For success the rider can't afford to let the horse take charge of the situation.

Perhaps the best expert to watch for a real understanding of the balanced seat is a dressage rider, for it is out of the dressage techniques that the balanced seat developed. "Dressage" is a French word meaning "training" or "schooling," and in horsemanship it means that the horse is taught to be supple, balanced, obedient, and cadenced. A well-schooled

dressage horse in motion is a thing of beauty, moving rhyth-
mically and with spirit yet perfectly under the control of the
rider, whose aids are so subtle they are virtually invisible. (See
page 38 for a more complete description of dressage.)

For those who like to intellectualize their riding and read
how-to books between rides, I can recommend one extremely
interesting title called *Centered Riding*. The author, Sally Swift,
has developed an effective approach to teaching the basics of
riding. She encourages riders to become aware of their own
bodies and to employ certain techniques (such as proper
breathing, centering, balance, and "soft eyes") to help develop harmony with the horse. She suggests the use of vivid
images ("Feel a spring pulling your center forward to the sky")
to enable the rider to achieve a natural position in the saddle.
Although Sally Swift is a dressage instructor, her approach is
valid for all riders, even those who are relatively advanced
and need help refining their skills. While her ideas are original and innovative, her basic philosophy is simple: Relax and
allow your horse to do the same. In the past, horses and riders
were trained, often in a military setting, through the use of
rigorous repetition and constant correction. No one has sufficient time, money, horses, or teachers today—to say nothing
of motivation and persistence—to become a perfect rider using these methods, but, thanks to the expertise of Sally Swift
and like-minded instructors, one may become an accomplished
rider in a far more natural and enjoyable way, by working
with the horse rather than against him.

STOCK-SEAT EQUITATION

Riding in a Western saddle is the easiest method of riding for
a complete beginner, not because riding Western is easy per
se, but because the shape of the saddle makes the inexperienced rider feel more secure than an English saddle, which
has a relatively low pommel and no horn. Actually, riding a
Western seat well can take as much work and skill as riding in
an English saddle, but because security and self-confidence
are important at the beginning, many novice riders prefer the
stock saddle. And, since most people who don't ride a great
deal have undoubtedly watched a great deal of television, they
may not even be aware of the English saddle at all. Most hacking stables that cater to beginners or occasional riders find
that they simply won't attract customers if they offer only
English tack, and thus it behooves the dedicated horseless

rider to learn at least the basics of Western horsemanship if he or she intends to spend holidays on horseback anywhere in the United States and Canada. If you are the sort who sneers at a horse in a Western saddle as a vehicle for a neophyte or drugstore cowboy, keep in mind that there is as much of a challenge in handling a cutting horse or a reining horse as there is in getting a hunter over a course of jumps.

Before mounting up, however, let's take a closer look at the saddle. The horn of the saddle was not, of course, designed as a handle for the rider, though it may come in handy if you lose your balance and is a far better brace than pulling on the reins. The horn is a device developed by roping cowboys to hold the end of the lariat when a steer or calf is being roped. Thus, the impact of the roped animal won't pull the roper out of the saddle but will be supported by the weight of the horse as well as the rider. And the high cantle was not designed entirely to keep the rider from slipping off behind. It

A typical stock-seat rider, with her weight back in the saddle, legs extended, and reins held in one hand with the right hand resting on the right thigh. The rider is properly dressed for the occasion, with suitable boots, chaps over long pants, a long-sleeved shirt, a neckerchief, and a broad-brimmed hat. These clothes are designed to provide comfort in the saddle and protection against the elements.

was designed for comfort—a necessity for anyone who spends long hours in the saddle—and also to keep the rider's seat well into the saddle rather than forward. The different kinds of stock saddles evolved out of the uses to which horses were put—roping calves, cutting cattle, riding broncs, or long-distance cattle drives—but the all-purpose saddle is the kind usually employed for pleasure and trail riding and is the one most commonly offered to horseless riders.

No less important than the saddle for Western riding is the bridle, which may be a bitless bridle or hackamore, a snaffle, a curb, or a spade, each involving a different approach, a different effect, and requiring a certain amount of dexterity and skill to use. The most common type found in a hacking stable is a curb bit, which is meant to encourage a horse to tuck its head (or flex at the poll behind the ears and keep its head lowered), so that the rider has the ability to command quick stops and turns necessary in chasing cattle or working in underbrush. Since neither of these activities is generally encountered by the renting rider, the curb should probably be switched for a less punishing bit, but most stable operators feel that it just doesn't "look right" and so their horses become professional bit-evaders, raising their heads, shaking them, or lowering them and getting behind the bit so that they are in control and preventing pain and injury to their mouths.

With a curb bit—as with a hackamore, which in spite of having no bit at all can be very painful if misused—the idea is not to keep a tight rein, punishing the horse constantly, but to keep a loose rein, tightening it only when necessary to get the horse to change pace and then releasing immediately when it obeys. Don't be tempted into believing that a loose rein is an invitation to gallop; most horses remain relaxed on a loose rein but will tense up and resist a tight rein, often by bolting off into the blue.

Changing direction is done by laying the reins—always held in one hand or the other—against the horse's neck, pressing in the direction you wish the horse to move. Neck-reining is a relatively natural cue, since the horse will invariably move away from the pressure, and I have found that it will work even on horses that have never seen a Western saddle let alone a cow. While one hand holds the reins (held as illustrated), the other hand should remain immobile on the thigh, even at gaits faster than the walk. Presumably, this style was

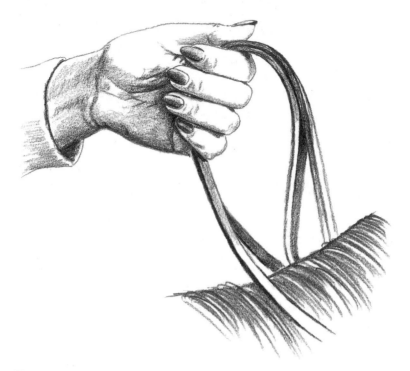

Use one hand (preferably the left) to hold the single pair of reins in stock-seat equitation. The reins may be open-ended or closed and may have buttons or knots for a better grip.

developed to keep one's hands free to work the rope, but for trail-riding purposes it is also practical, since one can brush branches aside, open gates, or whatever, without changing the position of one's hands. And, like a lot of other aspects of equitation, one-handed riding is traditional and that's reason enough in some circles.

Stirrups should be fairly long so that one's knees are not bent; this is as much for comfort as for any other reason, in order that the rider can maintain a deep seat in the saddle. Elbows should remain at the side and weight should be back rather than forward even at the fast lope (canter) or gallop. Although it is not traditional for Westerners to post at the trot, it is acceptable (even in most show rings) and far more comfortable than a bad bouncing. Many horses that wear Western saddles are not well trained to the proper Western jog, a very slow trot to which any rider may comfortably sit. The lope, too, is a slow version of its English counterpart, the canter, and a well-trained Western horse won't go into high gear without a good deal of encouragement. A friend of mine, renting a horse at a stable in Santa Fe, realized after a few strides of the lope that she couldn't turn the horse and that she was being run away with. Because she knew she could run twice as fast as the horse was going and that he would tire of the game in a hundred yards or so, she relaxed and enjoyed herself, delighted that standard forward gear in New Mexico was much different from what she was used to in New York.

One problem that riders accustomed to an English saddle generally have in a stock saddle is insufficient contact with the horse's sides. The ample amount of leather on the saddle does put a formidable barrier between human leg and equine barrel, which explains why spurs are often seen on Western riders. But for the beginner in Western equitation, spurs can be dangerous, and instructors will often recommend that the rider use a stick or the ends (or bight) of the reins to reinforce leg pressure and that weight be employed to reinforce the reins in turning. Whereas it isn't proper in an English saddle to lean from side to side to get a horse to turn, some experts feel it is perfectly okay in a stock saddle, just because one doesn't have enough "feel." Most horses will move under a rider to keep themselves in balance, and if the rider is leaning out to the right, they will move to the right to avoid falling over. Although leaning is frowned upon if it is overdone (it can cause a fall if exaggerated), it may be helpful if the horse isn't responding to anything else.

Stopping a horse is similar the world around: lean back, grip with your legs, and tighten the reins to achieve a firm contact, at which point the horse's head should rise and his hindquarters lower over the hocks. The moment the horse responds, drop the reins (to reward the animal by reducing the pressure), reapplying them only if the horse fails to come to a full halt. If you aren't experienced, don't attempt one of those screech-to-a-halt stops from grade-B movies. This kind of stop is the result of hours of patient training, not of brute force, and should be performed only by a skilled horseman on a trained animal. Once you dismount, you can—if the horse is trained—let the reins drop to the ground, confident that the animal will remain standing in place. If you suspect that the horse has not been so trained, don't take a chance but keep hold of the reins. Don't tie them to anything; if you plan a stop along the trail, take a halter and lead rope along for that purpose.

Highly trained Western horses are a joy to watch, especially the cutting and reining horses. The former, whose job it is to single (or cut) out a steer or calf and keep it from rejoining the herd, can do its work with just about anyone in the saddle, so long as that person has excellent balance and a quick set of reflexes—the cutting horse makes starts and turns and stops on its own and as fast as the animal it is cutting. A reining horse, however, is—like the dressage horse—at its best in harmony with the rider, performing rollbacks, pivots, and spins that take practice, correct cues, balance, and rhythm to perfect. The rollback, which is nothing for an inexperienced rider to attempt except under supervision, is a change of direction (180 degrees) at a fast lope, involving a change of lead as the horse "rolls over" or back on its hocks as it stops and turns. A pivot is performed at a standstill, and the horse turns on its hocks while lifting its front legs off the ground. A spin is a series of four pivots in succession so that the horse makes a 360-degree turn in place.

SADDLE-SEAT EQUITATION

Although use of the hunter (or forward) seat has become widespread throughout the United States, the saddle seat or its variations may still be the most popular form of equitation in the English saddle; it certainly is the most traditional American seat. Nowadays, saddle-seat equitation brings to mind high-stepping three-gaited or five-gaited show horses, but in fact this is only one facet—and the most highly developed aspect—of the style. Certain breeds, the Arab, Morgan, and Tennessee Walking Horse, for example, are shown in "park" classes, and it is still believed by many to be the style that best shows off a horse's action at different gaits. Some experts believe that this type of training has been refined to a point where it is detrimental to the horse, and it is true that some abuses have been perpetrated for the sake of fashion in certain breeds, but federal laws exist to prohibit the "soring" of horses for show purposes, and tail breaking and tail docking are also illegal. Some training methods that may be considered controversial are used to achieve the flashy, animated look that judges and the public love, but similar accusations could certainly be aimed in the direction of many other equestrian disciplines.

The saddle-seat rider on a three-gaited horse uses a broad, flat type of saddle and carries his weight well back to allow the horse's front quarters enough freedom for animated, high-stepping action. The horse wears a double bridle (curb and snaffle bits), and the rider wears a saddle-seat suit with a long jacket, Kentucky-style jodhpurs, and jodhpur boots.

Flashiness aside, the horseless rider should be able to cope with a saddle-seat or park-trained horse with an open mind, since riding one of these animals at an extended trot or a beautifully collected canter—to say nothing of the smooth slow gait or the brilliant rack—can be an incredibly exhilarating experience. Out of the show ring—with all its hot lights, screaming spectators, and competitive atmosphere—the saddle horse can deliver an excitement of its own and an immensely pleasurable ride, if you know how to handle the animal.

The first thing to note is the shape of the saddle. It is relatively flat with a long tree ending over the horse's haunches in a low cantle. This means, of course, that the rider's weight tends to be balanced toward the back of the saddle rather than the front, with the legs somewhat forward rather than directly under the rider's center of balance. Most saddle-seat riders nowadays ride a modified version of the balanced seat for the walk, trot, and canter, keeping their weight well back for the slow gait and rack, when the rider must encourage forward impulsion and free the horse's forequarters for the high-stepping action.

After the saddle, the next thing to note is the bridle, which will probably be a double bridle or perhaps a pelham, either one involving a set of double reins, the curb and the snaffle. If you have never held anything in your hands (or hand) but a single set of reins, the double reins will seem awkward at first, and it will take some practice to get used to them. The illustration shows the correct way to hold the reins, and once this has been accomplished, all you need to remember is to hold your hands upright, thumbs up. By turning your thumbs toward the horse's neck, you will apply pressure on the curb bit—which will bring the horse's head down and cause it to flex at the poll—and by pulling back in the straight-up-and-down position you will put pressure on the snaffle for signals to stop or slow down. Because the horse's head is carried higher than in a hunter or Western horse, your hands should be proportionately higher over the withers. The higher the hands, the more animated the horse, however, so if you wish to calm him, lower your hands. Unlike the Western horse, the signal for a turn is the use of a direct rein (putting slight pressure on the side toward which you wish to move) and the use of leg or heel pressure on that same side. Because the saddle is not

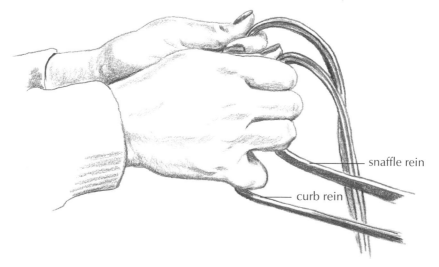

snaffle rein

curb rein

One of the correct ways to hold reins for a double bridle.

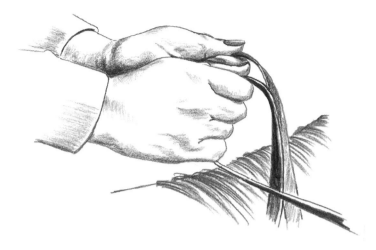

One way to hold snaffle reins.

built up like a stock saddle or even a forward-seat or jumping saddle, the rider's security is based on balance. Unlike the hunter-seat rider who must use a great deal of lower-leg pressure to retain control as well as grip, the saddle-seat rider's pressure point on the saddle is the thigh and knee, and cues are given with the heel rather than the calf. To move into a canter, turn the horse at an angle away from the side on which you wish the horse to lead, apply heel pressure on that side, and you're off.

One aspect of saddle-seat riding that non-enthusiasts write off as entirely artificial—the stretch stand at the halt—is actually a sensible solution to a perfectly common problem, that of keeping a horse standing still while it is being mounted. An animal whose legs are out from under it simply can't start off at the walk until the rider is safely in place—an important consideration for a plantation owner being watched by his employees or for the less-than-agile lady who must cope with more skirts than reins. Those who are still convinced that "shaky tails" are silly peacocks who belong back in the days when a fashionable turnout was more impressive than a "natural" style of riding should try to envision a loose horse voluntarily taking a course of artificially constructed fences or racing in a cloverleaf pattern around a bunch of barrels. And try to remember that William Steinkraus, the first U.S. Olympic gold medalist for show jumping, won some of his first ribbons on a gaited horse.

HUNTER-SEAT EQUITATION

In several parts of the country—the eastern states particularly—this form of riding is very popular, and yet it is, perhaps surprisingly, the most recent in its development. Unlike the Western and saddle-seat styles, the hunter seat was not developed for comfort during long hours in the saddle, so important in the good old autoless, trainless days. It was devised as the most efficient method of enabling a horse to perform certain short-term but intensive activities—racing at full speed and jumping over obstacles. For these relatively extreme movements, a horse needs as much freedom as possible to move its head and neck (essential to balance) and its hindquarters (essential for power). Thus, the rider, helped by the design of the saddle, remains forward in position at speed and in the air over a jump, keeping as little weight as possible on the hindquarters and giving freedom to the forequarters. The construction of the forward-seat saddle is, therefore, much different from those we have met so far: a relatively high cantle to keep weight from slipping back and a knee roll to give security and a steady position to the legs, which are in this style of riding the main source of control, since the seat is often a two-point rather than a deep three-point position. Stirrups are short to relieve the horse of the rider's weight—more so in race riding and less so in cross-country riding over jumps where security and control are more important than speed.

In addition to a special saddle, the average horse trained as a hunter will probably also wear a running or standing martingale (see illustration), a piece of tack designed to keep the horse's head relatively low to prevent it from rising too high and thus interfering with balance (and also with the rider's face, which is closer to the horse's neck than in other styles). Although there are always exceptions, most hunter-trained horses also wear snaffle bits rather than double bridles, which tend to force a high head carriage, although on jumpers it is not surprising these days to see any number of different bits, including the Western hackamore.

Most hunters and jumpers are Thoroughbreds or European warmbloods, long-bodied and long-limbed, with gaits that are naturally less collected than those of the high-stepping, collected breeds (and nonbreeds). These animals, because of the refinement of their breeding, are rarely found in a hacking stable, and their willingness to move ahead rarely

This is a typical hunter-seat rider, weight forward over the withers at the canter. The horse is suitably tucked in a forward-seat saddle, a single-reined snaffle bridle, and a running martingale to keep the horse from throwing its head and evading the bit. The rider wears a hunt cap, a jacket, breeches, and hunt boots.

requires the constant encouragement that the usual hack horse demands if one wants anything more than a slow trot. Nevertheless, even the occasional rider may be given a chance to ride a hunter type, and it is worth learning how this is done, just in case.

If your instructor does not know the fine points (or even the rough ones) of hunter-seat equitation, you can, by watching hunter classes at horse shows, gather important tips. Observe how the riders sit on their animals, adjusting the length of strides between jumps; keeping their balance directly over the withers rather than over the horse's back; and tilting forward once the horse has taken off for a jump, keeping contact with the horse's mouth yet allowing the horse freedom to extend its neck as it jumps. Note, also, that hunter-seat riders actually have several different seats—the forward position for moving ahead and taking off; the defense or safety position (leaning back behind the horse's center of balance) for landing over a drop fence, handling a resisting horse, or dealing with a buck or rear; and any number of seats in between. A useful description of these and many other aspects of this type of riding can be found in William Steinkraus's book *Reflections on Riding and Jumping* (Trafalgar Square).

DRESSAGE

The years since the first edition of *The Horseless Rider* was published have seen a dramatic revival of dressage, which has evolved from the classic tradition of horsemanship first written about by Xenophon, a Greek military leader of the fourth century B.C. and a disciple of Socrates. Originally a training method employed by the cavalry for use in battle, dressage (which means "training" in French) eventually became part of the basic education of all European noblemen and ultimately an art form, which can still be seen at the Spanish Riding School in Vienna. Dressage as a sport is one of the Olympic disciplines, where it is increasing in popularity, perhaps in part because the American teams have begun to gain on their European rivals, who have dominated the field for many years. Instruction in dressage is now offered at many schools and stables, for its own sake and as part of three-day eventing, or combined training. Whether or not one competes in the dressage ring, however, the education of every well-rounded horseman should include some schooling in dressage, for its principles apply to all forms of riding. An added advantage is that dressage is a relatively safe form of riding so that a novice with little or no experience can quickly gain confidence. Because dressage is as much a continuous learning process as a sport, progress is measured by more than just prize ribbons.

The traditional image of dressage is that of a straight-backed rider seated aboard an obedient horse performing balletlike movements with precision, an image familiar to anyone who has seen the "high school" horses of the Spanish Riding School demonstrate their airs above the ground. In recent years, a less rigid approach to training—one that promotes harmony and understanding of the horse rather than force and correction in obtaining obedience—has resulted in a far more attractive picture. Perfection is still the ultimate goal, but precision must be balanced with a willing obedience and spirit.

At first glance, a dressage rider may seem to be doing nothing at all, and one tends to admire the brilliantly trained horse performing subtle and intricate moves without a cue. Actually, dressage is an expression of perfect cooperation between horse and rider, the result of long hours of practice. Because the rider must have a deep, secure seat and an erect upper body, the stirrups are long and the saddle balanced in the middle of the horse's back (not forward as on a hunter or back as on a saddle horse). This position gives the rider

A classic dressage seat at the extended (long-strided) trot. Note how the other styles of riding have adapted certain elements of this fine, traditional form of equitation.

complete control with both seat and legs, so that only the slightest pressure or movement will indicate to the horse that a new movement is requested. The bridle is usually a double-bitted one, to ensure perfect collection. Ideally, the dressage horse is always on the bit (completely under the rider's control and responsive to every move of the hands, seat, or leg) and prepared to respond to whatever command may be given.

Dressage should not, however, be relegated to an elevated category of riding in which only a few may participate. Indeed, dressage has a great deal to offer even the most ordinary of horse and riders, for its basics are neither difficult to understand nor difficult to learn. I have often been surprised to find that the dowdiest-looking hack and school horses are familiar with certain dressage movements—the half pass, simple two-tracking or leg yields, and turns on the haunches (see glossary in Chapter 3). These movements may not be performed well—it often takes some doing to push the right buttons, in fact—but it is always a wonderful feeling to find

HOW TO START, STOP, AND TURN IN ANY LANGUAGE

The following instructions are not necessarily universal, nor will they work on every horse, but they are the most common cues used these days and well worth committing to memory in case you find yourself aboard a horse that refuses to tell you who his trainer was.

Balanced Seat

Start by giving pressure on both sides of the horse with your calf muscles, moving your seat bones forward in the saddle, and releasing slightly with the reins.

Stop by arching your back, giving pressure on both sides of the horse with your calves, and holding the reins firm to resist forward movement.

Turn by putting pressure at the girth on the side toward which you wish to move, putting your outside leg behind the girth, and pulling gently on the inside rein (the rein facing the direction you wish to turn).

Stock Seat

Start by giving pressure just behind the girth with both legs, leaning slightly forward, and moving the rein hand ahead to release pressure. (If that doesn't work, give a kick with both heels behind the girth or on the horse's shoulders.)

Stop by saying "whoa," leaning slightly back, and taking up the reins until you make contact with the mouth.

out that you and the horse have something in common, an appreciation for a motion that is neither straight ahead nor back but sideways or around. These lateral movements are invaluable in teaching the horse to be supple and obedient, but they are also useful to know when a gate needs closing, a jacket needs to be hung on a fence, or a move needs to be made to the side without involving a complete turn. Maneuverability is always important on the trail, in the ring, or approaching a fence, and the horse that can be maneuvered without dismounting is always worth rewarding. Collection and extension and bending on turns are part of all styles of riding, but they are the essence of dressage, and a horse whose

Turn by laying the reins (which are held in one hand only) on the side of the neck opposite the direction you wish to turn. Apply some pressure by pulling your hand across the neck; if the horse doesn't respond right away, you can also try leaning slightly in that direction.

Saddle Seat

Start by applying pressure with your legs at the girth, saying "walk," leaning back slightly, and, with your hands held relatively high, releasing pressure on the horse's mouth. If the horse doesn't respond, kick lightly with both heels and use a whip to reinforce the cue.

Stop by releasing pressure on the reins and leaning slightly forward, arching the back, and applying pressure at the knees. If the horse does not respond, lower your hands and apply rein pressure with a mild jerk (not a steady pull) to get his attention, and say "whoa."

Turn by using a direct rein on the side toward which you wish to turn holding the outside rein steady and applying pressure at the girth with the inside leg.

Hunter Seat

Start by applying calf pressure on both sides of the horse, leaning slightly forward, and releasing pressure on the reins. Make a clucking noise if the horse doesn't respond immediately and apply more pressure with the legs, using a crop if necessary.

Stop by applying pressure with the legs and resisting with the hands, saying "whoa."

Turn by applying pressure at the girth on the inside leg and using a direct or indirect rein on the side toward which you wish to move, keeping the outside rein steady.

gaits can be "rated" (speeded up or slowed down) without breaking stride is a useful animal indeed.

For the serious dressage rider, it can be frustrating not to have access to the same horse every day, because it is impossible to achieve a high level or even to measure progress in an animal one shares with other riders. But for the novice and intermediate rider, horselessness is a definite plus. Charles de Kunffy, a trainer, judge, and author of several books on dressage, advises that one "should ride as many different kinds of horses as possible." He does not recommend lazy horses,

STIRRUP LENGTHS

When you sit in the saddle with your legs relaxed and hanging down straight, the bottom of the stirrup should be:

1. At anklebone or just below for balanced seat

2. 1 to 1½ inches above sole of boot for stock seat

3. Just above sole of boot for saddle seat

4. Just above anklebone for hunter seat

5. Just below anklebone for dressage

which can stiffen the novice rider, or untrained animals, which can make an untrained rider anxious, but he does believe that horsemanship is based on a "sincere love for the horse. Not just a specific horse, but a love for all of them."

There are, of course, many other forms of riding—such as sidesaddle, race riding, polo, and fox hunting—but these will be dealt with in Chapter 9 as sidelines for the adventurous rider to explore. In this chapter I have tried to stick to the basics as you find them in the horse books, at horse shows, and in lesson programs at riding stables. In many parts of the country, you may not have a choice about the type of instruction offered or the way in which your horse-of-the-hour has been trained. The point is that, for the horseless rider, any style is suitable at the beginning so long as you develop confidence in the saddle (and out of it) and any horse is acceptable so long as you have sufficient confidence and some idea of what to expect. If you are one of those fortunates who has complete access to a single animal owned but unused by someone else, you can afford to specialize, but most of us must make do with various horses or with a horse ridden by various riders, and that calls for a generalist's approach. I am delighted to report that virtually every horseman and horsewoman I have met or read about can be typed as a generalist—capable of handling any equine that comes along regardless of experience or temperament. And so, to make our attitudes and ability as flexible as our riding muscles, let's apply to some generalists for some advice and instruction (see "How to Start, Stop, and Turn in any Language," page 40).

3

A CURVING GRAVEL DRIVEWAY leads you past white-fenced pastures shaded by graceful elms. The elegant chestnut Thoroughbreds grazing there lift their heads to watch you pass. As you near the large, freshly painted stable, you note that there is a huge indoor ring behind it and several sizeable outdoor rings alongside, where a number of well-dressed riders are schooling their mounts. You step into the stable manager's office where you are greeted with a friendly hello and asked a few questions about your experience with horses and your willingness to sign a release. After a quick tour around the premises, you are then escorted to the school-horse barn and introduced to a sixteen-hand bay gelding, a former equitation horse who looks you over with a wise and benevolent eye. As he is tacked up by a groom, you meet your instructor, an attractive older gentleman in riding garb who tells you in a soft European accent about his background and about his approach to teaching. After lending you a riding crop and making certain that your hard hat fits properly, he leads you and the horse out to an empty outdoor ring and proceeds to give you a private lesson. The horse stands quietly as you mount and adjust your stirrups and then moves forward at your command into a steady walk. Your instructor speaks gently to remind you about lowering your heels, explaining the reason for this position, and after gathering your reins to put the horse on the bit, you move him into a springy working trot. After a full hour of work, in which you have learned the basics of the balanced seat and your own strengths and weaknesses in the saddle, you are given an appointment for your next lesson and told that the billing will be arranged on a monthly basis.

A dream? Perhaps, considering your experience the previous week when you rode at another stable in your search for the ideal riding academy. On that occasion, you drove off a busy highway directly onto a rutted dirt road that soon ended in a crowded parking lot. In front of a shabby-looking barn, a few sleepy horses in Western saddles stood in the sun tied to a fence. Several young people in jeans and sneakers were hanging around the tack room and, feeling slightly conspicuous in your clean boots, you asked for the stable manager. "Aw, he's around here someplace. Try the feed room over there."

Making your way down the narrow corridor between the straight stalls on each side, you tried to get a look at the animals but decided to keep your eyes on those cocked hind feet, since the horses seemed to have taken offense at your presence. Finally you located the manager, who asked your name, remembered your phone call, and generously offered any horse in the barn. "Take yer pick," he said proudly. "Ya don't look like a beginner, so mebbe you'd like Brownie over there."

Brownie appeared not to like you much and promptly flattened his ears at your approach. Someone slapped him on the flank to move him over and grabbed his bridle to pull him out of the stall for your inspection. "He's no plug, this one," the kid announced, and pulled him out into the parking lot. Although Brownie danced about a bit, you managed to mount without completely losing your composure in front of the crowd, and then you inquired about the instructor who was to have given you a few pointers at ten o'clock. "Oh, Nancy's down in the ring. Just go back behind the barn there. You can't miss her." And so you couldn't. After picking his way through the stones on the path, Brownie reluctantly moved toward the ring—at least you assumed it was a ring from the boards nailed up on trees and posts surrounding a roughly circular mud puddle. You were just beginning to sympathize with Brownie when you heard a shrill, female voice yelling at someone thumping around the ring on an Appaloosa mare. "For God's sake, you're on the wrong lead again! Stop her and start over!" The rider yanked on the reins and the mare threw her head up to avoid the jab in the mouth. After a jolting trot around half the ring, the rider tried for a canter again. "Kick, you jerk! She can't feel that feather you're using!"

And so it went for another ten minutes. Finally Nancy turned to you and said, "Okay, put him on the rail and trot for a bit while I get a cup of coffee. I've been out here since dawn. What a lousy day, and it isn't even ten thirty yet." Assuming that she meant for you to trot around the ring, you proceeded to do so, trying to keep out of the way of the Appaloosa whose rider kept letting her come right up behind you, annoying the already irritated Brownie. Eventually six other riders on equally irritable animals showed up and joined you in the ring. Nancy finally returned, having regained her poise sufficiently to ask each rider for ten dollars and to tell you that you were on the wrong diagonal. When you asked what that was, she shrugged her shoulders and told you to post up when the horse's right shoulder moved forward. "Oh," you said and followed her directions, weaving around the other riders who seemed to be in as much of a muddle as you were. After thirty minutes of this, you became as depressed as Brownie and when someone came up and asked you to hand him over, you dismounted and escaped to your car, breathing a sigh of relief as you drove back onto the highway.

To those of you who have never ridden at a public stable or had a riding lesson, these stories will read like exercises in fiction. But they are both true, and I can vouch for every word. As it turned out the perfect instructor wasn't so perfect, because his real efforts were devoted to sixteen-year-old kids who had the money and talent to compete for hunter-jumper championships. He treated me as a sideline, canceling my lessons without warning when parents came to discuss their children's future in the show ring. And the awful stable did have another instructor, one who was articulate enough to explain what diagonals were and sympathetic enough to the likes of Brownie and me to set aside a special hour each week for a real schooling session that benefited us both.

In other words, the ideal riding instructor and riding school may not be so ideal on closer inspection. In fact, there may be no such thing as the ideal riding school. My very first teacher, with whom I spent a few hours at the age of seven or eight, was an old Irishman named Pat who used to take me out riding, paying no attention at all to my awkward attempts but spinning out terrific yarns about horses he had known. I learned a lot about horses from him but not much about riding, except that I loved it. My first serious set of lessons came along when I was thirty-two at a public stable in New Jersey an hour and a half from my apartment but well worth the commute, thanks to the quality of the instruction. In between I did a lot of seat-of-the-pants riding, but I never felt capable of entering a horse show, handling a difficult horse, or enjoying myself quite as much as I did after I had learned some of the principles of classical horsemanship under the tutelage of a good teacher.

FORMAL INSTRUCTION

Selecting a potential instructor can be as complicated and difficult as picking a family doctor, since a good personal relationship is almost as important as actual expertise. Someone who screams at a rider who takes criticism badly is probably not going to be able to teach much, while some riders can't learn anything unless instruction is delivered in the most forceful way. Many beginners need a good deal of reassurance from an instructor who builds a sense of self-confidence by progressing slowly on one or a series of well-schooled, well-mannered horses. More experienced but timid riders need encouragement and support to go beyond the basics to more demanding aspects of the sport, such as jumping, riding competitively, or simply getting onto more difficult horses.

A semi-private lesson in stock-seat equitation. The instructor is teaching his students how to bend their horses around cones placed at intervals in the ring, perhaps as part of an early lesson in barrel racing or pole bending.

You needn't like the person who is giving you a lesson, but you should respect him or her and be willing to handle criticism, since there will be some. There's no point in taking a lesson unless you plan to learn something, even if it goes against what you have been taught previously. If that happens, you should feel free to ask the reasons behind a particular piece of instruction—not by presenting a counterargument but simply by asking for an explanation. At one point in my checkered career, I overlapped lesson programs at two different stables, one where I was being taught the balanced seat on average school horses and another where I was learning hunter-seat equitation on a private horse. The first instructor insisted that I sit straight-backed with my weight in the center of the saddle, while the second kept trying to make me sit forward and use only my legs (not my seat bones) to move the horse forward. I was quite confused at first, but I eventually learned that each method has its reasons: the school horses needed the extra push and the private horse did not; the former instructor wanted to emphasize dressage movements and the latter wanted to prepare me for jumping. Thanks to the willingness of both teachers to explain the different horses and the different goals, I was soon able to sort it all out.

It goes without saying that riding instructors should know a great deal about horses and horsemanship, but for most students, an instructor should be a good teacher first and an expert rider second. It is very impressive to be able to tell your friends that your teacher was a former Equestrian Team member, but it doesn't do you much good if you can't understand a word he says or if he can't articulate his techniques. Many instructors fall into habits of using phrases that they can no longer define in plain English. The glossary on page 58 is intended to help out the confused rider, but if you're really having trouble, it might be a good idea to find another instructor.

But before we look for another instructor, how do we go about finding the first one? The initial step, of course, is deciding just what it is you want to learn. It would be a waste of time learning to ride a reining horse when you'd rather be able to handle a hunter. (Actually, for the horseless rider, *nothing* is a waste of time; sooner or later, you'll want to be able to take advantage of any and every riding situation that crops up!) Once you have selected the style that suits you, you must find a stable where instruction is available. Obviously, a stable that specializes in Western pleasure riding is more likely to have lessons in that than in hunter-seat equitation, but many stables have more than one teacher, while others have none at all.

The least reliable way of finding good instruction is the Yellow Pages, but if you are unfamiliar with stables in your area, this may be the most convenient way of finding out which stables offer instruction (or claim that they do). A telephone call will ascertain what kind of lesson program exists, whether there is room for you, and what the time and financial arrangements will be. An on-the-spot evaluation is much more effective, however, than a conversation over the telephone, so arrive a few minutes before your scheduled lesson and have a look around the stable and at any lessons in progress to see whether the investment will be worthwhile. (See Chapter 4 for advice about finding and analyzing stables.)

A better way of finding a good teacher—and getting yourself a good introduction—is to ask for a recommendation from a friend who rides. If that friend is a valued client, the instructor will probably welcome you with a special personal touch. And you will have the advantage of knowing ahead of time just what to expect from the stable, the horses, and the teacher—as well as what will be expected of you.

One excellent way of selecting a riding teacher is to visit a horse show and watch the competition—especially the equitation classes for both youngsters and adults in which riders rather than horses are being judged. Look at the winners and ask around for their coaches or teachers (who can usually be found hanging over the rail or at the ingate giving their pupils lavish praise or constructive criticism). Approach an instructor by offering congratulations on the pupil's achievement and asking whether he or she might be willing to take on another pupil—i.e., yourself. If you are a beginner or can only afford the time and money for a weekly lesson, a successful teacher involved in preparing youngsters or training young horses for top-level competition may not even be interested in your custom, but don't be put off by a refusal. Ask the instructor to recommend an assistant or a protégé who could take you on. You needn't be a pest—after all, the instructor has students to coach at the show—but if you show sufficient polite enthusiasm and interest, you should be able to get some helpful tips.

If you'd prefer to get your instruction stage over in one intensive swoop, rather than learning in weekly lessons for a month or two, you should look into the possibility of riding schools, camps, and other equestrian centers that provide resident programs in different aspects of horsemanship. These exist throughout the country and abroad, and, for a price, you can learn an enormous amount in a very short space of time. Look in the next chapter under "Schools and Colleges" and "Equestrian Resorts and Dude Ranches" for further information.

Once you have selected an instructor, you should ask for advice about how to approach your equestrian education. Should you have private lessons, and if so, should they be forever or only at the beginning? Would you do well in a group, and if so, how many people would that involve? Or perhaps a semi-private lesson, with one or two other riders, would give you the most attention for your money. (I tend to believe that groups of more than six are usually worthless and that private lessons are important only for the first few beginning lessons.) If you have your heart set on a group lesson with a friend or two who may be riding at a more advanced level, don't complain but do what the instructor suggests, so long as it is within reason. You'll learn more if you ride at your own level for a while, progressing at your own pace rather than at someone else's. With concentration and practice on your part, you'll soon catch up to your friends. If you must rely on your friends for a car pool, for instance, explain the situation to your instructor, who will probably try to work out a convenient lesson arrangement.

Lesson programs, prices, personalities, and the quality of school horses will vary considerably from one stable to the next, so you must be realistic about what you can afford and what you really want. No instructor is likely to be perfect in fulfilling all of your requirements, so you must judge for yourself which ones you are willing to sacrifice or compromise on. You may find that you will learn a great deal more in a very expensive half hour with the best coach in town than you will in a cheaper group lesson where you have to share the teacher with ten other riders. You may find that five lessons a week on a sour school horse gives you less than a weekly hour on a beautifully athletic private animal. Or you may find that the exact opposite is true, as I have on a number of occasions. I remember almost every word spoken by a fine instructor who taught at a county-run public stable that required him to teach as many as twelve students at a time on average school horses.

A group lesson in an indoor ring. In the foreground the instructor has set up a low vertical fence after a series of poles that have been arranged so that the horse will trot in an even-strided, steady approach to the obstacle.

In fact, I feel that every lesson I had there, cheap as they were, was worth far more than lessons costing twice as much at fancier stables where the owners were far more interested in selling me an expensive Thoroughbred than in teaching me to jump a crossrail. When you are starting out, a well-schooled "push-button" horse that does everything you ask (even if you don't ask correctly) can give you a good ride and some self-confidence, but after you have learned the basics, a difficult or sour horse is almost guaranteed to teach you more. And if you're paying for instruction over and above the price of a hack, that's the horse you need.

INFORMAL INSTRUCTION

If you can afford only one lesson a week, say, and you have reached the level where you can rent a horse to take out alone, there are several ways in which you can supplement your education by working on your own. Doing homework in this way will be successful only if you know what you are practicing, however, so ask your instructor at the end of each lesson what you can do for yourself without supervision. You can work on riding without stirrups, for instance, to improve your seat and balance, or you can practice collecting and extending the horse at different gaits, even on a trail ride. If you have access to a ring, work on more controlled exercises, such as any dressage movements you may be learning or the basic application of aids in asking for changes of gait, correct leads at the canter, and so forth. (See page 150 for more suggestions.)

If your problem is that your legs tend to move forward or flop around rather than stay in the proper place, or if your heels slide up rather than down, you may need someone to watch if you don't have a mirror to ride in front of so that you can give yourself an occasional check. But that someone needn't be your instructor; anyone who knows what to look for can help you here, and you can offer to help in return by watching for your friend's particular faults. I have often learned something while riding in company with better riders, listening to their comments when I asked for advice about particular problems encountered along the way. Many years ago, I rode in New York City's Central Park, and it was very helpful indeed to have an experienced friend along to tell me how to handle a horse that believed he was being attacked by joggers and nursemaids pushing baby carriages. Guides or wranglers on trail rides or pack trips can be good sources of information even if their primary function is to make sure that no one gets lost and not to improve your riding technique. Don't interrupt when the lead rider is busy reassuring a novice or making sure that everyone is aware of low-hanging branches ahead, but do take advantage of quiet moments to ask a question or two about the way he or she rides or about the way in which your horse may have been trained.

Remember, though, if you are asking for criticism without paying for it, take it in the proper spirit. Don't resent a helpful remark; if it is helpful, be grateful, and if you feel it is uncalled for, thank the criticizer for the effort and do what you think is best. Even in a situation where you feel that you know more than the instructor or trail guide, keep an open mind and a closed mouth. You'll learn something—a new trail, a horse's particular habits, or whatever—and you can always demonstrate your own knowledge by riding as well as you know how rather than by talking about it. (If you feel the need to instruct, read on to Chapter 10 about ways to earn extra money or free rides by becoming a teacher yourself.) The only time that I've found it necessary to speak up is when a horse is being abused by someone thoughtless or inexpert enough to cause needless pain or confusion. In such a case, you can adopt a relatively mild approach ("Aren't you scaring Horace?") or a firm one ("Please don't hold the reins so tight; you're hurting his mouth!") depending on the abuser, but do adopt *some* manner to avoid suffering, both equine and human. My only caution here is that you make sure that abuse is being committed; many expert horsemen use methods that may seem cruel to the novice but that are necessary if the horse is to become obedient. Whips, spurs, and severe bits are definitely harmful in the wrong hands, but they can be effective tools when applied by a horseman. The best way to learn the difference is to watch an expert at work, and this involves perfecting the technique of observation, whether or not you are paying for the privilege.

If, for instance, you take an occasional lesson, you'd be wasting your money if you arrived a few minutes before the lesson and left immediately afterward. One thing that every horseless rider must learn how to do is hang around, keeping your eyes and ears open the whole time. Watch other lessons in progress; observe the riders and listen to what the instructor tells them. You may not learn much from an "up-down" class in which beginners are learning to post at the trot, but you'll pick up valuable tips from more advanced classes. If no lessons are in progress, you can watch trainers schooling private horses, asking them any questions you have when the schooling session is over. Park yourself next to an instructor or a trainer at a horse show and ask him or her to comment on individual riding styles. If a rider uses a different technique than you do, or a special piece of tack with which you are unfamiliar, don't hesitate to ask someone who knows what it's all about. If a horse makes a mistake or if a rider you picked out as the best doesn't win, try to find out the reasons.

Another virtue in hanging around is that you can't help but learn something about horse care and stable management. If the instructor or the stable help allows it, ask if you can tack or untack the horse you have been assigned. If you don't know how to put a bridle on, watch it being done and then try it yourself. Make mental notes of grooming methods and techniques, and learn what the different pieces of equipment are designed to do. Offer to help by grooming horses, mucking out stalls, lugging bales of hay, or whatever needs doing. Walking a horse to cool it out, helping another rider to mount and adjusting the stirrups, or just remaining interested but out of the way will help convince the stable people that you are serious and considerate. The more time you can manage to spend being useful around a stable, the more you will be welcomed and the more you will learn.

BOOK LEARNING

During all those hours that you don't spend in the saddle or hanging around the barn, you can feed your hunger for equestrian knowledge by reading books and looking at the pictures. Here and there in this book I mention a few titles that are worth their weight in information, and below are listed some books on the different riding styles. But before you race out to your bookstore or library to stock up, ask your instructor to recommend books that will supplement what he or she has been trying to teach you. Actually, even the best-stocked superbookstore is unlikely to have much on serious horsemanship. Your best bet is your tack shop, or if you don't have one in the neighborhood, your tack-shop catalogue. There are a number of good ones that sell horse books currently in print;

many advertise in equine magazines and give their toll-free order number.

Since I have spent most of my adult life in the book-publishing business, I tend to collect books, read them, and trust what they say. So when I started riding seriously after a ten-year hiatus, I naturally sought the best books on the subject. One publishing colleague, an excellent rider, told me that the finest book around was Waldemar Seunig's *Horsemanship* and it quickly ended up on my bedside table. A fine book it is, but at that point in my education, it was more than I could handle, especially the part where Seunig, in the tradition of his place and time (Germany in the 1950s) described the configuration of the ideal rider, dismissing the endomorph (heavyset) and mesomorph (medium build) in favor of the ectomorph (thin). Since I was definitely an endomorphic type then, I was nearly convinced to give up equitation for crochet, but luckily my instructor intervened and sent me in the direction of Mr. Right—in this case Gordon Wright, former USET coach and author of *Learning to Ride, Hunt, and Show*, which is aimed at the novice rather than the sophisticated expert.

In spite of my bias for books, I must admit that reading may not be the most valuable way for the horseless rider to learn (with the exception of reading this book, of course). Books on equitation and training are very instructive and useful, but only if you are able to apply those written lessons to daily work, which usually involves having your own horse. Many instructors have their own methods of teaching and may be annoyed if they feel you are trying to outguess them by learning contradictory methods or if you get too far ahead of yourself by trying to understand technical matters beyond your ability. The most frustrating books for horseless readers, of course, are those devoted to horse-keeping. I call these "wish books" and collect them anyway, in preparation for the morning I find that pony tied up in my backyard, and I study everything in them just because I find everything about horses and horse care of great interest. The most useful books, however, and this includes some of the magazines as well, are those written by experts in the field who enjoy sharing their own experiences as well as their knowledge, and these are included among those listed below.

BOOKS ON EQUITATION

A good introductory book to both English and Western riding and the closest I've found to a manual for the balanced seat is *Basic Horsemanship English and Western* by Eleanor F. Prince and Gaydell M. Collier (Doubleday). In addition to its value as a guide for beginners, it is also an excellent textbook for would-be instructors. I mentioned in the previous chapter Sally Swift's *Centered Riding* (Trafalgar Square), which is well worth exploring, as is Pegotty Henriques's *Balanced Riding* (Half Halt Press), another valuable discussion of how to achieve a balanced seat in the saddle.

For stock-seat equitation, *The Art of Western Riding* by Bob Mayhew and John Birdsall (Howell Book House) addresses all basic aspects of the subject. *The Schooling of the Western Horse* by John Richard Young (University of Oklahoma Press) is the standard work in its field.

George Morris's *Hunter Seat Equitation* (Doubleday), now in its third edition, is the bible for hunter-jumper enthusiasts, and his most recent book, *The American Show Jumping Style* (Doubleday) is on its way to being the bible for jump riding. Peter Churchill's *Practical Showjumping* (Howell Book House) is good on the basics, and for those who enjoy personal experiences, William Steinkraus's *Riding and Jumping* and *Reflections on Riding and Jumping* (Trafalgar Square) offer great insights from a real master (who happens to be a good writer as well as rider).

Saddle-Seat Equitation by Helen K. Crabtree (Doubleday) is addressed to the instructor rather than the rider and assumes that the rider will have access to his or her own animal, but aside from that, the information is sound and the author is one of the most respected authorities on saddle-seat riding in the country.

Good books on dressage abound, each with its own theories, but the most accessible are Charles de Kunffy's *Training Strategies for Dressage Riders* (Howell Book House), Sally O'Connor's *Common Sense Dressage* (Half Halt Press), Jane Kidd's *Practical Dressage* (Howell Book

House), and Dominique Barbier's *Dressage for the New Age* (Simon and Schuster). Also worth reading are Alois Podhajsky's *The Art of Dressage* (Doubleday) and *The Complete Training of Horse and Rider in the Principles of Classical Horsemanship* (Doubleday).

The popularity of three-day eventing has spawned any number of fine books on the subject, but books on jumping and dressage will be as useful here as those on cross-country riding.

Other excellent books worth owning are Lt. A. L. D'Endrody's *Give Your Horse a Chance* (J. A. Allen), W. Müseler's *Riding Logic* (Scribner), and Vladimir Littauer's *The Development of Modern Riding* (Howell Book House).

There are books that provide exercises for riders and solutions to riding problems (*The Less-Than-Perfect Rider* by Leslie Bayley and Caroline Davis [Howell Book House] is one), and of course there are many books about training and keeping horses, all of which are probably worth looking at the next time you visit a tack shop or bookstore.

There are many horse magazines around, but if you are interested in more than just pretty pictures or specific breeds, you will want the journals that offer practical advice along with the rest. *Western Horseman* is a must for almost any rider, especially the stock-seat aficionado. *Practical Horseman* (for the hunter-jumper), *Dressage Today*, and other specialized magazines can be found in tack shops, along with more general publications. *Equus*, with its veterinary focus, is of particular interest to those who care for horses, as well as about them.

Tack shops and catalogues abound with videotapes about riding and horsemanship, and some of them are excellent, as they show not only experts at work but also teachers and students demonstrating basic skills and methods for achieving them. The tapes are expensive, however, so try to rent one first before investing; if your tack shop doesn't offer rentals, ask them to look into the possibility of instituting such a service.

AN ANNOTATED GLOSSARY FOR THE HORSELESS RIDER

Most horse books contain glossaries—one-line definitions of rather mysterious horsy terms that appear in the back of the book and are rarely given much attention by the reader. Because these terms are usually meaningless out of context and because the glossaries are usually out of reach when you are in the saddle taking a lesson, here are a few terms and phrases that you'll hear around a barn or in the ring that are worth reading, understanding, and committing to memory.

POINTS OF THE HORSE

Any horse book worth its salt block has a diagram showing an animal covered with tiny arrows, each one giving a name to a specific area. The terms defined below, however, refer to parts of the horse that one must care about while in the saddle.

Mouth, as in "keep your hands off his mouth": This may seem to be an odd expression for an instructor to use when your hands are several feet from the horse's head, but what is meant is to loosen the reins slightly to put less pressure on the bit, to use a lighter "contact." A horse with a "soft" mouth is responsive to the bit, allowing the rider to control him; this animal is a horseman's dream and deserves light hands from his rider. A horse with a "hard" mouth—usually found around hacking stables and riding academies—tries to evade the bit in order to control the rider, who will probably try to apply more pressure, creating in turn even more resistance on the part of the horse. This horse should probably be reschooled or fitted with a different bit if he is to be ridden successfully.

Poll, as in "flex at the poll": This word refers to the area just behind the horse's ears, the point where the horseman wants his horse to flex, thereby lowering his head somewhat, indicating that he has accepted the bit, or is "on the bit," ready to do whatever the rider wants.

Forehand, as in "heavy on the forehand": This has nothing to do with the horse's tennis game, but refers to the front half of the animal (specifically shoulder and forelegs). Since a horse's "motor" is in the hindquarters, a horse who is heavy on the forehand tends to be a bit out of balance and tends to pull on the reins, forcing the rider forward. This tendency is acceptable in some horses (those who pull vehicles, run races, etc.) but not in jumpers or cutting horses, for instance, where the impulsion—or power—must come from behind if the animal is to be able to leap a fence or stop and turn on a dime. A horse who performs a "turn on the forehand" is making a 180-degree turn in place, keeping his forelegs in place and moving his hindquarters around.

Withers, as in "keep your hands down by (or above) his withers": This word refers to the top of the shoulder joint just in front of the saddle. A horse's height is measured from the withers to the ground—not in inches but in "hands" (equivalent to four inches). A horse that stands 60 inches high at the withers is referred to as a 15-hand horse, not a five-footer. Some horses have low withers, which are comfortable for bareback riding but sometimes incapable of keeping a saddle in place, necessitating the use of a breastplate. Horses with wide or high withers may require a special saddle or pad to prevent saddle sores from constant pressure and rubbing. If you hold the reins too far above or below the withers, your hands may not be able to control the bit (or the horse) effectively.

Girth, as in "put your foot behind the girth": This refers to the area of the horse below the saddle where the cinch or girth can be touched by the rider's foot. A schooled horse will respond to pressure at or behind the girth in different ways—taking the former as a sign to move ahead and the latter as a sign to keep the hindquarters from swinging out to the side.

Near side, as in "mount on the near side": This is the left side of the horse, from which a horse is always led, mounted, and dismounted. (The right side is the off side.) This tradition, which is nearly universal today, once had a practical purpose—to keep the rider's sword, which was suspended from his left side, from swinging over the animal as he mounted or dismounted.

Inside, as in "inside rein" or "inside leg": When a horse is moving (or bending) around a turn, the inside is the side of the animal closer to the direction in which he is moving; the outside is the other side, or, in a ring, the one

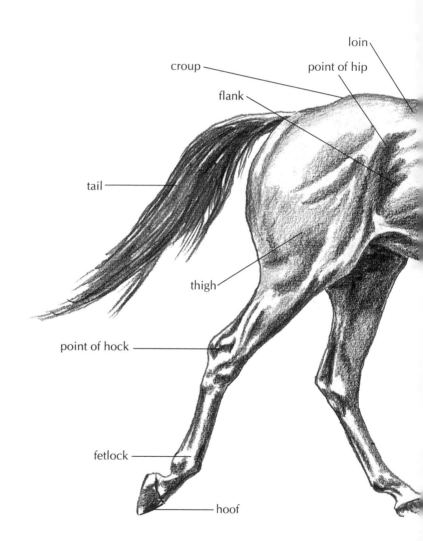

loin

croup

point of hip

flank

tail

thigh

point of hock

fetlock

hoof

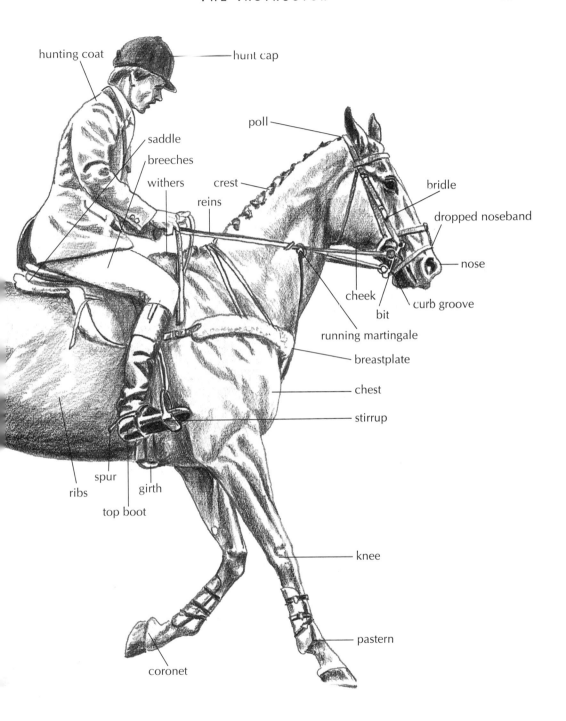

The points of the horse and rider.

that faces the outer edge of the ring. If you are moving around a ring to the left, the right side of the horse is the outside. During the counterclockwise trot, one posts on the left diagonal (moving up as the horse's right or outside leg moves forward), and during the counterclockwise canter the horse should be on the left lead, which means that the left leg is the leading leg.

Hindquarters or *haunches:* This is the origin of the horse's moving power or impulsion and is the area that the rider controls with legs and seat. Many horsemen can successfully control a horse using no reins, indicating that to the rider the most important part of the horse is the hind end. A turn on the haunches is a 180-degree turn in place in which the hindquarters remain still and the forelegs move around.

Hocks, as in "keep his hocks under him": This refers to the part of the hind leg comparable to the human heel; when the hocks are under the horse, this means that the horse is moving forward properly, springing from his hind legs rather than pulling himself with his forelegs.

POINTS OF THE RIDER

Few instruction books have diagrams of the human figure with little arrows defining parts of the rider, but these are no less important to successful riding than points of the horse.

Hands, as in "light" hands: Many beginners assume that the horse is controlled with the reins and that a good pair of hands must be strong. Since a horse is far stronger than a person and a hack horse is usually smarter in the use of the bit, the use of force on the reins can only lead to trouble, unless properly applied. If a horse is not on the bit, the reins are virtually useless and the horse must be outsmarted if control is to be regained. This may involve a quick jab with the reins, not steady pressure, but it also involves getting control of the hindquarters and other methods too complicated to describe here. The point is that light hands, applying pressure properly and only when necessary, are far more effective than heavy hands, which have ruined many a good horse with a soft mouth.

Eyes: Since the name of the game in riding is balance, and since balance can be affected by even the turn of a head, you should always keep your eyes up and in the direction you wish the horse to move. If your eyes are down, your head is down and your weight is too far forward; if you are looking to the left and wish to move straight, you may be confusing your horse.

Elbows: These are of very little use to the rider unless they are at your sides and flexible. Too many beginners flap their elbows, bringing their hands out of the proper position and causing their wrists to "break" or bend when they should remain relatively rigid. The hands are more effective if they are positioned with thumbs up, and keeping one's elbows at one's side is the best way to ensure that.

Legs: These are perhaps the most important aids that a rider has, since they help to control the horse's forward movement. A horse will move away from the pressure of the leg on its sides—forward (or back) if both legs are used, and to the side if pressure is given on only one side.

Heels, as in "heels down": Riders often wonder why it is important to keep heels down if they are not even touching the horse. Note, however, that as you lower your heel, your calf muscles enlarge; this means that without moving your leg, you can apply constant pressure on the horse's side, keeping him moving forward. This is more effective in the long run than constant tapping or kicking with the heel in the horse's side, which can sour a responsive animal. Horses that are insensitive to leg pressure may need a kick with the heels, but this is not a regular practice in good horsemanship—just a quick, effective way of getting a horse to move. A better method is to apply calf pressure first and, if there is no response, to reinforce that pressure with the crop or stick behind your leg. A horse will quickly learn to connect the crop with the application of the leg aid and should begin to respond with only the leg pressure. Many instructors will ask students to keep their weight in their heels—this is to make sure that the rider's weight does not move too far forward but stays balanced over the center of the horse's own balance.

Ball of the foot: This is the strongest part of the human foot and is where the stirrup should be placed, even in a Western saddle. The reasons for this are several: First, the foot will be less likely to slip through the stirrup (or go "home"), which can be dangerous if the rider is thrown, leaving the foot caught in the stirrup. Second, the heel will remain freer to move down if the stirrup is on the ball of the foot rather than the arch. And, third, the stirrup won't be as likely to slip off the foot, as it would if it were on the toes.

Seat: This can refer to the position of the rider in the saddle as in having a good "seat," or it can refer specifically to the "seat bones," which are an important aid in riding. There are also, as we have seen, several different kinds of "seats" or types of equitation. When an instructor speaks of a two-point seat, he or she means to keep your fanny out of the saddle; a three-point seat means that you should sit down (the three points being the two upper thighs and the rear end). The two-point seat is sometimes called the forward or half seat.

MOVEMENTS OF THE HORSE

There are many different movements that a horse can make, some natural, some man-made or artificial, but all requiring a degree of training if the horse is to perform them at the rider's command and with the proper amount of rhythm and control. The names for these different movements and gaits differ considerably from place to place, from breed to breed, and from trainer to trainer so it behooves the horseless rider who travels in a wide circle to learn the names as well as the movements themselves. There is no room here to list all of the variations that exist (these abound in the other horse books I have recommended), but the following tips will, I hope, be of some use to the novice.

Walk: This is the basic four-beat natural gait at which the rider can establish his or her position in the saddle, either at the beginning of a ride or between the other, faster gaits. The walk can be collected or extended, like the other gaits, meaning that the length of the stride is shortened or increased. As dressage trainer Charles de Kunffy points out, "relaxation will come most easily at the walk. . . . It is the slowest gait and is the only one without a period of suspension, allowing the horse to adjust to the foreign weight of the rider. Being the smoothest gait, it allows the rider to sit in harmonious balance and apply a minimum of aids."

Trot: There are several types of trot, a two-beat natural gait that is the best gait at which to learn the use of various aids or to school a horse, although one must first be sure that the horse is relaxed, best achieved at the walk. The slow trot or jog employed by Western riders (also known as the eight-mile-an-hour trot) enables one to sit in relative comfort; the collected or sitting trot used in dressage is similar but more highly controlled by the rider. The working or rising trot, which is the most common type of trot, requires the rider to post (or move up and down in the saddle) for comfort as well as for control. The post is often a difficult technique for the beginning rider to learn, but it should be a simple motion made in rhythm with the horse's movements, which will push the rider naturally out of the saddle. The rider can post on one of two diagonals, and these are part of the basic vocabulary of equitation. The extended trot, used in dressage, is not simply a speeded-up version but a lengthening of the horse's stride.

Canter: This three-beat gait is the third natural gait of the horse (although in Europe it is called a gallop and in a Western-schooled horse it is termed a lope). The horse canters with one or the other foreleg leading (or on the left or right lead), and the rider can learn to put the horse on the lead he or she wants by using proper cues. A well-schooled horse can be made to change leads without breaking out of a canter (a flying change); most horses can manage a simple change—dropping back to the trot for a stride or two in order to rebalance for the other lead at the canter. A collected canter looks and feels like a rocking-horse gait; an extended canter is one with a longer stride.

Gallop: This is a four-beat gait (not just a fast canter), the fastest a horse has. A hand gallop is a controlled gallop where the rider (in a two-point seat) maintains contact with the horse's mouth; a full gallop is all-out with only enough contact to enable the rider to slow the horse when he or she wants. Although a hand gallop is permissible in cross-country riding (indeed necessary in certain equestrian events), a full gallop belongs only on the race course. Many hacking stables and bridle trails post signs that say "No galloping," and these should be obeyed. Even racehorses are allowed to run full out only occasionally during training (as in a "breeze" or "workout") when they are not actually in a race.

Pace: Although some horses have been known to perform this gait naturally, it is an artificial gait invented by humans in which the horse's foreleg and hind leg on each side move forward and back in unison rather than on the diagonal as in a trot. A fast pace is used in harness racing, but because it is very uncomfortable for the rider, who is swung from side to side in the saddle, the pace is rarely taught to saddle horses. A very slow pace, or amble, may be found in the occasional riding horse, usually a member of a breed in which the gait is a natural one (a Paso Fino, for example). A variation—called a stepping pace or slow gait is one of the required gaits in a Five-Gaited saddle horse. The horse appears to be trotting with its forelegs and walking behind, and the resulting gait is comfortable to sit to as well as attractive to watch. Speeded up, the slow gait is known as a rack.

Reinback or *backing up:* All horses should be trained to move backward, whether they are expected to do so in the ring as a pleasure or equitation horse or out on the trail when movement ahead is impossible. Oddly enough, getting a horse to move back is just like getting it to move forward, except that the reins are held firm to resist the forward motion. Some horses have been trained to move back only with a gentle see-sawing of the reins.

Lateral movements: A leg yield is accomplished when a horse moves away from the rider's leg pressure, and this may be as simple as bending around a turn or as complicated as moving sideways. Two-tracking, in which a horse moves ahead on the diagonal with forelegs and hind legs on two different sets of tracks, can be done at the walk, trot, and canter. A half pass is a move diagonally toward one side or the other; a side pass is directly sideways. In performing the movements called "shoulder-in," "shoulder-out," "haunches-in," and "haunches-out" the horse moves straight ahead but with the body bent in different ways.

Turns on the haunches and on the forehand are 180-degree turns in place when the horse holds either his hindquarters or his forelegs still and moves around them to change direction.

Rollback, pivot, and spin are reining-horse movements that are described on page 32.

4

THE STABLE

IF YOU HAVE found a stable that provides good instruction, you may not need to read this chapter all the way through, but for those of you who already know how to ride or who are looking around for a new place or a different kind of riding, read on.

There are two basic types of stables to which the horseless rider can apply—public and private—but within those categories lie many different variations on the theme. Learning to understand and play those variations to your satisfaction needn't take years—as it did me—so long as you approach the problem with some forethought and a bit of information about what to expect and how to analyze what you find. Stables vary considerably in quality, appearance, and cost, but this is one situation in which a beggar can be a chooser even if limited in time, money, and talent. It would cost a bundle, of course, to fly to France for a week or two of riding at the famous cavalry school at Saumur, compared to an investment in a couple of hacks down the road at the local hacking stable, but those aren't the only alternatives if you know where and how to look. First, where.

PUBLIC STABLES

Establishments that specialize in renting horses to the general public have been around for thousands of years. Before the advent of the horseless carriage, the livery stable functioned like Hertz or Avis, and the rented horse was expected to get its rider wherever he or she wanted to go without breaking down along the way. I suspect that the public stables were run with some efficiency in those days, treating their animals with a degree of intelligence so they remained in good working order, although Anna Sewell's *Black Beauty* reveals that the care was not always humane, particularly on the part of the riders. Often they were not horsemen at all, nor were they even sensitive to the fact that horses, like humans, were capable of feeling pain. Nowadays, of course, public stables do not serve the same function in providing transportation, but there are still many thousands of them throughout the country that exist to provide enjoyment to people with an hour or two to spend on the back of a horse. Unfortunately, the pleasure involved in a ride at one of these places is sometimes minimal, even at the best-run stables, which are all too often in the minority.

There are many reasons why public stables should be approached with great caution. There are very few regulations governing their management (with the exception of the state of Maryland), and except for cases of cruelty that can be prosecuted by humane societies or lawsuits for negligence when a rider is injured, there is no way in which standards of care can be supervised or controlled. In most areas, anyone with a couple of horses can open a public stable by advertising as such. There is no regular inspection by the authorities, let alone a veterinarian; no stipulation that the stable manager must have any knowledge of horses; and no guarantee that the horse you rent is in good health, let alone safe to ride. The Uniform Commercial Code does contain wording to the effect that a horse owner warrants the "suitability" of a horse when he or she turns it over to a renter, but it is usually difficult to prove breach of warranty if the horse turns out to be unsuitable, whatever that may mean.

While visiting many public stables, I have found situations too horrible to imagine—starving horses, broken tack, filthy stalls built from packing crates with nails and broken glass well within reach of their occupants, and fully tacked animals waiting for hours in 90-degree heat with no access to water or even adequate ventilation. I have seen kids who have never ridden being allowed to gallop down the median strip of highways with no control over their mounts, and on one occasion I saw a boy thrown into the middle of traffic because the cinch broke or slipped, causing the saddle to slide and the horse to bolt. Another boy, galloping his horse cowboy style, so terrified the animal by flapping the reins and kicking the spurs that he ran into a bus, which broke the horse's forelegs. I have known stable managers who deliberately underfed their horses—not just because it was cheaper and produced less manure to clean up, but because it also made the horses weak enough to be handled by beginners.

Not all public stables are that bad, but it is true that, even at attractive, well-run stables, the inexperienced rider may have difficulties getting a satisfactory ride. Even more difficult is the situation of the experienced rider who will want to ride a good horse and won't be able to get it the first time out. The stable may have one or two good horses, but the new rider will usually have to cope with slow movers before he or she will be trusted with a livelier animal. There are various reasons for this, and few of them have to do with bad management. Indeed, most stable operators try their best to do well by their clientele and their horses both, but the problems of running a public stable are often insurmountable.

For one thing, running a stable—no matter how primitive—costs money, and that investment is very difficult to recoup by simply renting horses on an hourly basis. If the weather is bad or if one or more horses are lame, the income goes down but the horses must still be fed and shod; the stable and the tack must still be cleaned and repaired; and taxes or rent on the property must still be paid. One of the best public stables I know—with a full lesson program, an indoor ring for bad-weather riding, and an enthusiastic group of regular customers—loses money each year. It stays in business because the stable is subsidized by the county park system, and the manager told me that the only way he could make money would be to deal in buying and selling horses, which the park commission could not allow him to do. Stables that are not subsidized in some way (as tax write-offs for wealthy owners or as government establishments such as those run by counties or national parks) must cope with this financial situation in some way, either by scrimping or by offering a less-than-elegant service.

Another major problem faced by public stables is that of safety. No matter how many warnings a rider is given or how many "ride at your own risk" signs a stable posts, there is always the possibility of a lawsuit in case of injury. If a plaintiff can prove that he or she was given a horse that was known to be unsafe or unsuitable to ride, the stable owner can be

An ideal public stable facility, with a roomy barn, a sizeable outdoor ring for lessons, an indoor ring (above right) for inclement weather, and an office/clubhouse (upper left).

liable for damages. Even though these cases are difficult to prove, the stable must bear the court costs anyway. This situation has resulted in expensive insurance premiums on the one hand and an overcautious attitude on the other—which means that any rider new to a stable is likely to be given what we tend to call a "plug," a horse that has to be pushed hard to do more than walk. One stable operator told me that there were only two things a hack horse had to be: "four-legged and safe." Such a horse is unlikely to provide much of a ride for anyone, but at least it won't bolt at the first opportunity. Until a stable gets to know an individual rider, that's about all you can expect to be given when you ride. A good stable will require an evaluation test for each new rider and constant supervision unless or until that rider has proven that he or she can handle a horse at the walk, trot, and canter. That kind of individual attention costs the stable money, which is why a good stable will charge more than a poor one, but in this case you are far more likely to get a ride with less likelihood of injury. It may take two or three rides before the manager is convinced to let you have a lively horse, so don't be too impatient and run the risk of ruining your image. Keep in mind that an advanced rider should always be able to get an "advanced" ride out of any horse, even if it means that you have to push rather than pull. If you've been accustomed to willing, headstrong horses, it's a good experience to get on a slow mover every so often—if only to remind you what your leg muscles are for.

Many stable managers have told me that their worst problem is the new rider who claims to have ridden all his life and can handle any horse the stable has. (All horsemen have categories of riders—beginners, intermediates, and advanced—but the experienced stable operator has a fourth category—the wise guy.) Although the wise guy's self-evaluation usually recedes somewhat when the horse is brought out for him to mount, all but the most timid will usually try to perpetuate the image by brandishing a crop and giving a good imitation of John Wayne by trying to gallop off into the distance. Any experienced hack horse knows how to handle this type even before they get into the saddle, but all too often the episode is an unpleasant one for both horse and rider.

Because inexperienced riders don't usually know enough about riding to handle a horse properly, the average school or hack horse must develop various defense mechanisms to avoid the punishment that their riders invariably deliver. If the horses become too defensive or sour, they become unsuitable for their jobs, and so the turnover in public stables is often rapid, unless the horses are ridden and reschooled by advanced riders once in a while.

We will discuss in more detail the relative merits of the public-stable horse versus the private horse in the next chapter, but the point here is that horses cost money, and good horses cost more than bad ones. Any horse in reasonably good health has some monetary value, because of the market for horse meat, so even the poorest riding horse will cost a stable a few hundred dollars unless he can be obtained through trade. And a good hack horse, one that will stand up under abuse (inadvertent or not) and still give a good ride or a lesson, is worth his weight in pure gold. In a public stable, "good" has nothing to do with looks or athletic ability and everything to do with temperament and endurance. If you should find a hack horse that has had the benefit of good breeding and careful schooling, you should consider yourself very fortunate indeed.

Stable operators who take care in selecting their horses are wise enough to know that if they can provide good rides to their clients, they will quickly build up a regular business. Some of these stables for the same reason will offer lesson programs in addition to hacking, so that their regular clients will learn enough to enjoy each ride more the next time around. Though there may be no polished brass on the stable door and the tack may be old and well worn, such an establishment may be just what you are looking for (so long as the place is clean and the tack in good repair). The quality of the lessons will also depend on the experience and personality of the instructor, as we have seen, in addition to the quality of the facilities and the horses themselves. Learning to ride at a public stable is not the only way to go about pursuing an equestrian education, but it is usually the most convenient, and it's worth the extra effort to pick out a good one. Toward the end of this chapter, I will give some suggestions for analyzing a stable, but first, some hints about how to find one to analyze.

The simplest way to locate a hacking stable is to look in the Yellow Pages under "Riding Academies" (called that even when lessons are not offered) or "Stables." You can also check the local newspaper for ads or inquire at a tack shop, which may know about smaller establishments that don't advertise. Perhaps the best way is to ask a friend who rides for a recommendation. Not only can the friend describe for you what the place is like and how good the horses are, but you will have the extra advantage of a personal contact. As the old saying goes, "It's not *what* you know but *who* you know that counts," and it's as true in the horse world as anywhere else. As I have said, stable operators tend to be cautious about sending out a new rider on one of their better horses, but if a reliable client recommends you and provides a realistic analysis of your ability, there's no doubt that you will be given a better horse than the usual first-timer. Don't risk destroying whatever reputation has preceded you, however, by acting as if you deserve special treatment or overestimating your ability. Impatience or dissatisfaction with a slow horse the first time out may lead the stable management to believe that you haven't got the proper attitude.

Whether or not you know anyone at the stable, make a telephone call ahead of time to find out what kind of riding the stable offers, what sort of facilities they have (ring, trails, indoor ring, and so on), whether they require an appointment, and how much they charge. Costs will range from $10 to $30 an hour for a hack, depending on the stable and its location, and lessons will be more expensive, but ask about them anyway. You will probably have to pay cash in advance for the hack. Ask also whether you will be allowed to ride by yourself or if you must pay for the services of a guide and be accompanied by several other riders. Make an appointment and, when the time comes, get to the stable at least fifteen minutes ahead so that you can look around. The extra few minutes will give you a chance to size up the stable (see "Stable Analysis," page 87) and fall into conversation with other riders or with members of the stable staff.

PRIVATE STABLES

A private stable can be as enormous and elegant as an estate where fine racehorses are bred and trained or as simple as the backyard facilities operated by your next-door neighbor. It may be impossible for you to penetrate the former, but the latter is often available to the horseless rider, especially if you are willing to do a bit of work around the stable or exercise the animal when its owner is not around. Riding someone else's horse under these conditions is usually an attractive opportunity, since it is free for the asking (if it's not, you've gotten yourself into a public stable setup). But there are a good many things for the horseless rider to keep in mind if the opportunity arises.

First of all, some horse owners may not be receptive to your offer to muck out the stall in exchange for a free ride. This isn't selfishness on their part so much as caution, since they could be held liable if you were to fall off or be kicked. Also, they may not feel that you have had sufficient experience to handle the animal properly. Anyone who spends the money to keep a private horse has probably also invested time and energy in schooling it, and allowing an unfamiliar person to ride that horse can result in the animal acquiring some bad habits or regressing in its education. If you are refused, don't be insulted or assume that they are acting like a dog in their horse's manger. Learn more about riding to convince them that you are capable of handling the animal, and be prepared to sign a release indicating that you will ride at your own risk, not theirs. On the other hand, if something should happen to the horse while you are riding, *you* may be held liable for damages, a risk you may not be willing to take. It would be a shame to lose a good friend just for the sake of a free ride, so be sure that you and the horse's owner, friend or not, are in clear agreement about the responsibilities involved. (See Chapter 6 for further information about such legalities.)

While interviewing private owners for this book, I found that some of them were reluctant to hire people on a "work for a ride" basis, if only because of bad experiences in the past. It takes time and energy to teach someone the proper way to behave around horses and the methods of caring for them, and some people simply don't have that kind of time and energy. Also, because of the risk involved in being around horses—especially high-strung animals that don't become accustomed to strangers quickly—some owners fear the incidence of injury in their stables to people who are not on their paid staff, or who don't have written permission from parents to ride.

Happily, there are a few stable owners sympathetic to the plight of the child (or adult) in need of a horse, since they were in that situation themselves before they had the money to own their own. One of them, a woman in California with a boarding stable of about fifty horses, told me:

There is nearly always one horse who needs some loving attention because its owner is away or in college or some such. I do believe that horses need attention over and above the stable care—someone to groom them, chat with them, ride them, etc. Maybe I am sentimental, but I do think that a horse taken care of and loved by a kid looks better. Anyway, when I notice a child hanging around a lot. I try to encourage her* and involve her in the stable care. If I get a sense she is really sincere and has the obsession, then I am done for and of course I have to find a horse for her to lease or borrow. I really don't care how well the child rides, for I feel I can always teach that part as well as how to take care of the animal. What really impresses me and persuades me to take on a child is knowing that she is obsessed. As for money, if the child can't afford even half the board, then we usually work out some arrangement—help with the chores or baby-sitting for my children. I even have one older girl making me a stained-glass window in lieu of several months' board. I much prefer this to money, actually.

Needless to say, such understanding and generous souls don't grow on trees, but if you can find yourself a horse owner who has once been horseless, you may be able to win a heart if not a ride or two. Finding a private stable is not as simple as locating a public stable, since it probably won't advertise unless it offers a lesson program or boarding facilities. Knowing someone who owns a horse or works for such an owner is probably the only way you can get your foot in the stable door. For this reason, veterinarians, blacksmiths (who liked to be called farriers, incidentally), and tack-shop owners are good people to get to know, although I have myself used any number of other devices (mostly trying to get my friends to buy horses!).

Although I am not particularly aggressive, I do recall one unusual incident that occurred when I was a child. I once found myself wandering down a strange country lane trying

*Her use of the feminine pronoun here indicates the high percentage of female enthusiasts in this activity. The age-old affinity of girls for horses is still true, even past the age of girl-hood, but many stable owners and instructors tell me that the percentage of male riders (and adults in general) has increased over the past five years. Men's lib at last?

to keep busy while my parents were visiting friends nearby. Naturally, I found myself drawn like a magnet to a field where a black mare was grazing. She came over to greet me, and while we were in conversation, a woman came out of the house next to the field and asked me if I liked to ride. It seemed that her daughter had recently sprained an ankle, and Inky had been left to languish in the field, unexercised and unloved. Needless to say, I generously offered my services as the lady generously offered me a pair of jodhpurs, and before long I was happily riding along that country lane aboard the deprived Inky.

(Of course, that kind of story is the stuff of which horseless riders' dreams are made, and, although it involved pure luck, the moral should be clear: Anyone for whom horses are a magnetic force will find a riderless horse sooner or later if one can develop a sixth sense about sprained ankles.)

SUMMER CAMPS

Any camp directory or newspaper advertisement can tell you whether a camp offers riding, and those that do usually make a big play to attract the horse-minded camper. Some offer riding every day; some even offer one complete horse to each complete camper along with a course in stable management, rated horse shows, special clinics with well-known horsemen, and advanced instruction. Some even throw in swimming, tennis, and arts and crafts as a bonus. For those city kids who don't get a chance to ride during the rest of the year, summer camp can be heaven on earth. One woman I know who now teaches riding at a college and owns two beautiful hunters never had a horse until she graduated from college herself, but learned everything she knew at an eight-week summer camp program over a period of several years. Many an undirected child has become an obsessed horse lover thanks to the chances afforded by a good summer camp.

If you are looking for a camp for yourself or for your child, don't be misled by an attractive brochure, but do a bit of research before you make a commitment to spend the one thousand dollars or more that a camp program can cost. Some camp directors, to attract business, will throw together their riding programs on a shoestring, renting horses they have never seen let alone tried, and hiring instructors they have never met let alone watched in the saddle. If you cannot visit a camp yourself to investigate the facilities and the animals, try to find someone who has been there in previous summers. Check with the American Camping Association (12 East 31st Street, New York, NY 10001), and ask for the names of riding camps in whatever area interests you; specify whether you prefer an all-girl, all-boy, or coeducational camp, and ask for the winter addresses of the camp directors. Write or call for camp information, a personal interview if possible, and follow up on at least one former camper who may live in your neck of the woods.

Tuition will vary considerably, just as the facilities will, from cheap to lavish, and you should always make sure what activities will cost extra (riding sometimes falls into that category), but don't stop asking questions when you have learned the cost. Ask the camp director if the camp owns its horses; if so you can be fairly certain that the animals are treated consistently, if not well, and that the camp cares about what animals it provides from one summer to the next. (You might also inquire about where the horses are stabled during the winter; it may be nearby so that you could take a look.) Some camps simply rent their horses from hacking stables, taking whatever shows up, and while this may not be a bad thing, it might be worth checking into the hack stable for the quality of their stock. Ask about the riding program that is offered— is riding available daily (if so, how many hours) or only once or twice a week? Is there only one instructor? Are lessons given in large groups or small ones? Is advanced instruction available or is it a basic program? Do the facilities include a real ring, a field, trails, or an indoor ring? Is stable management part of the program and, if so, is it truly a course of instruction or simply a way of getting the campers to do the counselors' work? Most camps offer at least one horse show a season (usually on parents' weekend), and some will provide other kinds of activities—overnight pack trips, day-long trail rides, jumping, barrel racing, and such. Ask about the flexibility of the program—whether the curriculum can be custom-designed for the individual camper or whether it is the same for everyone. Don't forget to ask about other camp activities, of course, as well as the types of lodging, ratio of counselors to campers, medical care, and so on.

If you are over eighteen, beyond the age of camperhood, don't despair. If you have a free summer and know something about horses and horsemanship, you may be able to get yourself a job as a counselor, if you are capable, or as a riding assistant if you have had little teaching experience. Don't tell the camp director in applying for the job anything that isn't true; the truth will come out the moment you meet your first beginner. And don't expect that such a job will be as full of fun as it is of horses. Standing in the hot sun surrounded by a group of beginners learning to post can be very tiring work, especially when their parents are expecting trophy winners by horse-show time. The responsibilities will also be immense—not only for the children but for the horses as well—and you'll have to enter into other phases of camp life, which can include everything from short-sheeted beds on nights when you least expect them to teaching table manners and cabin cleaning along with the walk, trot, and canter.

In addition to short sheets, you should also expect to supervise the care of the horses; if you don't quickly figure out how to make mucking out and cleaning tack an attractive pursuit for enthusiastic campers, you'll end up doing it all yourself. Experience in stable management, and some first-hand knowledge of horse care (including first aid), should be considered a must.

If you are intrigued by the idea of teaching at summer camp and the camps you know don't offer riding, look into the possibilities of developing a program. Before you do, however, read Molly Sivewright's *Thinking Riding* (J. A. Allen), which addresses the training of riding instructors, and Werner Habermann's *Teaching Better Riding* (J. A. Allen), which will give you a good leg up to the various problems and pleasures you are likely to encounter, as well as some invaluable advice. You should also become familiar with the ins and outs of running a horse show.

No matter how much you like kids and horses, be prepared to supply the camp director with letters of recommendation attesting to your knowledge of riding and horse care. And apply early; these summer jobs are often filled soon after Christmas.

SCHOOLS AND COLLEGES

Although public schools and colleges don't often offer riding as a form of physical education, many private institutions do. Some of them even have special programs in horse-related subjects and encourage students to take part in stable management and showing, in addition to providing riding lessons. You will probably have to pay something beyond regular tuition to join the riding program, but depending on the amount of riding you do, the cost will undoubtedly be less than the cost of boarding your own horse at the school. Private preparatory schools that specialize in riding will usually advertise their programs in horse magazines, as will private colleges, but again the best way to be sure about the quality of the facilities and of the program is to investigate the situation yourself, either in person or by inquiring of someone who has attended the place. State agricultural colleges and extensions usually offer courses in animal husbandry, and many universities offer veterinary technology and horse management as well as riding opportunities.

The Intercollegiate Horse Show Association provides a nationwide program for competition on the college level, and many thousands of students and alumni associated with more than a hundred colleges and universities participate in every level from beginner to advanced horsemanship, including hunt teams. IHSA shows take place throughout the academic year, and privately owned horses are (hooray!) ineligible. Most schools arrange with local stables to supply the mounts and the riders draw them by lot. Regional finals are held each year, followed by national finals judged by prominent riders and trainers. For information about which colleges are members, write the Intercollegiate Horse Show Association, Box 741, Hollow Road, Stony Brook, NY 11790-0741.

If you are over sixteen and looking for an intensive education in horsemanship without the usual academic setup of the college or university, you may be interested in one of the various institutions that teach only riding and horse-related subjects. These schools advertise in the horse magazines, and many of them are well worth the cost of tuition. Most of the people who attend these schools are headed in the professional direction—as trainers, stable managers, professional riders, and such—but you needn't have a specific goal in mind when you apply.

One of the largest of these schools is Meredith Manor in Waverly, West Virginia, which maintains a large stable of school horses and offers a series of courses in everything from dressage (a specialty of Kay Meredith, the noted dressage rider) and Western riding (a specialty of Ron, her husband) to horseshoeing, business, and teaching. This and other similar schools offer resident programs in various aspects of horsemanship, and a certificate or diploma from one of them will be of great value if you decide to turn professional.

If you would like to combine education with travel, you could follow in the footsteps of Michael Page, former U.S. Equestrian Team Three-Day rider, by studying abroad. As a youngster, he applied to an English school through an advertisement in a British magazine, *The Light Horse*, and spent a summer there. Eventually he went on to year-round study in Neuchatel, Switzerland, Westphalia in Germany, and finally at Saumur, the French cavalry school. Needless to say, it took a great deal of talent and perseverance—as well as money, time, and a command of two languages other than English— but if you feel qualified, there's no harm in trying to get into these schools. Write to the American Horse Shows Association (220 East 42nd Street, New York, NY 10017-5806) for the names of international federations to which you can apply for information. Or check the horse magazines for advertisements. Cross Country International and other firms that offer equestrian vacations often include excellent educational opportunities, such as driving in Scotland, dressage or cross-country training in England, and hunter-seat instruction in Ireland. (See the section on equestrian resorts below.)

CLUBS

Whether you are eight or eighty, there is probably a club that you can join to pursue your horsy interests with like-minded companions, even if you don't have a horse of your own. Some clubs are local, involving very few members and a single stable facility, while others are national with chapters or local clubs in various areas throughout the country.

The United States Pony Club, modeled after the British Pony Club, was established in 1954 "to produce a thoroughly happy comfortable horseman, riding across a natural country, with complete confidence and perfect balance on a pony equally happy and confident and free from pain or bewilderment." Children up to the age of twenty-one are eligible to join, and although membership was originally designed for pony owners, it is now possible for horseless members to lease or borrow animals, which may be either ponies *or* horses. Write to the national headquarters at 4071 Ironworks Pike, Kentucky Horse Park, Lexington, KY 40511, for the name and address of the chapter nearest you. Each chapter determines its own programs under the directorship of volunteer officers, and most provide instruction at minimum cost, as well as horse shows, lectures and demonstrations, films, and practice sessions for the various activities, which include stable management, dressage, cross-country riding, stadium jumping, drill teams, trail riding, polo, and mounted games. There is a national set of rules for each level of competition and a rating system for individual members from D, the most elementary, to A, which is so demanding that there are only a few dozen members given that designation each year. D and C levels are rated locally, but B, HA, and A involve an extensive test given by a nationally sanctioned examiner.

Pony Club competition centers around the rally that tests all levels of horsemanship, usually in teams rather than individually. These rallies include written tests, inspections, and three phases of riding, modeled on a combined-training event (dressage, cross country, and stadium jumping). Individual accomplishment is not emphasized so much as sportsmanship, teamwork, and concern for the welfare of the horse. (Howell Book House publishes the three *United States Pony Club Manuals of Horsemanship*. The second and third manuals, on intermediate and advanced riding, should hold the most interest to you.)

The 4-H Club concentrates on animal care, though not all chapters involve horses exclusively and some require that members own animals. Check with the Cooperative Extension of the U.S. Department of Agriculture in your county for the name and address of the 4-H Club nearest you, or check the Yellow Pages under "Youth Organizations." Many clubs have now relaxed the rule about ownership and can make arrangements for buying or leasing horses, dividing costs among the members. (There is no regular membership fee.) Children between ten and nineteen are eligible, and instruction in stable management, horse care, training, safety, first aid, and other aspects of horsemanship is given. Other activities may include trail rides, gymkhanas, horse shows, and field trips to breeding farms and such.

Clubs for adult riders are often a kind of disguised public stable where the idea is to keep liability to a minimum. A group of horse owners may decide to pool their resources and run a cooperative stable to house their horses, sharing maintenance as well as initial costs. They will, if the facilities are large enough to warrant it, also hire a stable manager and a trainer to work with the horses, give lessons to members, and scout for likely show prospects. Such a club obviously has its advantages for horse owners, since it is unlikely that members will sue their own clubs (i.e., themselves) in case of an accident, but a club can also have a great deal to offer the horseless rider if the club committee is willing. The usual arrangement is for a new member to pay an initiation fee or buy a bond in order to join and then to pay a certain amount in dues or expenses for lessons or rides. If the club officials do not permit non-owners, it might be possible to become a co-owner of a horse, sharing expenses with a willing owner for the privilege of becoming a member (see the last chapter for a discussion of co-ownership and leasing arrangements). These clubs may be large enough to support regular horse shows, and many will also offer other activities, such as lectures, films, and clinics given by visiting experts. If you don't know any clubs, you can find them by watching for horse-show announcements, asking at tack shops, and following the usual stable-finding route. Once you get a name and address, you can simply call for information or drop in to talk with the stable manager.

Another sort of adult club that may be attractive to working folks with limited time is an organization formed under the aegis of the company for which one toils. Many businesses with large numbers of employees are located in suburban areas, some of them having fled the high-tax, high-rent, high-rise, and low-horse cities for the relative comfort of the countryside nearby. Such companies often support clubs for tennis and golf, and I know of at least one corporation on Long Island that has recently begun a riding club. At this particular firm, the management put up a small initial sum to help advertise the inauguration of the group, and when enough employees signed up, one of the horsy members of the staff approached a friend at a nearby stable, proposing two weekly series of ten group lessons, one for beginners and one for more advanced riders. Because the stable manager was guaranteed a set number of riders for a specific period of time with cash in hand for the first five lessons in each series and the balance payable before the next five, he was willing to make a special arrangement with his instructors and school horses. Any rider who decided not to continue could drop out with a refund after one or two lessons, but drop-outs were minimal and enthusiasm was very high. Although that program is still in its infancy, it shows all signs of increasing its members the next time around, and many adults who had never had the impetus to ride seriously became thoroughly hooked.

EQUESTRIAN RESORTS AND DUDE RANCHES

Although most of these establishments are not designed for regular weekly riding, they can be a wonderful experience for the horseless rider on vacation or escaping for the weekend. Here, too, the facilities and opportunities run the gamut from simple one-horse affairs to vast equestrian centers where the instruction is first rate and the horses highly schooled. Room and board are provided along with other vacation activities, such as swimming, and costs will vary according to the programs and facilities. Some are family-style affairs where meals are served at specific hours with little variation in the menu but a good deal of camaraderie at the table and in the barn, where guests can enter into all phases of farm or stable life. Others are elegant places with formal programs of instruction and special activities, room and laundry service, and restaurantlike dining rooms. And most are just resorts where riding is offered as an attraction, like golf, tennis, swimming, and the rest.

Before you go to any resort, you should check as you make your reservations just how much time you will be able to spend riding or around the horses and just what the level of instruction (if any) will be. I know of several people who have been disappointed by too little riding or too elementary a program, although some were able to convince the management to give them special treatment. Riding centers that specialize in instruction and high-level activities such as hunting, eventing, and such will require skill and experience; this can be very satisfying indeed for advanced riders but rather terrifying or at least demoralizing for beginners who arrive unprepared. And dude ranches that cater to people who have never ridden bend over backward to provide a safe, slow trail ride on quiet animals that would quickly frustrate anyone beyond the beginner level. Be frank and honest over the telephone about your experience and judge the place by their response to your questions. Ask, too, if you will need to take any special apparel or equipment and whether extra charges will be required for any activity. Club Med, for instance, offers intensive riding programs at some of their facilities, and if you are lucky, the quality of the horses and the instruction can be quite good.

The cost is generally extra, over and above the usual swimming and tennis activities, but for the rider who wants to indulge daily while the others are snorkeling, the expense can be well worth it.

If you really want to spend your vacation learning, be prepared for work as well as pleasure. A friend of mine had the great privilege of being able to visit Saumur and looked forward eagerly to enjoying the delicious meals and wines along with the fine-blooded horses in the beautiful stables. He relished the idea of hacking through the lovely landscape of field and forest surrounding the chateau and picking up a few tips from one of the resident cavalry instructors. It turned out, however, that his equestrian ability was found wanting by the instructor to whom he was assigned, and he spent his first forty minutes in the saddle practicing the sitting trot. By the time he finally got back to the chateau, he was far too tired and sore to drink in all the beauties, to say nothing of the wine.

A comparable experience in a stock saddle might be had by signing on as a cowhand for an authentic cattle drive, which involves a week of hard riding through Wyoming as you move cattle to winter pasture and a few days spent roping, branding, and such. For information, write High Island Ranch & Cattle Company, Hamilton Dome, WY. Champion Cowboy Experience in Ardmore, California will teach you cowboy skills (including singing and dressing) with some competition thrown in for the best team and for individual riders. *Horseback Adventures* (Howell Book House) provides detailed information on all kinds of vacations involving horses.

If you simply want to relax, however, by taking comfortable and undemanding trail rides through the countryside, there are plenty of fine places that offer same—both here and abroad. Check your local tack shop for travel brochures or your horse magazines for advertisements and other sources for information about resorts, dude ranches, pack trips, and other types of equestrian vacations. Most of our national parks have public riding stables nearby or on the premises, and there are many organizations throughout the world that specialize in holidays on horseback, some involving overnight pack trips or week-long treks into wilderness areas led by experienced guides. Most of these trips take place in the West or Midwest, but there are wonderful opportunities in Canada, Mexico, Spain, Norway, Hungary, and other countries as well.

Pony-trekking is a specialty of the British Isles; if you prefer an English saddle you may find marvelous trekking trips in the eastern United States (especially Vermont and New Hampshire), as well as in England, Ireland, and Scotland. These do not usually involve camping out but offer overnight accommodations in homes or country inns along the way. Equestrian travel agents offer wonderful trips of this kind. Write to Hoofbeats International Inc. at 162 Cambridge Avenue, Englewood, NJ 07631; FITS Equestrian at 685 Lateen Road, Solvang, CA 93463; Cross Country International, P.O. Box 1170, Millbrook, NY 12545; and Equitour, P.O. Box 807, Dubois, WY 82513.

Tourist associations or visitor bureaus in most states can provide you with information about equestrian opportunities in this country, and tourist boards in different countries will be able to supply similar details for those interested in foreign travel. Your travel agent may be able to steer you in the right direction, if you explain that you want your tour to include not only a bit of riding but also trips to breeding farms, famous schools, and so on. Even if you don't plan to ride, your interest in horses should certainly lead you to attractions such as the Spanish Riding School in Vienna or major international horse shows and games on horseback. You may need tickets to these events, but the tourist bureaus in the nations you visit will be able to arrange matters for you.

If you are not the organized type and have difficulty planning ahead, do what most horseless riders (like myself) do: Stay alert to all possibilities and take advantage of them when you can. A couple of years ago, a sightseeing trip through the American Southwest was made even more memorable by seeing Monument Valley at sunrise from the back of a Navajo pony and riding down Bryce Canyon on muleback (which amazingly eliminated my fear of heights, presumably because four feet are better than two and I could look around without worrying about stepping off the edge). On a recent trip to India, in the region of Udaipur, I noticed a young man showing off his pinto horse to a group of tourists. I admired the animal and before I knew it, I surprised even myself by asking if I could ride. My guide quickly fixed a price (about a dollar in American money) before the young man could change his mind, and within minutes I was pacing along a Rajastani road with a lively group of horsemen on the back of a Marwari, the proud descendant of a Rajput cavalry horse.

THE HORSELESS RIDER ON VACATION

Over the years I have learned never to leave home without stowing my boots, breeches, hard hat, and crop in the back of my car, even if I have no particular plans to ride. Whether I am heading for the seashore or to a friend's house for the weekend, I have been surprised too often in the past by a sudden offer of an afternoon on horseback to be caught with my boots off. Even on a business trip to another city, I stick my rubber (i.e., lightweight) boots and breeches in my suitcase, just in case I find myself with a free afternoon to sample the local hacking stable. You may be horseless, but you don't have to be bootless!

STABLE ANALYSIS

Although it hardly seems worth the effort to analyze a stable if all you're investing in is an hour's ride, a quick look around the place to size it up can make the difference between an enjoyable ride and an indifferent or poor one. Even if a stable is the only one in town, your decision about *how* to approach it rather than whether to approach it at all can influence your rides there, since the first is not likely to be the last if it is a good one. Even if the ride or the horse or the stable is lacking in some important way, you might be able to do something to improve the situation your next time out.

Handsome is as handsome does, and the attractiveness of a stable is only important if it is supported by an efficient management. Beautiful rolling pastures and spanking clean stalls with polished brass nameplates are lovely to look at but not altogether necessary. I know of several good stables where the paddocks are relatively small and the barns are in need of paint, and yet the horses are turned out regularly and the stalls are cleaned thoroughly each morning. What a stable may lack in terms of money for property and superficial improvements it may spend wisely on knowledgeable help, a good management program, and decent horses. When you tour your prospective stable, look for the following:

1. A well-lighted barn with sizeable stalls (straight or box) that are sturdily built and safe, with no visible hazards, such as broken glass, protruding nails or boards, and pitchforks lying about.

2. A staff of grooms or stable people—at least one to every ten horses—who are working at something as you pass by, whether it be mucking out, grooming, feeding, cleaning tack, or anything horse-related.

3. An array of tack in good repair. The saddles don't have to be expensive but they should be well made and well fitting (to the horse if not to the rider). Before you mount your steed, look under the saddle's skirt to make sure that the girth or cinch is whole and that the billets are securely fastened to the saddle. The saddle pad should be clean and not stiff with caked-on dirt or dried sweat. Check the stirrup leathers as well. Signs of repair aren't necessarily bad, but the repairs should have been done well, not with baling twine or pieces of wire. Check the bridle, too, to make sure that there aren't pieces of leather about to break, especially on the reins.

4. A collection of horses standing in stalls with relatively fresh bedding underfoot, good ventilation, and buckets of water available. If the animals are in straight stalls, they should be tied by a lead rope attached to the halter, not by the reins. If they are tacked up, the girths or cinches should be loose. If you notice that your eyes are watering from the stench, you will probably notice that the horses are suffering too. Point this out to the stable manager, and if he or she reacts angrily, don't ride there but report the situation to your local humane society.

5. Notice whether the horses themselves appear to be in good condition—groomed and generally healthy looking. Saddle sores, a sign of ill-fitting tack, should not be in evidence, but if sores exist, they should be obviously medicated or somehow protected if the horse is to be ridden. Overgrown hooves, loose or missing shoes, untreated open sores or cuts, and general filth are signs of neglect and poor management. Don't leap to conclusions if you see some ribs showing or a few small scars here and there, but if the horses are in obvious distress because of poor treatment, report the situation to authorities.

6. The stable manager or an assistant should be present to supervise the renting procedure and be available for any questions, which ought to be answered with some degree of care. The manager of a stable is a busy person and does not always have the time to spend on what he or she considers minor details, but you should be able to get some satisfaction from the person in charge—especially where it concerns your own ride. If no one on the staff takes the time to see that you are properly mounted on a horse you can handle, beware.

7. Are there signs posted in the stable about safety? "No Smoking" signs are critically important, as are warnings about riding too fast or recklessly or bringing a "hot" horse back to the barn, regulations about footwear and headgear, and so on.

8. Look around at the people who are riding at the stable. Are they properly dressed? Ask one or two people who look like regulars how long they have ridden at this stable and how they like it. You can also ask about the horses and which ones are the favorites. Remember always that someone's favorite may be another person's runaway, but it's always good to know—if you have the choice—which are the problem animals and which ones will give a pleasant, safe ride.

9. One sign of a good stable is the questioning process the management gives the prospective rider. Are you asked to sign a release? Do they write down your address (in case of accident)? Your experience? If so, the management is probably right-minded. If you are asked to perform an evaluation test, be grateful rather than insulted.

10. Does the manager insist on a guide for trail rides? If you are new to the stable, you will not know the trails, so this is a sensible rule from your point of view, but it is also a necessary safety precaution on the part of the stable owner who has never seen you ride before.

11. Do the people on the stable's staff seem to know how to handle the horses they are caring for? Don't confuse firm handling with abuse if you see someone swat a horse's rump to get him to move, but be alert to abuses such as yanking on reins to lead a horse, hitting a horse unnecessarily, or letting a horse stand in the sun for an extended period of time without any water and laden with tack as he awaits the next rider.

These questions are the essential eleven, but there may be others that will come to your mind as you look around the stable. If you have made a reservation for a ride at a certain hour, be sure to arrive early to give yourself a chance to take this all-important tour. If you are not pleased by what you see, you can always cancel the appointment. If you are not allowed to walk around the stable, find out why. If it's a question of convenience to the staff that is busily readying the horses, ask if you may look around on your own, assuring them that you will not get in the way. If that request, reasonably tendered, is refused, you may have to limit your analysis to what you can see as you wait for your horse. On one occasion—at a truly awful city stable where we suspected ill management—my husband and I were rudely refused permission to see the stalls where the hack horses were kept. Happily, the soda machine was near the stable door, and we were able to take a look while innocently finishing our drinks near the machine. A stable hand did try to shoo us away from the door, but we managed to get a good look at what were intolerable conditions for horse or human. In this case, the real tip-off was the attitude of the stable manager.

If you are visiting a private stable—especially if it's just a barn with a horse in it—you will undoubtedly have a better chance to look around, but the investigation will be much different, if indeed you can make one at all in any obvious sense, especially if the ride is going to be a free one on a friend's horse. Pointing out broken tack or a messy stall would most definitely not be a polite response to the offer of a free ride, but you can couch those observations in an offer to muck out a stall or get the rein repaired yourself. That way the owner will be aware of the problem and might even thank you for pointing it out. Even if you end up with the responsibility of following through, you'll at least have the satisfaction of knowing that a wrong has been righted and that you'll always be welcome in this particular stable.

The old saying "Don't look a gift horse in the mouth" (which was referring to the animal's age and the fact that a free horse, regardless of age, was a bargain) does apply to some extent in accepting a free ride. If the stable where the gift horse is kept looks pretty shabby and the horse looks out of condition and poorly cared for, you would probably not enjoy yourself much, no matter how enthusiastic your friend is about getting you to ride. But casual appearances can be deceiving. I remember going once to a stable on the recommendation of the owner of a small hotel in an unfamiliar town and being allowed to make myself at home without any supervision. The owner's son, who was busily raking the lawn, said "Sure, you can ride. Just take a bucket of oats up to that pasture there and catch the first horse who comes to you. The saddles and stuff are in the barn."

Luckily for both me and the horse, I knew enough at that point to ask the kid what the horses' names were so that I could match the right saddle and bridle to the right horse. And I knew enough to groom the horse, pick out its hooves, and put the tack in the proper places before heading off into the woods for what turned into a delightful afternoon. Most owners aren't quite so cavalier about their animals, but if they are, you are obligated to be even more responsible about using the animals than you would be riding under the owner's nose.

On another occasion, a woman whose daughter was away at college was delighted to let me exercise the horse that had been virtually abandoned in the backyard. Before I could ride, I had to repair the neglected bridle, and during the ride, I noticed that the horse was breathing very heavily even after a slow trot. My husband, a veterinarian, watched the animal move and, taking the horse's lack of conditioning into account, was able to diagnose a case of emphysema (or heaves). Luckily for the horse this time, we managed to convince the woman to put the horse on medication and to change his diet of hay to a dust-free pelleted feed that would not aggravate his already stressed lungs.

After you have looked over the prospective stable and made your analysis of the management, the general condition of the building, the horses, and the equipment, you should look a little beyond the stable itself to see what kind of facilities there are for riding. Is there a ring in which you can school a horse, warm it up before a trail ride, or get the kinks out, as the case may be? Is the ring large enough for several people to use at once without getting on each other's nerves—or tails? If there is a lesson program, will individual riders not taking lessons be able to use the ring? Is there an indoor ring that can be used in the winter, at night, and on rainy days? Is it lighted or heated? (One indoor ring I knew was constructed like a plastic bubble, and while it was light, it also was extremely cold on winter days—at least ten degrees below the outside temperature. Another ring, a temporary tent affair, flapped so much in the wind that nervous horses shied at every corner.) If there is no ring at all, is there an area near the stable that can be used as an improvised ring—a level, relatively large piece of ground with good solid footing?

If the stable specializes in trail riding, are there several trails or only one? Are those trails relatively open or are they narrow and overhung with trees? Have woodchuck holes, rocky areas, and other potential dangers been spotted and marked? Are there parts of the trail that come close to or cross highways or paved roads? Have large branches been trimmed so that they don't interfere with the horses and riders? One stable I know in New York City is adjacent to a lovely park, but unfortunately the park is filled with abandoned cars and the occasional mugger who awaits the unsuspecting single rider. Another city stable rents horses for riding in Central Park, which has some very nice old trails where riders must share the space with joggers, baby carriages, and kids on bikes, to say nothing of people who enjoy frightening horses by throwing rocks or jumping into the path unexpectedly. These urban hazards may not bother the experienced urban horse, but the rider should be prepared for sudden fits and starts. Riding in company is always better in these cases than riding alone.

If there are several trails and the stable does not offer a guide, is there a map you can use to make sure you don't get lost and that you can get your horse back on time? Are there jumps set up along the trail, and will you have permission to take them? If you don't want to jump, are there paths around the obstacles so that you'll have a choice?

Private stables may well have training rings, fields with hunt courses set up, or lovely trails around the property, but in suburban areas a backyard horse setup may involve riding across property belonging to other people. Before you set off on your borrowed horse, make sure that you find out where you will be allowed to ride and which areas are off-limits. People who do not own horses may not appreciate hoofprints in their backyards or across their newly seeded fields and gardens, and you may do yourself and other horsemen a disservice by disobeying the rules of polite conduct by riding there without permission. In many communities horse owners have formed associations to protect and maintain riding trails— not only clearing away fallen trees but also negotiating with landowners and politicians who may have the power to block access to trail systems. Membership in these organzations is sometimes required of riders, whether or not they own horses, but they can provide the horseless with useful contacts and enjoyable horse-related activities. (See Chapter 6 for the etiquette of trail riding.)

5

THE HORSE

THE RIDER WHO approaches a stable for a ride, whether or not a fee is involved, may not have any chance to select the animal that is going to be his or hers. Public stables worth patronizing will probably select the horse for you based on your experience (or on what you tell them and what they can tell of you), and a free ride on a private horse is probably offered for that animal alone. Although an instructor may allow a pupil to pick a favorite mount, most teachers will assign horses according to what they are attempting to teach. Nevertheless, there is some element of choice involved on the rider's part, even if it's to change horses in midstream or not to ride at all. In other words, analyzing the stable is not the whole story in deciding whether or not you want to ride (or be taken for a ride, as the case may be). The horse needs some analyzing, too, before you put your feet into the stirrups, as well as a special on-the-ground approach.

SELECTING A HACK

Most horse books start off with a chapter called "Selecting a Horse" covering the fine points of breed, conformation, color, and so on. None of these aspects of horse selection, practically speaking, will matter to the horseless rider, but there are a few points worth noting. Whether you are offered one of those members in poor standing of the equine set—the hack or school horse—or a carefully tended private horse, which can be anything from a sour pony to a grandson of Secretariat, keep your eyes and your mouth open. In other words, look carefully at the horse and ask a lot of questions.

The horseless rider's choice: a sleepy "plug," an under-exercised, overexcited nag, and a calm, well-mannered animal.

BREED

Generally speaking, the average public-stable horse is a grade horse, the equine equivalent of a mutt, where experience and past history are more important than pedigree. A private horse, on the other hand, is likely to be a better sort of animal, perhaps a purebred with papers, perhaps not, but undoubtedly the object of better care, which can make him a superb performer, a spoiled brat, or something in-between. Exceptions to this general rule abound, of course, for I have found many public stables with one or two fine purebreds in the wings for advanced riders, and I have known any number of private mongrels, if you will. But the public purebreds are usually long in the tooth, with their best years behind them, while the private grades can run the gamut from sassy youngsters to wise old dobbins. Nevertheless, if you are offered a purebred to ride, you should approach it in a somewhat different manner than you would a grade or a crossbred. Finely bred animals will have certain characteristics of their breed and may require relatively delicate handling on the part of the rider.

A Thoroughbred may (or may not) have been bred for the track, and he is likely to be high-spirited and fast, given his head (which is not a good idea). An American Saddlebred Horse or Tennessee Walking Horse is likely to be highly animated in gait though comfortable to ride, if one knows how to handle him. A Morgan will probably also be animated, especially if he has been park-trained, although he is also capable of excellent performance on the trail and behind a carriage. A Standardbred, or trotting/pacing horse, may be uncomfortable to ride, although I know of several that were excellent trail horses. A Quarter Horse is an equine for all seasons—wonderful on the trail, superb as a reining or cutting horse, and capable of winning ribbons as a hunter or jumper. But in many specimens of that breed, there is more than a hint of Thoroughbred, and you can't assume anymore that a Quarter Horse is just a cowpony. Arabs are Arabs, trained in many different ways—as dressage horses, as hunters, as park horses, and as contributors to most other light-horse breeds—and any purebred Arab is likely to be a handful. Finely bred European warmbloods, such as the Trakhener and Hanoverian, most often used for dressage and driving, have become popular in the United States as jumpers, and Appaloosas, the spotted horses of the Nez Percé Indians, are seen all over the place these days doing well at any number of equine duties. Ponies come in all shapes and sizes, of course, so long as the size doesn't go over fourteen and a half hands (fifty-eight inches from ground to withers), and each one of them has a different attitude toward life and people, usually spiced with insubordination.

Crossbreds, where the breeding has been planned for particular reasons, may be treated like purebreds in that they will have certain identifiable, built-in traits. The Irish hunter, for example, is a cross between a Thoroughbred—full of speed and athletic ability—and a heavier, almost draft-horse type—full of the strength so necessary to carry big riders over treacherous ditches and uneven terrain.

Grade horses may show some breed traits, and since most of them are raised in the West, the Quarter Horse is probably the dominant contributor to their genetic makeup. But for the most part, they are the mutts of the horse world—and while that may mean "low class" in the social department, it also means unique and adaptable in practical terms, to be judged on the basis of experience and personality rather than looks or innate characteristics.

SEX

Unless you are at a breeding farm, sex isn't a subject that usually rears its interesting head around a riding stable. Most hack horses are geldings (castrated males), which tend to be steadier in temperament than mares or stallions, which often have each other on their minds rather than the business of obeying human commands. I once had my ankle broken by a mare who was in heat and so frustrated with the gelding I was riding that she kicked out at him and got me instead. Many experts feel that mares are more sensitive than geldings and make wonderful competition horses for that reason, but even they will admit that a mare in heat just before an important event can be a disadvantage to the rider. I have ridden many mares as school horses and in private barns, and I would agree that they are more alert and perhaps even smarter than the average grade gelding, but if you want to be sure of a relatively safe ride, a gelding is your best bet. They aren't all angels, of course, since a bad experience can make a rogue out of any horse, regardless of sex, but they are far more predictable than mares and far less complicated than stallions, who should probably not be handled except by expert riders who know them well.

CONFORMATION

According to one stable manager I talked with, the only point of conformation or horse anatomy worth noting by the horseless rider is that a horse have four sound legs. And it's true that the rider setting out for a short ride needn't concern him- or herself with the horse's appearance unless there are a lot of obvious faults. Roman noses are traditionally worn by stubborn horses, and high-withered equines won't be very comfortable to ride bareback, but beyond this, the average horse needn't be looked at too closely if you're not planning to invest in his future after your hour is up. Very short or tall people may want to ride relatively short or tall horses, and heavyset men should obviously aim toward heavyset horses capable of carrying them out of sight of the barn. But most riders of average size should be able to deal with average-sized equines, whether they are fifteen hands or seventeen. On the other hand, signs of illness or previous injury that may result in a bad ride should be observed and noted, even by the occasional rider. Saddle sores should be treated and protective padding used under the saddle; a horse that breathes heavily after only a little exertion should not be worked very hard, if at all; a horse with a very shabby coat, an oversized belly, and a listless disposition may be infested with internal parasites (worms) and may not be strong enough to manage anything more than a gentle walk-trot session. Any symptom of lameness should be checked immediately, and if no obvious cause is present (such as a loose shoe or a stone imbedded in the hoof or frog) and if the lameness doesn't work itself out within three or four minutes of walking, the horse should be led, not ridden, back to the barn. (I admit to knowing one hack horse who was clever enough to invent a lame foreleg every time he felt a saddle touching his back; the threat of being sent back to the dealer's managed somehow to cure him, though we still can't figure out how he knew.)

You don't have to read a veterinary manual or insist on a veterinarian's presence before you ride, but you should make a point of watching normal horses at work so that anything unusual in a horse's appearance or gait is obvious to you at a glance. If you do notice something amiss—or if the animal is wearing what seems to you an unusual assortment of boots and bandages on his legs—ask the owner or manager about his condition and follow their instructions about using him (or not). Some busy stable managers may miss slight problems, and they will (or should) be grateful to you for noticing or taking the trouble to care. If the management doesn't seem to care as much as you do and brushes you off with an unsatisfactory explanation, you should—if you are certain that the horse is suffering pain—report the case to your local humane society. But don't jump to conclusions unless you are sure; be persistent enough to check the situation with the groom who tends the horse and to have an expert horseman confirm your findings.

COLOR (IN MORE WAYS THAN ONE)

People in the market for a horse often have preferences about a horse's color ("I just have to get a chestnut, Mom, because it will go so nicely with my new jodhpurs" and stuff like that). Except for a few genetic experts who have determined that some colors are dominant traits in certain breeds, and accounting for the fact that some public-stable operators tend to avoid white horses (because the dirt shows more readily), almost everyone would agree that color is only skin deep. For the purposes of a rider looking for a comfortable, pleasant ride, the only color that matters to the horseless rider is green. An inexperienced (green) horse will probably know less about the fine art of equitation than you will, and if you are a beginner, you should avoid that animal. Most experts agree that the best horse on which to learn the basics is one that knows more than the rider, and a well-mannered, well-schooled horse is a treasure to any instructor. Some friends of mine, green as grass but enthusiastic as they come, bought a seven-year-old Morgan gelding right out of the show ring and soon realized that they had to take a few lessons to catch up with the horse. Once they learned about collection, extension, and leg yields, their appreciation for the horse grew with every ride. (The nice part of this story, actually, is that they were able to teach King about trail riding, for he was accustomed to travel only on well-combed paths, preferably in the shape of a ring. He ignorantly plowed through the brush, stumbling over rocks and being frightened by deer until my friends gave him sufficient exposure to the horrors of the wilderness. At last report, he was still teaching and being taught.)

If you are about to take a lesson or be led out on the trail by a guide, you needn't worry too much about getting into trouble, since you will be under supervision, and, if you are at

a good place, you will have been given a horse whose manners and habits are well known to the person in charge. If you
are going out on your own, however, you should try to find
out as much about the horse's past history as possible before
getting into the saddle.

Some useful questions to ask are:

- Has this horse been trained in any special way—to a saddle or park seat, a hunt or forward seat, a stock seat, or
  dressage? Knowing how a horse has been trained will affect
  how you sit in the saddle, use the reins, and apply cues for
  different gaits (see Chapter 2). The tack may be a giveaway
  here, since a horse that comes with a stock saddle will
  probably respond to neck reining while a horse in a double
  bridle will not, but you can't always be sure. Some horses
  in Western tack will do better if you keep contact with the
  bit rather than hold the reins loose, and one Morgan I
  know always wears a forward-seat saddle yet must be
  ridden as a park horse.

- Does the horse go best with light contact on the reins,
  strong hands, or a loose rein? (Remember that some horses
  speed up with a tight rein and slow down with a loose
  rein.)

- Does the horse have any bad habits, such as kicking,
  shying, bolting, wheeling, rolling into puddles and ponds,
  and so on? If so, you'll have to keep clear of other horses,
  avoid or be prepared for scary spots, keep a good firm
  hand and leg on the animal, and otherwise stay alert to
  trouble.

- Does the horse have any special phobias? Some horses are
  afraid of dogs, of certain spots along the trail, of crossing
  bridges or going under them, of walking through water,
  or of horses that come too close behind or get ahead of
  them. Some even have special aversions to one or two
  stablemates. I once spent a delightful summer schooling a
  pony at a zoo and found, to my surprise, that he shied
  away from one particular corner in the camel-riding ring
  that we used. It turned out that this pony had a real terror
  of elephants (not camels) and that this corner abutted the
  elephant house. We soon taught him to treat that corner
  like any other, but riding in parades was never a real
  pleasure unless we could get a camel between us and the

elephants to give zoogoers the impression that domesticated animals were easier to handle than wild ones!

- Does the horse have the habit of eating grass or leafy branches along the trail? This isn't a particularly serious fault, although I've known several people who have been pulled right out of the saddle because of piggy horse behavior. It's always best to be prepared to keep a firm rein if you are going through succulent-looking farm country.

- In jumping, does the horse tend to run out, stop, or jump willingly? Even if you know that a horse has been jumped, don't try it on the trail the first time out unless you are in company with an experienced rider. I remember once trying to leap a log on an old grade gelding only to find that the experience triggered in him some old memory about chasing something or other, and off we went. Another time I tried to get a healthy, otherwise willing cowpony over a small fence between pastures only to find that he had been trained never to cross such a barrier. After one spill, a lot of soothing encouragement on my part, and a number of cuss words, I gave up and we went off in search of an open pathway.

- Is the horse a "barn rat"—reluctant to leave the barn alone and determined to race back to it the moment he is turned in the direction of home? Such a horse needs reschooling to break the habit, but for the occasional rider, one needs a firm sense of determination (and perhaps another horse and rider) on the way out and a firm grip on the reins on the way in. I've known horses who could put on a tremendous act of exhaustion until they were headed homeward, at which point they would suddenly develop a whole new interest in life and a new spring to their step. (This, incidentally, is not altogether a bad fault if you are riding an unfamiliar trail; chances are that the horse will be able to find his way home even though you are convinced that the two of you are completely lost.)

If the answers to all of these questions lead you to believe that you're about to board the worst-mannered, least agreeable animal in the world, or even if they make you a bit apprehensive, don't fret. And try not to let your apprehension show, because you will risk transmitting some nervousness to the horse, making disobedience likely. If you know that a horse has a habit or two that may show up during a ride, you will always be in a better position (literally) to prevent it if you are prepared, or to deal with it if you get into an unavoidable situation. Sometimes such questions cannot be answered, either because there is no one around to do so or because there isn't time. One friend of mine, while visiting a farm in Ireland, had the good fortune to be there when the pack of hounds, which was being shown off to him, caught a scent and began racing off to follow it. The owner and his staff quickly saddled up a few of the horses for their visitors and our friend was led up to a mare he had never seen before. "Anything I should know?" he nervously asked the groom who was giving him a leg up. "She'll take care of you" came the reply and off they went. It soon became apparent that the mare knew much more about the whole business than our friend, and she carried him safely for an hour's gallop (or so it seemed) over terrain that she knew as well as her own paddock, over ditches and hedges that were four times as imposing as the crossrails he was used to at home. All he had to do was stick to the saddle, keep his balance, grab a handful of mane, and let her do her thing with as little interference as possible. After the experience, he breathlessly admitted that he had never before felt more exhilarated and more terrified at the same time.

With the average hack horse, naturally, you can't always consider yourself on such a capable, willing animal. But don't underestimate the ability of any horse, especially a hack horse. Some people maintain that horses aren't even as intelligent as pigs, but hack horses are as smart as you are—and with good reason. All those jabs in the mouth—inadvertent or not—from riders of every shape and ability (or lack of it) haven't gone unnoticed, and such a horse invariably picks up a whole array of tricks to avoid getting hurt. Throwing the head up or lowering it to evade the bit, grabbing the bit in the teeth to get control of the situation, and keeping a stiff neck or a rubbery one to avoid bit pressure are only a few. Some horses when they anticipate abusive treatment will bolt off at the first chance, taking a buck as they go to put the rider off balance, and others will just not go at all—or at least not at any perceptible speed. A few horses I've met will do just as they please, disobeying commands as rapidly as they are given. It isn't only a mule that is stubborn, and it isn't only an elephant that remembers. A hack horse who doesn't want to do something can be pretty determined not to do it, and once he gets away with something (which is usually the case with novice riders), he'll remember that for a long time and get away with it until an expert gets hold of him.

But the approach to take with these animals is not anger or rough handling. Respect the horse and try to figure out why he is that way. Disobeyed commands may be the result of many confused hours suffering at the hands and legs of riders who pull and push at the same time. Bolting off into the blue may have become a habit of the horse who has had more than one two-hundred-pound rider plunk himself unceremoniously into the saddle. Such horses deserve reschooling as well as respect, but if you are only aboard for an hour, you can count on getting a pretty good lesson, even if there isn't an instructor in sight.

I remember one particular animal, a rather fine mare who had a considerable knowledge of dressage movements and a pronounced dislike of people who sat too far forward. She had had a sore on her withers a few years before I rode her and never forgot the pain, even though the injury had healed long ago. My instructor had not been able to convince me in words that leaning forward was a bad habit of mine, but one short hour on this mare cured me forever. Every time my center of balance got ahead of hers, she would stop short and back up until I got into the proper position. Believe me, one hour of backing around a ring when all the other riders were going forward was a very embarrassing experience, though a pretty effective forward step in my education!

Another horse I remember had a real hatred of heels in his side, especially on the near (left) side, I suppose as a result of a spur-dragging rider in his past. My instructor used Arizona to teach her pupils to rely on calf pressure rather than heels and to keep their lower legs from flopping around in the stirrups. That lesson I spent going sideways in a series of side passes that would have done a Lipizzaner proud, except that I had never given a deliberate cue for that particular dressage movement and quickly learned to be aware of the position of my feet.

Some hack or school horses aren't nearly as predictable, however, and that's because they are subjected to many different riders. One horse whose name (Sneakers) will remain permanently engraved on my mind (and knee) was an honest

if not talented jumper whom I used to ride regularly in weekly
lessons. One session, however, he started running out to the
right at every fence and eventually sent me careening in a
rather spectacular fall that wrenched my knee. Obviously
someone had "taught" him in a previous hour how to drop
his right shoulder and wheel to the side by letting him get
away with the trick once and then again, so that by the third
time the running out had become a pattern. The horse was
successfully reschooled by my patient instructor and a more
severe bit, but *I* learned a lesson, too, which was never to take
a school horse for granted.

Private horses also have their special habits—and though
they may not be sour from years of poor or ignorant riders,
they are perhaps even more of a challenge for the first-time
rider, especially if they have become accustomed to one particular person in the saddle. It seems as though they act like
school kids with a substitute teacher and try to make as much
trouble as possible just to see what they can get away with. It
is more likely, however, that the unfamiliar rider has aroused
their suspicions just because he or she is unfamiliar. Obviously one must ask the owner or regular rider for any tips,
but even so the horse should be approached with special care
and no rough handling, if only because giving a private horse
bad habits or a bad experience will soon make you a *persona
non grata* around that stable. Sometimes the owner may not
even be aware that there is a problem. A horse owned by a
friend of mine always—without fail—broke into a canter at
one point in the trail near her house, and simply wouldn't
stay at a walk, no matter what I did. It turned out that this
spot on the trail was the first safe place to canter and that my
friend invariably asked for a canter at that point. It wasn't
until she saw me having such trouble with her suddenly headstrong horse that she realized how well the horse had trained
her. (Reschooling the horse, incidentally, was not too difficult: we simply took a different route away from the barn and
after a half hour of good exercise tried the usual trail. By this
time the horse had gotten the kinks out and was agreeable to
walking past the critical spot. A few days of this, first walking
and then trotting, was sufficient to keep the horse under control and responsive to deliberate cues rather than automatic
reactions.)

Generally speaking, private horses tend to be more athletic and willing than hacks, needing less of a strong hand

and more of a delicate contact with the mouth, less of a strong leg and more of a secure, balanced seat. If a horse has been trained to specific cues, you should know this before you start out (or you may not be able to stop); if a horse should be ridden on a loose rein rather than with constant bit contact, unless you know this you may find yourself on an animal that will resist every cue you give, running ahead when you think you are asking for a slower gait or a halt. The under-exercised private horse can also be full of high spirits that feel a lot like bad manners if those spirits involve bucking or heading off for the hills. Horses that haven't had regular exercise, however, shouldn't be worked hard until they are conditioned sufficiently to handle it. Make your first few rides short and easy, gradually building up the length of the ride and the amount of exertion until the horse is fit.

APPROACHING THE HORSE

All of this talk about breed, sex, conformation, and experience covers only part of your analysis of the animal you are about to mount. Obviously, if you are presented with a feisty little Arab stallion, complete with a lame foreleg and a decidedly green color, you would be advised to say "No, thanks." And if someone leads out an experienced, well-seasoned Quarter Horse or grade gelding who knows his way around, you should probably feel privileged at the chance to ride him. Your choice won't, of course, be quite so dramatic, but you should be able to get some impression of a horse's way of going long before you mount up by taking a good, hard look before you make a commitment and by asking some of those penetrating questions if you have a chance to do so.

If the horse presented to you looks like a handful that you're not prepared to handle or confident enough about, you are perfectly within your rights to refuse. Busy stable managers with only a limited number of horses at their disposal may object or refuse your request for a substitution, claiming that they don't have any other animal to offer. This may be true, and you may not be able to ride, but if you feel insecure enough to make the request, you'll be better off not riding at all than risking a bad experience. Most stable managers—like headwaiters at busy restaurants—can usually come up with a suitable alternative, however, and it is their obligation by law to provide just that. Although stable signs may insist that the renter agrees to ride at his or her own risk, the management is liable if it puts anyone who requests a "quiet, safe horse" on one that is neither quiet nor safe. (See the section on "Legal Considerations" in Chapter 6.) Since public stables tend to cater to a clientele that has never set foot in a stirrup, their barns are (or should be) full of horses that are accustomed to novices, and chances are that you will be able to find yourself a suitable mount.

Now you have reached the moment you've been waiting for. You have studied the stable and found it and its instructor acceptable; you have studied the horse and found him rideable. But before you get into the saddle, take another moment or two on the ground and forget the generalities you've just read. Look the horse in the eye and let him know right from the start that you are fully prepared for whatever lies in store. At this point, self-confidence (even if you feel none) is more important than the fit of your boots. For during the time that you've been analyzing him, the horse has undoubtedly been sizing you up. It is impossible to put oneself into a horse's pea-sized (or, rather, polo-ball–sized) brain, but his internal analysis may be going something like this:

"This rider is going to be a real winner. She's a bit afraid of me I can tell, because she's nervous about getting into the saddle. She's not really sure how to hold the reins and, wouldn't you know, she's going to stick me in the side with her left foot when she mounts! I wonder if she knows about Weight Watchers . . . . This is going to be fun—I think I'll wait until we get around that bunch of trees up ahead and then I'll show her what it feels like to land hard—right on the ground!"

Or, perhaps in your case, it will go like this: "That's nice, this guy really knows what he's doing. He doesn't seem to worry about whether I'm going to step on him, and his reassuring pat on the neck is definitely a good sign. He seems pretty thoughtful about seeing that the girth isn't pinching me on the belly, and he can adjust the stirrups without asking for help. I might give him a buck or two just to be sure, but this is going to be a pleasure, I'm sure."

Let's hope that the equine aspect of your test doesn't work as follows: "Oh boy, here's another Clint Eastwood. Lookit those duds! The blue jeans may be faded but not in any of the right places, so I know he's never been in a saddle—at least not enough to handle the likes of me. And look at him swagger over to me, full of confidence and empty of horse sense. Yep, there he goes, grabbing the reins, pulling them tight, and kicking the daylights out of me. He wants to gallop? Okay, fella, here we go! This won't take a minute . . . ."

If all of this seems far-fetched—we all know horses aren't very smart—think again. Horses are very sensitive creatures, having spent so many hundreds of years in human company, and they are probably more expert at sizing up potential riders than we are at figuring them out. Don't let this equine superiority get the best of you, however. You are, after all, a member of a presumably more intelligent species, and even if the horse may be stronger and wiser in his ways than you are, you can be master of the situation if you use your head and approach the animal with a positive, confident manner. It will be worth convincing him that you are on the side of the angels—not a potential devil on horseback.

Some time ago, I read a curious book by Henry Blakely called *Talking with Horses* (Dutton). The author is well known in England for taming ornery horses and for communicating with the animals he rides, and over the years he has devised a method by which people can understand what it is that horses "say" and what it is that they like to hear. Of course he is referring to gesture as much as to actual sound or language, but his discussion of horse talk is very interesting indeed, mainly because he has a real insight into the way the species naturally behaves. Some of his observations are very useful for humans meeting a horse for the first time, since they are based on what horses do when meeting each other. When you approach an unfamiliar horse, for instance, breathe gently into his nostrils and let him breathe into yours. Silly as it sounds, that tends to have a soothing effect, rather like a human handshake, indicating that you mean no harm and can be trusted. Another reassuring thing to do is to lay your arm across the top of a horse's neck, somewhere between the ears and the withers. If you watch friendly horses in a pasture, you will notice that one will occasionally lay his neck across the neck of the other. This trick isn't guaranteed to work on a rogue who is dead set on kicking you into the next county, but it's worth trying on any animal you suspect of distrust or uneasiness in your presence. (Also, you are standing in a place where a kick is difficult, if that's what is on his mind.)

Even rank novices around horses know that flattened ears mean trouble and that a cocked hind foot should be given as much room as possible to avoid a kick. But there are many other signs of equine disturbance that an eager horseman should learn to interpret. A horse that paws at the ground while standing is impatient to be doing something else; if he "nods for rein" and keeps wanting you to loosen up, he's probably bored and needs to be taken in hand and encouraged to work harder. If he shows you the white of his eye, he's nervous or frightened by something or other, and if he swishes his tail while you are riding—even though the fly season is long gone—he's disturbed by something that you are doing, such as giving an inaccurate or confusing cue, using a rein that is too tight, or simply making him do something he doesn't like to do. You'll pick up these signals and more just by being around horses, but even at the start, it's important that you take a "learning" approach toward every horse you meet. Even more important, however, is that you let the horse know that you are confident, for like dogs, horses can quickly sense fear or insecurity in humans. If you let yours show, the horse is likely to take advantage in some way. Don't allow self-confidence to be displayed as bravado or macho behavior, because a horse can also sense the insecurity that lies behind it. Just be quiet and self-assured and deliberate in your movements, handling the horse with as little fuss and hesitation as possible. A hyperactive or dangerous-looking horse will need a different approach, but if you don't know how to deal with that, ask for another horse.

A more recent book, well worth reading, is *Getting in TTouch: Understand and Influence Your Horse's Personality* (Trafalgar Square, 1995). The author is renowned equine behaviorist Linda Tellington-Jones, who specializes in rehabilitating difficult horses through a method that uses touch and exercise to eliminate pain and to establish a rapport that can build self-confidence and improve performance. The author claims it is possible to read a horse's personality through physical characteristics as well as gestures, and her analysis of ears, nostrils, and other equine parts is fascinating.

THE FIRST RIDE

Now that we have selected the horse and analyzed him, let's get aboard. Chances are that the first few minutes in the saddle will be a continuation of the testing process that was begun on the ground, so keep alert to the situation. You may have to undergo a couple of unpleasantries, such as the horse's moving on while you are mounting, refusing to go forward once

William Steinkraus, formerly Chairman of the U.S. Equestrian Team, participated in the Olympic Games six times and was the first individual rider to win an Olympic gold medal for the United States. He did that in 1968 aboard Snowbound, who was owned by the Princess de la Tour d'Auvergne. In his first Olympics in Helsinki in 1952 he rode Velco's Duke, owned by Norman Coates; in 1960 at the Rome Olympics, he rode Riviera Wonder owned by Mr. and Mrs. Bernie Mann and Eleanora Sears's Ksar d'Esprit. In 1964 in Tokyo, he rode Sinjon, and in 1972 in Munich, he again rode Snowbound to the gold medal, as he had in 1968.

In recent years, because of the increased cost of good jumpers and the fact that good riding is not guaranteed by the existence of a healthy bank account, many of the best jump riders today ride other people's horses. Leslie Burr Howard rode Gem Twist, the usual mount of Greg Best, to a Horse of the Year award from the American Grand Prix Association in 1992 after Greg broke his shoulder, and rode him again in 1993 on the winning U.S. Nations Cup team. Margie Goldstein-Engle, Michael Matz, and Anne Kursinski regularly ride horses that they do not own, a trend that seems to be on the rise.

you are in the saddle, resisting your commands, or even delivering a buck or two—not enough to unseat you but enough to upset your balance and unsettle your peace of mind. As soon as the horse figures out that you know how to handle these tricks of the trade, he'll probably give up and let you take charge. But instead of going through this initiation, you will gain the animal's respect a lot more quickly if you take charge from the start—and that includes the attitude that you are the tester, not the testee. You'll save valuable time (which for an hour's ride may be worth as much as a dollar or two) by preparing yourself right from the time you leave the ground. Here are some tips:

• First, make sure the cinch or girth is tight.

• If the horse moves away from you while you are mounting, hold the reins properly to prevent this by keeping pressure on the off (right) side of the horse. If this doesn't work after a couple of tries, ask someone to hold the horse for you or to give you a leg up. If you only have an hour to ride, don't waste time schooling a horse you may never see again, and don't feel embarrassed about needing assistance. If no one is there to help you, use a mounting block, if there is one, or any convenient object to get you into the general vicinity of the left stirrup.

- While you are mounting, don't stick the horse in the side with your left toe, which will only give him an excuse to move ahead before you are ready. And when you sit, do so as lightly as possible. Most horses resent having a hundred pounds or more flopping unceremoniously down on their backs or banging their kidneys.

- When you get your stirrups adjusted to the correct length (and ask for help if you need it), double-check the girth or cinch. And then get yourself—your position in the saddle, your legs at the horse's sides, and your hands on the reins—together and ask the horse to move off at a slow walk.

- If it becomes apparent at this point—or even earlier—that the horse is going to be a handful and that you're not quite prepared to manage his high jinks, don't feel shy about asking someone to lead you for the first few minutes. Horses that haven't been exercised in a while—such as neglected private animals or hack horses that have been rested because of injury or lack of business—are quite likely to act up, usually out of high spirits rather than ill temper. If you feel at all anxious, put common sense ahead of bravado and save yourself a possible fall by being led or by dismounting and lunging the horse, if necessary, to get the kinks out. (See page 144 for lunging advice.) If neither alternative seems possible, stay aboard but take things very easy. Ride the horse on a relatively loose rein—being ready to pick up contact if the animal shows signs of bolting—and be very gentle with your aids. Instead of applying leg pressure, for instance, simply think "walk" or "trot" and chances are that the horse will respond. If things still look bad and there is no ring to contain your fiery steed, ask for another horse or don't ride.

- Use a ring if possible for the first few minutes of your ride. If there is no fenced-in ring, aim for an open, level piece of ground and work in a large circle. While you are walking the horse, which you should do for at least the first five minutes, see how he responds to more or less contact on the reins and establish the proper amount to keep him responsive to your signals for turning and halting but not resistant. As noted dressage trainer Dominique Barbier puts it, "For knowledge, walk; for rhythm, trot."

- The trot is the best gait at which to test a horse, so once you have your bearings, put the horse into a steady posting trot. It may take a couple of turns around the ring to get the gait as steady and rhythmic as you like, but don't give up. There's no point in trying anything else until you and the horse have reached a good working relationship in both directions at this gait. If the horse seems to be pulling on the reins, indicating that his weight is on the forehand rather than the hindquarters where it should be, work him at the sitting trot, bringing him to a halt every so often and even backing up once in a while.

- Once you have figured out the trot working the full circumference of the ring, trot half the ring and in occasional small circles to see whether the horse "bends" properly. Work on collecting and extending the gait, and alternate your route once in a while so that the horse doesn't anticipate your commands.

- Once in a while you may come across a horse with more gaits than just a walk, trot, and canter—or with gaits that seem to be somewhere in between the basic three. Some American Saddle Horses and Tennessee Walking Horses, for example, have a long walk or slow gait that involves trotting with the forelegs and walking behind; it is a peculiar gait that one cannot post to, but over long distances it is efficient and comfortable. Paso Finos have an interesting amble, and some horses have a natural singlefoot, a four-beat gait in which each foot hits the ground at a different time. Occasionally you will come across a pacer, and you may even find yourself, as I did not long ago, on the back of what was presented to me as a "shuffling Morgan." While riding him at a sitting trot, I found myself extremely comfortable indeed but realized eventually that it wasn't my skill but the horse's rather curious motion. Since his action wasn't at all animated, I felt sure he wasn't a real Morgan or an American Saddle Horse or Tennessee Walker. After a while, one of the people watching me said, "Oh, that's one of those Missouri Fox Trotters!" I was tempted to shrug this off as a horseman's joke, but in doing some research, I found that there was indeed such a breed and that this breed did just such a "shuffle." I still can't figure out what cue I used to get him to shuffle, or what it took to get him into a full-fledged trot, but this sort of problem is always a pleasure, since the horse is doing the teaching.

- After ten minutes or so at the trot, try a canter in one direction and then in the other. If the horse takes the wrong lead, although you have given the appropriate cue, stop him and start again until you get the correct lead. (Remember that some horses have been trained to obey different cues.) If the horse seems very strong and you are planning to take him out of the ring for the rest of the hour, you might think twice about cantering on the trail where he is likely to get even stronger.

- When you are outside the ring, the horse should have your respect enough not to take you for a ride you won't enjoy. But don't take chances. Don't gallop, jump fences, or canter up or down steep hills, and be sure to walk the last mile home so that the horse is completely cooled out when you get back to the stable. If the day is hot and the horse is still wet from the exertion, you should offer to untack him, sponge him off with cool water, and walk him on a lead rope until he is completely dry. Anyone who brings a hot horse back from a ride will be considered something a good deal less than a horseman by the stable management and may be charged a (justifiable) penalty fee.

6

THE LIST OF responsibilities faced by the average horse owner seems endless—from the health and well-being of the horse to the maintenance of the stable in which the animal lives. The horseless rider, by comparison, is a blithe spirit who can sleep late on rainy mornings while others muck out stalls or tote bales of hay and whose mailbox is blissfully free of bills from farriers, feed stores, and veterinarians. But every rider has some responsibilities—to him- or herself, to the horse, and to the others in whose company he or she rides—for the sake of both pleasure and safety. Being alert to potential danger or discomfort is the first step in avoiding problems, but it isn't the whole story. Knowing how to behave in certain situations will help prevent trouble or at least keep it from getting worse. This chapter, then, is devoted to the rules of riding behavior, the handling of difficult horses, first aid in emergencies, and some of the legal aspects of horselessness.

The art of horsemanship is an ancient one, and there are more rules, regulations, formalities, and traditions connected with it than with almost any other sport. But if you remember that chivalry—another art in which proper behavior and etiquette play a great role—derives from the French word for horse, it may not be surprising to find that what follows are a series of dos and don'ts for those who ride.

RING ETIQUETTE

At a glance, there isn't much involved in ring riding, but in practice, especially if there are other people in the ring, there is a certain form to follow if order is to be kept where chaos can easily erupt. First of all, even when you are alone in the ring, it behooves you to display good horsemanship by keeping your mount well into the corners as you circle rather than cutting them and to use discipline as you ride so that the horse will know you mean business. A horse that takes advantage of the informal, uncaring rider by heading into the center of the ring without being asked to or by repeatedly taking the wrong lead at the canter will be no pleasure for the next rider. So when you are in the ring, keep on the rail (the edges of the ring) unless you intend to make a circle or some other deliberate movement. Pay attention to your diagonals at the trot and to your leads at the canter, for the sake of the horse's education as well as your own. Remember that in dressage the ring is called a school—and a school it should be considered, a classroom in which the horse should be encouraged to do his best at all times. Loose-reining is all right if it is part of the educational or cooling-out process but not if it is done carelessly.

The usual program for a session in the ring begins with the walk for a few minutes in both directions and then a good working trot, first in one direction and then the other. Once a steady pace is achieved, you can work on extending along the length of the ring and collecting in the corners, but don't attempt this during every round. The horse will quickly pick up the habit of speeding up on the straightaway (which may not be correct extension in any case, since the number of strides should remain the same and only the strides themselves should lengthen) and slowing down or even breaking pace at the ends of the ring. Make half-schools (using half the ring) and smaller circles or figure eights occasionally to make sure that the horse has his hindquarters in gear and is sufficiently bent to make a smooth circle without ballooning out or cutting a corner. (Don't forget to change diagonals as you change direction.)

At the canter, make sure you start out on the correct lead (left lead going counterclockwise; right lead clockwise) and that you work on your inside and outside aids. Keep your hands level if you are using both hands, not one raised above the other; keep your legs in the proper position; and keep your balance over the center of the horse's balance. The whole point of the lead is that the horse can maintain balance while turning; counter-cantering (cantering on the wrong lead) will only invite a fall unless it is done by someone who knows what he or she's doing, such as schooling a horse in making a flying change of leads. When you practice halts or changes of gait, do so at different points of the ring each time, preferably away from the ingate (entrance) so that the horse won't get into the habit of stopping there whether you want him to or not.

If you are alone, you may, of course, set your own pattern in the ring, changing direction and pace when you like. But when there are other people riding, you will have to be alert to what they are doing and conform your own routine to theirs to keep confusion to a minimum. If other people are trotting in one direction, don't try to canter in the other without asking permission (especially if the other horses are hard to handle or are ridden by beginners). If you wish to walk while others are trotting, keep to the inside rather than on the rail. If, conversely, you want to trot or canter while others are moving at a slower pace, move in their direction but keep to the outside; if anyone is on the rail in front of you, call out "Rail, please!" to signal that you are coming through. If that person doesn't move, don't scream and yell but circle or otherwise attempt to avoid the horse in front without letting your horse know that anything is out of order. If everyone is cantering and your horse's stride is longer or faster, don't run up on the rumps in front of you but call for the rail or make a circle to avoid a collision. A rule of thumb to follow: You are responsible for the horses ahead of you, not behind, and if they don't (or can't) move at your request, give them right of way. Another rule to keep in mind: If you are schooling your horse using voice commands, keep your voice low when others are in the ring or you will confuse other horses or riders. I have often been in a ring while lessons are going on and without thinking have obeyed the verbal instructions of the teacher when they weren't directed at me at all. What's worse is having your *horse* obey those commands, breaking into a trot when the teacher calls out to his or her students even though you're trying to stay at a walk. If you find yourself in a similar situation, "auditing" a class when you're riding on your own, you should do whatever the instructor suggests—stay out of the way or change direction—since he or she may be working with beginners who don't know the rules of the ring.

If you feel that you have been going in one direction long enough, suggest to the other riders that they change direction so that you can do so as well. But don't just turn around and run into them. If you want to practice halting or backing up, or if you wish to stop to adjust a stirrup or tighten the girth, don't do so in the path of other horses but move into the center of the ring or to some area where horses are not traveling. If you want to practice a special movement, such as a leg-yield or a turn on the haunches, be sure that the path is clear and that your horse won't interfere (or be interfered) with others.

Should your horse act up, kicking out or bucking, stay calm and settle him down as quickly as possible. In a confined ring situation, nearby horses are all too likely to take another animal's disobedience as an excuse for a general riot. If another horse acts up while you are riding, keep a firm rein and anticipate disobedience in order to stop it before it starts. Some horses have a real antipathy to others, so keep those animals separated if at all possible. A buckskin mare I once rode regularly was convinced that a fellow school horse (well-named Jughead) was out to kill her, and she stopped dead in her tracks if he came within twenty feet of her. (She had reason: Even his groom admitted that he would rather fight than eat.) The only solution was for me to tell his rider, whoever that may be, to keep him at a good distance no matter what. Horses that kick are occasionally made to wear red ribbons in their tails but not always, so it is up to the rider (or the stable manager) to be sure that everyone knows about this vice before they learn in a more painful way.

The only thing to do if a horse bolts or throws its rider is to stop and remain standing until the runaway has stopped or until the rider has remounted. Such an event will excite and alarm everyone in the ring, and it may take a few moments of steady walking to get the atmosphere back to normal.

If you are jumping in the ring while others are working on the flat, you will have to be especially careful to make sure your course is clear before you start. As you begin, call out "Heads up for the gate" (or oxer or in-and-out or whatever). If you find that someone is in front of or behind the jump as you head toward it, simply circle and try again. In a ring full of beginners, you may discover that the other riders aren't exactly sure what a gate or an oxer is, so don't be impatient. Explain what you want and be as cooperative as you expect them to be. Don't expect too much of your horse in this situation, however. If there are many riders around, a well-schooled horse should be able to mind his business (or yours, rather), but some horses are easily distracted, especially if they must weave around other animals while keeping a steady pace on a course of jumps. It is up to you to reassure your horse and keep him under control.

ROAD ETIQUETTE

In rural parts of the country, trail riding is just that, but, unfortunately, as humans expand their population, they also expand their highway systems, and all too often trail riding in suburban and urban areas means road riding—at least for part of the time. In many places it will be necessary to ride along paved roads or to cross them in order to get to trails, and even in some rural areas, it is often a good idea for riders to use roadways rather than fields. In the spring, farmers resent riders who trample across plowed and seeded fields, and in the autumn the game-hunting season can be as dangerous for horse and rider as it is for deer. In many areas, a horse will be much safer confronting a ten-ton truck than a mindless gunslinger who shoots first and looks second. And so, before we get to the bridle path or park, let's cross the paved road.

Macadam or concrete are fine for rubber tires but not for horses' feet, and if there is a soft shoulder wide enough to walk on, do so. (In some states the laws are specific about which side of the road one must ride on—toward the traffic or with it—so be sure you know what your state's law is before starting out.) Pounding on pavement at a trot or canter is not only hard on a horse's natural shock absorbers, but it's also a risky business since the surface invites skidding, especially if one tries to make a sudden turn or halt. Horse owners who ride regularly on the streets usually take the precaution of having their animals shod with borium calks on their shoes for grip and leather pads to help absorb the pounding, but hacking stables may not take these expensive precautions. Unless you know that the horse is shod properly, keep to a walk on pavement at all times. Make sure that you are wearing protective gear even if your horse isn't. A hard hat—the kind used for jumping—is an extremely good idea, and should be considered as much a part of the riding uniform as a motorcyclist's helmet is part of his or her outfit. One man I know rented a horse from a stable in the heart of Brooklyn, New York, and while crossing a street on the way to the park, the horse shied for some reason and the man was thrown and knocked unconscious. When he came to, he looked up and saw the sign for a funeral parlor. It took him a few anxious moments to realize that he was really alive!

Most horses that are ridden regularly in traffic become accustomed to it, which means getting used to loud noises, blinking lights, blowing papers, cans, bottles, and all kinds of distractions. Although you can assume that a public stable near a roadway will offer you a horse that has become streetwise, you shouldn't take chances, which means that you should keep the horse under complete control at all times. An inexperienced horse may shy or refuse to negotiate such threatening obstacles as bridges or railroad tracks, and even an experienced horse can become alarmed if he lacks confidence in his rider. It is usually a good idea to ride with other people, not only for help in case of an accident but also because the presence of other animals will have a calming effect on your own mount. If you are in a group, however, don't ride abreast down the middle of the street, but ride single file along the same side. No matter how sure of yourself or your horse you are, never take any oncoming vehicle for granted and always prepare yourself for the unexpected. Most drivers will slow down and behave courteously, but some won't, either because they don't realize the danger or because they take a sadistic delight in scaring horses. Be sure to wave your thanks to any driver for slowing down or stopping. New York City police horses are probably the most streetwise animals that exist, having been trained to ignore open umbrellas and spray cans stuck in their faces, hoses snaking along the ground, and gunfire, but even the Police Department was impressed some years ago when an ice-cream truck blew up, throwing a police horse named Pride and his rider completely off their feet. Because Pride remained standing calmly after the accident (in spite of the bits of glass that were stuck in his back) while his rider helped out injured pedestrians, the city gave him a special commendation for courage.

Take particular care in crossing streets to watch for traffic and to gauge its speed as well as to note the condition of the road before you cross. If you start to cross and a car appears, it is usually safer to keep going rather than to attempt a turn or a halt. If you are in a group, the leader (or you) should stand in the road, holding up traffic with your hand, until everyone is safely across. If traffic is heavy and your horse is nervous, it may be wiser to dismount and lead him, putting yourself between the horse and the cars. It goes without saying that you should obey traffic signs just as any other driver must and use hand signals whenever necessary.

TRAIL ETIQUETTE

Once you reach a nice, unpaved road or trail, your troubles aren't entirely over, but life will be somewhat simpler. You must remain in constant control, of course, for even the calmest of horses can always shy or bolt, but at least you aren't likely to run into trucks or cars, although motorbikes and snowmobiles all too often find their way onto bridle trails. Nevertheless, your most likely companions on the trail will be other animals. If you come across other riders on the trail, be sure that your own horse is moving at a similar or slower pace. Since horses are herd animals by nature, one horse galloping past a group of walking horses can cause a stampede, especially if the riders in the group are beginners. If the trail is narrow and you wish to pass, call out "Passing, please!" before you barge ahead. You have the right of way and the rider being passed must move over. As you pass, don't use your crop or whip since it may startle other horses; if you must give your horse something more than simple leg pressure to move it faster, use the crop on the side away from the other horses so they can't see it. If you are being passed and the trail is very narrow, move your horse's hindquarters off the trail.

If you encounter a dog along the way, slow to a walk and ride past without much more than a "go home" to the dog. Most dogs will give up barking once you have passed "their" property line, since they tend to be territorial. If you come across the rare dog who may attack a horse, keep going and make a note to avoid that route in the future, or plan to carry a water pistol (filled only with water, please). Horses will usually treat the presence of other animals—cattle, deer, and such—without much more than a second glance, and you should behave the same way rather than trying your hand at rodeoing. Although many people enjoy taking their dogs along with them when they ride, it's not a good idea for the horseless rider to do so, unless the animals know each other and you know that the trails you are going to take are not lined with other dogs, chaseable deer or rabbits, and similar attractions (or hazards) for your pet. When in doubt, leave your dog at home. Loose dogs around a stable can be a pain, barking at horses, fighting with each other, and generally getting in the way.

Trail riding is not as formal as showing and a good deal more relaxing, considered by many as the best possible way to view the countryside.

If you are riding with a group of riders, make sure that everyone is prepared ahead of time for a change of pace. When there is a beginner or timid rider in the group who may not wish to canter or gallop, don't bolt off and expect his or her horse to remain walking. Either pick a spot where the beginner's horse may stand quietly as you circle around him, or ride on ahead and canter back toward the standing horse. When you ride single file, keep at least one horse's length between each horse. A horse that walks too close to the one ahead is likely to stumble because it can't see where it's going or isn't paying attention to its rider. Tailgating is also a good invitation for a swift kick. Don't hold branches aside for a rider who is following you; because of the distance between the horses, the branch will probably swing back just in time to knock the rider behind you out of the saddle.

If you know or suspect that the horse you are riding is likely to shy at this or that, don't ride in front but let the other horses go first. Many spooky horses will follow another animal past some rock or other that it would take an hour to pass on its own. Although riding in groups may be an advantage in this situation, don't get carried away in conversation or let your attention stray from your own horse. As on the roadways, ride defensively, anticipating trouble and keeping in control at all times. Once you have gotten to know the horse you are on, this attitude can become second nature, so that trail riding will be more pleasure than work, but if you are on an unfamiliar horse going over unfamiliar terrain, don't assume that the animal is going to behave well unless he respects his rider.

Stay alert to trail conditions, and don't attempt to lope or canter over rocky ground, through low-hanging branches, or down steep hills. Slow to a walk if you come upon any patches of ice, mud puddles, or sandy areas, and pay special attention to holes or rocks. If you are in a field, don't just gallop across heedlessly but stay on the trail or path around the edge. If you notice any particular hazards, point them out to other riders. If the trail takes a sharp turn downward or up, stay at a walk, and don't lean back but remain over the horse's center of gravity (the withers) to help maintain traction.

If the trail is owned and managed by the stable, be sure you know ahead of time where you are going, how to get back, and what the boundaries are. In many areas, bridle paths are public property and marked as such (often with other rules, such as "no reckless riding"), but sometimes you may find yourself having to use private property. Some property owners may be kind enough to allow riders to cross their land, but don't do so without being sure that you have their permission. A number of communities have trail associations or committees that obtain this permission and maintain good trail conditions, and if you are heading off into private land, it is a good idea to check with such an association ahead of time. Rude or thoughtless riders can try the patience of any landowner, and if you are granted permission to cross, be sure to behave yourself. Don't allow your horse to walk on lawns or gardens, and in cultivated fields, keep to the very edge. If a crop is growing right up to the fence, stay outside the fence, and if the ground is wet, avoid the field altogether. If you come across bridges or streams, make sure that the footing is good before you proceed and that the horse is relaxed. Some animals will try to jump their way across, spilling you or getting themselves into trouble, and if you suspect any fear on the part of your animal, it may be best to dismount and lead him. (Don't pull the reins over his head, though, since he might get away and trip, and be sure to stay out from under his feet if the going is tricky.) If you come to a gate, don't jump it. The footing on the other side may be poor, but more important, the horse may not be capable of negotiating an obstacle over three feet high (most gates are four feet or more). If you must open the gate, always close it after passing through.

While you are paying attention to the condition of the trail and its hazards, don't forget about your horse. Whether you are riding for an hour or all day, remember that horses aren't machines and must not be overused. Western movies may show horses galloping over the Rockies all day long, but most of these running sequences were filmed over a period of days, not in an hour. If you enjoy a good canter, your horse probably will too, but don't keep it up for more than a few minutes, and don't even try it unless you are sure that the horse is in fit condition. Change gaits frequently, spending most of the time walking if you expect to be out for any length of time.

If you stop along the way for a picnic, let the horse have a rest too, but don't tie him by the reins; be foresighted enough to take along a halter and lead rope when you pack your lunch, so that the animal can enjoy grazing on his own without a bit in his mouth. If you think that the pond or stream water on the trail may be less than spring-fresh, or if the horse is in any way overheated, don't allow him to drink. Take along some water for him and allow only a few swallows. (I don't have to say, do I, that you should pack up any bits of trash you make along the way?)

If for any reason you have an accident or a fall while you're out, don't panic. Just be sure you read the rest of this chapter before you go out.

On your way home, make certain that you obey the cardinal rule about walking the last mile. This will not only cool the horse down in preparation for his next ride or for a safe drink of water; it will also prevent the horse from becoming a barn rat, racing to the stall, and it will save you some embarrassment back at the stable. Even if the horse picks up some speed knowing that he's heading home, don't give in but keep him at a walk.

THINGS TO TAKE ON A TRAIL RIDE

If you are planning to go out on the trail for more than an hour over countryside that you don't know as well as the back of your hand, you'll need more than just the horse. Here's what else to fit into your pack or take along with you:

1. Another horse and rider (it's always risky to ride alone)

2. A halter and lead rope (especially if you plan to stop along the way for a rest or a picnic)

3. A knife or wire cutter (or both)

4. A water supply for you and the horse if you're going where water is scarce or suspect

5. A blanket (you may get caught in bad weather or overnight)

6. A first-aid kit (for you and the horse)

7. A map of the area

8. A slicker or rainproof poncho

9. A hoof pick

10. A flashlight

SPECIAL CONDITIONS

Riding in a city park is something between road and trail riding. Bridle paths are usually well kept and suitable for equine feet, but they are all too often filled with traffic in the form of joggers or trail bikes, and riders should remain alert to any contingency. Onlookers ignorant of horse psychology may frighten an animal by crying out in delight or running up behind it to "pat the nice horsie." Children are especially dangerous in this respect. It's nice to be admired as you trot along in front of an audience, but don't let it go to your head. And don't show off your horse's speed by doing anything more than a collected canter. A horse that bolts in a park doesn't have too many directions in which to go, and bursting out into traffic or running into a baby carriage is too much of a risk to take. Morgans, Arabs, and other saddle horse breeds are often "park-trained," and this isn't just for show purposes; that high-stepping, highly controlled set of gaits is ideal for riding in parks where the extended gaits of a hunter or cowpony would look (and be) rather out of place.

Riding at night is one of the most dangerous sports of all, especially if you are going across unfamiliar country or near roadways. Visibility is poor for both rider and automobile driver, even at twilight, and the rider should wear light-colored clothing and carry a flashlight (or put a red reflector on the left stirrup and a white cloth on the horse's tail).

Riding during wintertime can be great fun but the special conditions do require a certain amount of caution. Borium calks or Easyboots should be worn by the horse on hard surfaces, but these are not necessary in soft snow, though you must stop occasionally to remove snow from the hooves to prevent a buildup of icy snowballs. Don't overwork the horse so that he builds up a sweat or has difficulty breathing, and do avoid any unfamiliar spots that may actually be snow-covered ditches with poor footing. Don't bother with a special blanket for the horse unless you plan to stop for any period of time along the way, but do be sure that you wear enough protective clothing—long underwear, lined gloves, and warm socks, as well as a suitable parka or down vest and a warm hat.

PROBLEM HORSES

As we saw in the last chapter, every unfamiliar horse should be approached with a certain amount of caution—by asking questions about any habits he might have and by keeping alert to whatever may arise while you are in the saddle. Private horses may be high-strung, under-exercised, or spoiled by indulgent riders; hack horses may be temperamental as a result of poor riders or abusive treatment. Reschooling or trying on new bits or special types of tack, such as draw reins, checkreins, and such, are not within the capability of the occasional rider, of course, because such things take time and expertise. Any horse ridden by several people can pick up bad habits very quickly, especially if the animal is a sensitive one, and it may take a long time and a good deal of knowledge and patience to undo the damage. But even the occasional rider should know how to deal with trouble when it does occur, or, even better, *before* it occurs. Knowing how to anticipate trouble takes experience, as does applying the remedy, since some of the cures for bad habits are not necessarily the most natural response. But it is worth studying the following tips before you get into the saddle so that you will have some idea about what to expect and what to do.

BOLTING

Being run away with is a common fear among novice riders, and though bolting is a bad habit that should be eliminated in any school or hack horse available to a beginner, some horses may bolt out of fear or the misapplication of aids, and every rider should know what to do. The first thing to remember is *not* to pull hard with the reins, for the pressure will only cause the horse to resist and run faster. Try to sit back in the saddle and lift your hands to keep his head up. If a sawing motion (giving and taking with alternate hands) does not work, your best bet is to pull up and back on one rein very firmly so that the horse is forced to make a circle. (Don't make the circle too tight or you'll risk falling off or making the horse fall over.) Gradually make the circle smaller until the horse has to slow down and you can regain control. Or you can turn the horse toward an obstacle too high to jump—the side of a barn or a huge wall—so that he will stop of his own accord. If you are on a trail where circling is impossible, you can try to lean back, weight in the saddle, and give a single sharp pull on the reins and then release. Some horses will be startled enough to let go of the bit, at which precise moment you must reclaim it. If all else fails, simply let the horse run until he tires; if you head the horse uphill, he'll slow down from the exertion rather quickly. Speak to the horse all the time in a firm tone, saying "Whoa"—but don't yell, for that will only give him more reason to run. If the horse is running blindly into traffic or some obstacle and you fear a crash, your only recourse may be to bail out (see page 132).

SHYING

Leaping sideways or ducking away from a scary object can be the result of real fear on the horse's part or simply a manufactured fright that a sour horse uses as a ploy to unseat the unsuspecting novice. Theories about dealing with this vary, as do the causes, but the most sensible immediate response is to sit back, keeping a firm hold on the reins, and to regain your balance as quickly as you can. If the horse still seems wary of whatever it is that caused him to shy, keep him moving forward with your legs firmly on his sides and constant contact on the reins, speaking reassuringly but without any hesitation on your part. Let the horse know there is nothing to worry about and don't let him sense any nervousness on your part or he'll react the same way again. Don't try to pull the horse's head away from the object, for his peripheral vision will enable him to see the object anyway. If your horse is truly frightened, let him look at the thing and see that there is nothing to fear; dismount if necessary and, holding the reins tight under his jaw, walk him by. If you are riding with someone else whose horse seems calm, have that horse precede you. If you have a feeling that your horse is refusing to move ahead out of stubbornness, do whatever you can to get him to proceed—even circling back and tricking him past the object—but do not give up, or that horse will take advantage of the next rider at this same spot.

I have found that on a windy day horses are more likely to spook than on calm days, and I gather that this is caused by a natural equine inclination to be wary when the wind is blowing rather than the noise of rustling leaves. Wild horses use flight as their primary defense, and when the wind is coming strongly from one direction, they have to remain on alert for signs of danger since they will not be able to sense it against the wind. Rather than refuse to ride on a windy day, you need only be prepared for the possibility and keep a reassuring voice and firm control with legs and hands.

BUCKING

A horse that bucks is probably doing so out of high spirits rather than nastiness, although bucking can be caused by a sharp tap with the crop, fear, or a burr under the saddle. Whatever the reason, you can feel a buck coming on when the horse's head drops down and his hindquarters rise beneath you. Immediately pull the horse's head up and sit back. Although sitting forward may come more naturally for you or be unavoidable if the buck is already in process, do your best to get back in the saddle and keep a firm grip on the reins, pulling up rather than down. Keep your legs strong on his sides to force the horse ahead. A horse whose head is up in the air and who is moving forward cannot buck. If the buck was caused by high spirits, you might consider lungeing him before going out on the trail or giving him a session in the ring to use up some of the excess energy. If the source of trouble is a burr or a badly fitting bridle, check for discomfort and

A couple of tricks of the hack-horse trade. The rider on the rearing horse (left) is doing just the wrong thing by panicking and letting her weight fall back, which could pull the horse over on top of her. She should be holding the reins with both hands and leaning forward. Bucking (right) is best prevented by keeping the horse's head up, but if the buck is already well under way, the rider should react as this one is doing by keeping weight back and trying to make the animal move ahead.

remedy it. A horse that bucks out of bad temperament in an effort to dislodge his rider will need reschooling by an experienced rider, but one that bucks out of fear or pain may just need reassuring.

REARING

This is a dangerous vice, since it is possible for the horse to fall over on top of the rider; even without falling, the horse's neck can hit the rider in the face. There are several schools of thought on the subject, but all experts agree that a horse with a tendency to rear should be handled only by an experienced rider. If a horse should rear up under you, the first thing to do is to get his head down and move him ahead. You may find it easier to lean forward, grab some mane, and pull down as hard as possible with one or both reins; other experts recommend trying to slide one rein beneath the stirrup and pull as hard as possible using the stirrup as a pulley; yet another suggests leaning back, letting go of the reins, and urging the horse forward. Whatever method you use, don't pull on the reins if you lean back, for you'll probably force the horse over on top of you.

WHEELING

This is similar to shying or spooking in that a horse will suddenly change direction and unseat the rider. This can occur during a canter or gallop, going into a jump, or when a horse rears, and the only warning the rider gets is when one shoulder drops below its normal level, giving the horse sufficient balance to wheel around without falling. Here again, prevention is the best medicine; keep contact with the horse's mouth and keep your balance over his center of gravity, with your legs firmly in position to discourage disobedience. If you have any reason to suspect that a horse is going to give you trouble, you should be prepared for it, especially if the animal has any aversion to jumping or to a particular point on the trail. General nervousness, signaled by tail-swishing, head-tossing, and such, may be a sign that something more troublesome is about to erupt.

The following vices aren't as serious as the ones I've just described, but they are bad habits that can interfere with a comfortable ride. Horses that kick, graze along the trail, pull, and are otherwise difficult to control, can cause accidents as easily as ones that buck and rear.

KICKING

Horses that kick are bad-mannered, and people who own them should be sure that everyone knows it, either by a verbal warning or by tying a red ribbon to the horse's tail. A horse that kicks at people should be given a wide berth, as should any unfamiliar horse who might be startled by a sudden move behind him. Some horses reserve their kicks for other horses and these should be put at the end of a trail ride or otherwise prevented from getting their hindquarters into the range of other animals. If a horse lowers his head and flattens his ears, a kick may be in the offing; pull the horse's head up and turn him to avoid trouble or simply move ahead. If you are riding in company with a kicker, make sure that you don't ride up close behind him (not a good idea in any case, regardless of a horse's habits).

GRASS EATING

A horse that constantly stops to eat grass along the trail can be prevented from doing so by a strong, alert rider but can cause a beginner enormous frustration and even an occasional fall over the horse's head. If you suspect that your horse is more interested in nibbling than in getting exercise, keep a firm hand on the reins to keep his head high, and keep him moving forward with your legs.

PULLING

A horse that is heavy on the forehand and seems determined to pull your arms out of their sockets is a puller and needs reschooling if that habit is to be broken. These horses are really using their rider's strength as a fifth leg, to give support that should really be coming from their hindquarters. If you've gotten yourself a puller and want to enjoy your ride, you can save your arms by trying a few tricks of your own. Keep the horse moving ahead but let go of the reins suddenly; once you have removed the support, he may be surprised into letting you have control of the bit. If the pulling continues, lift your hands up to keep his head raised and maintain strong impulsion with your legs to get his weight back on his hindquarters where it belongs. As you ride, stop from time to time and make the horse back up. Use your back to brace yourself rather than letting your arms take the brunt of the pressure. You won't be able to change the horse's habit in an hour, but you'll have a more comfortable ride.

STARGAZING

A horse that carries his head high to avoid contact with the bit can be difficult to control. Try riding the horse in circles at the sitting trot, allowing his haunches to swing out beyond the circle. Eventually the horse will lower his head to keep his balance and you can reclaim control of the bit.

RIDERS IN TROUBLE

If a horse's high-jinks should lead to an accident, despite all of your efforts to the contrary, you should be prepared to deal with the situation, whether or not you are hurt. It is always best to ride in the company of other riders or with someone looking on, just in the event of such an emergency, and you should also be able to deal with problems that arise when you are the onlooker rather than the victim. The following suggestions are in no way intended as the last word on the subject; anyone who plans to spend a lot of time around horses should be familiar with the basics of first aid—both for humans and for horses. First, humans.

FALLING OFF

If you find yourself completely unbalanced and heading for the ground, try to remember to go limp to avoid landing in a tense, breakable heap. If the horse is going fast, try to roll up your body so that you do not risk hitting your head or the loose arm or leg as you fall. Professional riders fall as much as anyone else and it's worth asking your instructor for advice about how to fall or even to practice falling on your own (from a chair onto a mattress or at the local gym), just to make sure your reactions are automatic. Obviously, the occasional rider needn't go to these lengths, but anyone who is taking up cross-country riding or jumping would do well to learn the technique before an accident teaches you a lesson you'll never forget. Most important for all beginners and for anyone who jumps is to wear a hard hat just in case. Everyone who rides falls off sooner or later and the sooner the better if one is going to learn to do it properly. I once had a friend in a riding class who had ridden for several years without falling off; one evening she took a tumble, and instead of panicking, she jumped to her feet saying, "Thank God that's over! I used to be terrified of falling off but now I know it's not as bad as I thought!"

Some falls, of course, can be bad, causing serious injury—especially if the horse steps or falls on the fallen rider. Don't try to hang on to the reins as you fall and do try to fall as clear of the horse as possible. Horses will do almost anything to avoid stepping on something in their path so you needn't worry about this too much unless the horse falls too. If you are riding under supervision, the instructor or guide should be capable of giving the necessary first aid, but it's always a good idea to know some of these yourself if you plan to ride out alone or in company with someone less experienced than yourself. (See below for first-aid measures.)

LOOSE HORSE

If you fall and your horse heads for home, you have nothing to do but to follow on shank's mare. If the horse should stop to graze, don't run after him assuming that you can catch him. Walk calmly, speak softly, and carry a big bunch of attractive-looking grass to catch his attention so that your horse forgets he's loose. If you are riding with other people, don't have all your friends try to play roundup, for that will only cause the horse to become excited and run off. If reins are dangling in front of him, your horse can injure himself or break the reins. Some years ago I learned a marvelous way to catch a loose horse from someone who realized that horses have a natural curiosity about anything unusual so long as it doesn't seem to threaten them. If you are trying in vain to catch an animal and buckets of oats or handfuls of grass aren't effective or available, pay no attention to the horse but go off in a direction away from him—staying close enough so that he can see what you're doing. Sit down, fool around with a stone or whatever, and make interesting noises, concentrating thoroughly on that stone. Before long the horse's curiosity should get the better of him and he'll try to figure out what's so interesting. Don't make a move in his direction until he is standing right over you, and then—quickly but deliberately—catch hold of the rein or halter and the horse is yours—puzzled but definitely yours.

INJURED RIDER

If you do get hurt in a fall or otherwise, and you are out on the trail alone, your best bet is to take it easy until you know that you can move without doing yourself further injury. Most horses will find their way home, and the sight of a riderless horse will galvanize everyone at the stable into action on your behalf. If the horse does not leave you, don't worry about catching him until you are safely on your feet and can manage it. Lie still until you get your wind and your wits back and can determine whether or not you have broken anything or have simply been bruised. Only when you are calm—even if you are in pain—should you make a move to get help.

If you are with a rider who gets injured, you should, of course, try to get expert help, but you may have to apply first aid as well if the injury is serious. If someone is knocked unconscious, immediately make sure that he or she can breathe; using your hand or your crop, open the mouth and clear it of any dirt or other debris and hold the head so that there is an air passage to the throat. Apply appropriate CPR techniques as necessary. If there is excessive bleeding, use a pressure bandage by placing a clean piece of cloth directly over the source of the bleeding and holding it firm until the bleeding stops. Don't try a tourniquet (both dated and dangerous as a form of first aid), and don't worry at this point about infection, since loss of blood is more serious. Elevate the bleeding area and treat the victim for shock by having him or her lie down on a blanket to prevent chilling (or overheating). If you suspect a fracture, do not move the victim unless you have to and until you have immobilized the injured area with a splint of some sort.

If you or another rider with you gets kicked or bitten by a horse, wash the injured area with cold water to reduce pain and to clean it, and treat as you would any other injury, getting medical attention if it seems necessary.

Severe sprains should be treated like fractures; a minor sprain should be given a cold-water bath to reduce pain and swelling and then bandaged (for support) and elevated. Don't be too brave and try to deny that a sprain or a bruise hurts; I once had my ankle kicked by a horse and treated it like a bruise by simply hoping that the pain would go away. It wasn't until a week later, when the bruise didn't seem to be healing, that my mother insisted on an X ray, which revealed that the tibia bone had, in fact, been dealt a hairline fracture.

There is an old saying that you should get back on a horse the minute you fall off, on the theory that you will eliminate whatever psychological damage the accident may have caused. There may be some truth to this with beginning riders who aren't seriously injured, but sometimes the pain caused by remounting is worse than staying safely on the ground. The jarring that a few more minutes in the saddle can cause may have serious consequences if an injury has occurred. Sometimes injuries are not immediately apparent. After one of my falls, I got right back on the horse and finished up my hour in the saddle; then I drove home, took a cold bath, and went to bed. When I awoke the next morning, I couldn't move my knee, since the muscles and tendons had discovered during the night of inactivity that they had been severely sprained. I had to wait at least three weeks before I could ride, though I found—to my delight—that my reluctance to cause pain by jarring the knee kept my legs in the proper position after I was back in the saddle again. Nevertheless, it isn't worth doing yourself physical damage just for the sake of psychological health, no matter what the old wives and horsemen say.

HORSES IN TROUBLE

If an equine accident or sudden illness should occur and neither the owner nor an expert is available, you may find yourself having to cope with the situation on your own. The first and most important step to take if you have any doubt about whether the symptoms are serious is to get back to the stable as fast as possible and to see that a veterinarian is called. If the stable manager or the horse's owner is not around, call a vet yourself. Every stable should have the vet's number posted prominently (usually inside the first-aid kit or on the medication shelf in the barn), but if you have any trouble finding it, consult the Yellow Pages or telephone information service for the nearest veterinary clinic. If the vets there do not handle large animals, they will refer you to someone who does. Large-animal veterinarians usually work out of traveling vans or mobile clinics and are reachable through a cellular telephone or beeper system, although it may take an hour or so to get the vet to your particular problem. Follow whatever instructions you are given over the telephone and use whatever first-aid techniques seem appropriate, depending on the problem. There are several good books that outline these techniques (*Dr. Kellon's Guide to First Aid for Horses* by Eleanor Kellon, VMD [Breakthrough Publications], *How to Be Your Own Veterinarian (Sometimes)* by Ruth B. James, DVM [Alpine Press], and the chapter on "Horse Health" in the *Whole Horse Catalog* [Simon & Schuster]), and it's worth committing these methods to memory if the books are not on hand in the stable. The most important thing to keep in mind is to reassure the horse and keep him calm to prevent the situation from getting worse.

LAMENESS

If your horse comes up lame when you are riding, dismount immediately and check each hoof for a lost shoe, an imbedded stone, or some other foreign object. Don't check only the foot you think is causing the problem; it isn't easy to diagnose the problem correctly unless you are an expert. If you do see something in the foot that is causing pain, try to remove it as gently as possible with a hoof pick, but if you can't dislodge it, don't fool around until you get some help. Often the removal of the object will improve the situation enormously, but don't just remount and ride off into the hills until you are certain that there is no further pain. If you have any doubts, lead the horse back to the barn and ask for another horse or call it quits for the day.

If there is no obvious cause for the lameness, leave it to an expert or a vet to diagnose the source of the trouble and put the horse away in the stall or paddock until the expert arrives. Lameness can be caused by any number of injuries or illnesses—from pulled muscles to digestive troubles to inborn weaknesses—and treatment will vary considerably, depending on the cause. Rest and recuperation will cure many ills, but some horses may require special medications or even surgery. Your primary responsibility as rider is to notice that there is a problem, to get help as quickly as possible, and to become a pedestrian immediately.

ACCIDENTS

If a horse should fall or be injured in some way, approach the animal with caution, since you may put yourself into danger if he is upset or afraid or flailing around trying to get up or away. Speak reassuringly to him, try to figure out what the injury is, and get help immediately. If first aid is required, see the box below for some hints, but consult a veterinary manual or an experienced rider for further information. If you are alone on the trail, you may have to leave the horse to get help if he cannot be led home. Don't tie the horse or he may cause himself further injury. If the animal has been caught in wire, you should obviously try to get him free, but if you can't rescue the horse yourself from mud, a ditch, or some more complicated situation, call the local fire or police department for assistance. If an electrical wire is involved, don't touch the horse or the wire (or any water that may be nearby). Stay away and call the electric or telephone company.

ILLNESS

Most rental horses are relatively healthy and the renting rider is rarely in a position to determine whether a symptom exists or not, let alone a serious illness. But in the interest of developing a degree of horsemanship and for the sake of the conscientious horse-sitter, I have included below a very brief summary of symptoms to note and first-aid techniques to master.

Colic is the most common ailment that requires first aid at home before the veterinarian comes, so it is worth learning its symptoms and what to do about them. If a horse lies down and rolls in obvious pain, you must keep him on his feet and walking constantly; intestinal twisting or torsion may be aggravated or caused by the rolling, and walking the horse will prevent this and also help distract the animal from his pain. A veterinarian may treat the horse by feeding him mineral oil or some concoction to loosen the bowel, or he or she may inject a muscle relaxant, but these remedies should not be undertaken by a novice.

Because it is difficult for anyone but an expert to diagnose the actual illness, your responsibility will be to notice the symptoms and get help. The following symptoms deserve a call to the vet:

> Refusal to eat or drink for 24 hours
>
> Repeated coughing
>
> High temperature (over 103°F)
>
> Shivering or excessive sweating for no obvious reason
>
> Diarrhea or constipation for more than 12 hours
>
> Frequent lying down and rolling
>
> Persistent lameness

LEGAL CONSIDERATIONS

Being aware of the potential danger in working around horses and knowing how to handle emergency situations should keep accidents and injury to a minimum. But, as any horseman will tell you, accidents can happen even in the best of all worlds, and any horseless rider should understand the legal responsibilities involved in riding other people's horses. The question of actual liability is not an easy one to answer, for state and local laws vary and court cases are judged on the basis of specifics that may not apply in other, similar cases. Nevertheless, keep in mind the following generalizations.

If you simply walk into a public stable and ask for a horse without making any special request for a "beginner's horse" or a "gentle animal," you are agreeing to ride at your own risk, even if you do not see a sign posted to that effect or sign a release. Most public stables do have such signs and do insist on the signing of a release (usually at the urging of their insurance company), but some do not. One stable manager told me that he did not get his clients to sign a release because it frightened them about the potential danger and lost him some business. Another manager admitted that the releases weren't really worth much in a court of law, especially if

FIRST AID FOR EQUINE ACCIDENTS

Open Wounds

Abrasions—Surface scrapes or sores: Clean the area with water or a mild saline solution and keep it free of flies and dirt; do not bandage or use disinfectants, and do not allow any tack to come into contact with the affected area. Medication or veterinary attention should not be necessary.

Incision or puncture wounds—Clean with water or saline solution but do not bandage. If the wound appears to be deep, get a vet to look at it, since infection can set in if the skin heals over the injury. The vet will probably give a tetanus shot as well as antibiotics.

Lacerations or tears—These may require suturing, which should be done by a vet. You may clean the area if the horse can be handled but don't use disinfectants, only warm water, and try to pull any loose flaps of skin back into place.

Excessive bleeding—If the bleeding doesn't stop after a minute or two or if the blood is bright red and spurting, you will have to apply a pressure bandage to stop it. Put a clean piece of cloth around or on the area and hold it tight until the bleeding stops. Keep the bandage in place until the vet arrives, and don't bother with a tourniquet, which will only complicate matters.

Strains and Sprains

These are injuries to muscles and tendons and may be caused by overwork or accident. Mild injuries can be treated with an alcohol rub or a mild liniment, but more serious injuries should get a vet's attention. Keep the affected area cool (by using a hose) to avoid swelling; only after the area has cooled and stopped swelling should one apply heat treatments to increase circulation and promote healing.

Bruises and fractures—These are injuries to the bone and may, of course, be very serious, requiring a vet's attention. Some fractures are obvious and some are not, so don't try to diagnose the problem yourself. Keep the horse calm and relaxed in a darkened enclosure until the vet arrives. If the horse is trying to move about, you may have to apply a splint to keep an injured leg immobile. Wrap a thick cloth or pillow around the leg and tape it as securely as possible, supporting the leg by taping sticks or poles to opposite sides of the pillow.

In case of accident:

Don't hesitate to call a vet.

Don't apply medications without instruction from a vet (tranquilizers are especially dangerous to a horse in pain).

Don't panic, but reassure the animal as much as possible to keep him calm (a quiet, dark place makes a good waiting room).

Don't try to diagnose anything and treat it yourself unless the injury is obviously minor.

Don't approach an injured animal except with the utmost caution.

injured riders could prove negligence on the stable's part. It is this area of negligence that keeps insurance premiums high for stables, since almost anything can constitute negligent behavior when an accident results, although all possible precautions have been taken. Even in the best stables, a piece of tack can break, a normally placid horse can shy or enjoy a moment of high spirits, a rock or two can roll into a trail, a pitchfork can fall prongs up, and so on. An injured rider with an aggressive lawyer might easily be able to prove negligence where there seems to have been none. And such a case, even if won by the stable, can still cost both parties a great deal of money just to cover the court costs. On the other hand, a stable that doesn't care for its tack, routinely rents kickers and buckers to beginners with no supervision, and fails to maintain its trails or to put away stable equipment, might very obviously be negligent and truly at fault if an accident occurs, yet the injured rider might assume that he or she had no rights because a release had been signed.

If the rider makes a special request for a suitable mount, the stable that selects and offers the horse takes on a greater responsibility in the eyes of the law, since by providing that horse, they are making an "implied warranty that the horse is to be fit for such a purpose," according to the Uniform Commercial Code. If the rider finds that the horse is not at all suitable as a beginner horse, the stable may be found guilty of breaching the warranty, assuming that there is sufficient evidence to convince the court that the owner failed to exercise reasonable care in determining the suitability of the horse.

The position you take, if such an accident occurs, should depend on various things: the condition of the stable and its horses, the attitude of the management toward its customers, the circumstances that led up to the accident, and the damage that resulted. If the stable is poorly run and careless in renting its horses (no testing of riders, no supervision of beginners, no releases, no posted signs, etc.), then a lawsuit or the threat of one might improve the situation for future riders. If the stable is a good one, or if the accident resulted from the rider's own mistake in judgment, either in selecting the horse or in riding it into a situation where there is a known risk (such as jumping, galloping cross-country, etc.), then the accusation of negligence may be misplaced, and the stable would only suffer unfairly as a result.

One lawyer friend told me of a suit against a day camp where a young camper fell from a horse, cracking several ribs and severing a nerve in her hand that took several years to mend. It seems that the child's horse—a big, placid, but hungry creature—had wandered off to graze and pulled the child right over his head. The parents tried to prove negligence on the part of the camp for having let so young a child ride the horse, but the court ruled in favor of the camp, saying that the parents had in effect given their consent to the ride by allowing the child to attend the camp and to participate in all activities offered. The horse's suitability for the job as "beginner's mount" was not even questioned, since the animal had done nothing "unsuitable to the purpose for which it was selected."

Borrowing a horse from a friend or a private stable is less complicated if only because the lender is not being paid for the privilege and it is understood (even if never said) that the rider is going at his or her own risk. The rider's risk could even, in some cases, be greater than in a rental stable because if anything happens to the horse and the owner can prove negligence on the rider's part, the rider might be responsible for damages.

Another area in which the borrowing rider might be liable is if the horse should run into or be hit by an automobile. In such a case, the driver of the car may sue the horse owner for damages to the vehicle and its passengers, since in most states horses, like dogs, are considered pleasure animals (if the rider were on a cow, an "economic animal," the driver would be liable, regardless of actual fault). If the owner of the horse can prove that the accident was the fault of the rider rather than the horse, the liability might end up with the rider rather, not the owner. Only if the owner and/or rider prove that the driver had gone out of his or her way to hit the horse or shown negligence might the decision go otherwise.

Accidents don't always happen when people are in the saddle. Horses can bite, kick, or otherwise cause injury, and working around a stable has its hazards as well. Again the liability may rest with the owner or stable management if negligence can be proved, and I know of several cases in which suits have been brought on these grounds. One very cautious, conscientious horse owner I know used to hire enthusiastic youngsters to work in her stable, paying them a small weekly salary or allowing them to ride for nothing rather than putting them on her official payroll, since most of them were too young to have working papers. One of her grooms fell from the hayloft, breaking a leg, and the parents sued for damages, revealing in court that the child was not a legitimate employee. It took several years for the owner to pay off the damages, and it put a great many young horse lovers out of a job or a chance to ride. The problem here was that the parents believed the horses and the stable to be an "attractive nuisance"—compelling children to hang around in spite of the potential danger. Even if the owner had not employed the youngster, she might have been sued in any case, just because the parents didn't like the idea of their child spending time on the property and had not consented to it. Obviously, this is an extreme case, and one that I personally feel is unfair to horse owners and horseless riders alike, but in cases like this, one must be put at the mercy of lawyers, judges, and juries who may not be sympathetic to horse people.

In spite of the legal precedents and interpretations of the law, my recommendation to horseless riders is that unless negligence is obvious and provable, you approach every horse and every ride with the idea that the responsibility is your own. If you borrow or rent an animal that has been presented as a gentle, safe creature, and it explodes quite unexpectedly, the lender may be negligent in not having warned you, but you may be at fault for having inadvertently mistreated it— by giving it a confusing signal or forcing it to do something it refuses to do, such as take a fence, go through a stream, or under a bridge. Sometimes the cause is something that could not have been foreseen by either horse or rider: a bee sting, a thoughtless driver, or a suddenly awakened memory of something frightening in the horse's past experience. Even if a piece of tack breaks or slips while you are riding, you should count yourself at fault for not having checked everything before you started out. If you are a real beginner and the lender knows that, you may have some justification for placing the fault with him or her if sufficient precautions were not taken. But anyone who mounts a horse must realize that the possibility of falling off or otherwise being injured is always there. In these times of numerous malpractice suits against doctors, managers, and other professionals, the ones who are getting richer are the lawyers and only the occasional client. If it's money you want, there are more pleasant ways to get it. In the meantime, I can only repeat what it says in most stables I know:

"Ride at your own risk."

7

MAKING THE MOST OF YOUR RIDE

SOONER OR LATER, usually sooner, the average horseless rider begins to get restless. The hack horses at the local stable aren't much of a challenge anymore; the instructor has taught you the basics but you want to explore different types of equitation on more highly schooled horses; you've been bitten by the bug of competition; or you want a chance to try some advanced kinds of equestrian activity. But you still have the same old limitations of time, money, and horselessness. What to do? Believe it or not it is perfectly possible to improve the quality of each ride without completely changing your lifestyle (if you're prepared to do *that*, skip right to Chapter 10 for advice), and even without changing stables. Here are some tips.

IMPROVING THE HORSE

If the horses at your stable are nice, plodding animals that have lost their charm for you, don't despair and don't start looking elsewhere . . . yet. Any horse, regardless of conformation or past experience, will benefit from a change of pace, and it is definitely worth trying to change that pace for them, if you can convince the stable manager to let you do so. If you are a regular customer, ask if you may be allowed to school one of the horses in some new discipline. Study the books on dressage, for example, or elementary jumping, and learn what is involved in training a horse. You may have to adjust your schedule to a time when the stable facilities are not busy, and you may even have to get some new equipment to start, but perseverance will usually win out. A dressage whip and access to a ring is all you'll need for dressage schooling; jumping will also demand a ring—or a level piece of ground—and a few rails and standards. If the stable management can't be convinced to invest in these or to lend you some rails from which you can fashion some jumps, offer to buy the lumber and undertake the labor yourself and trade them for a few free rides. A plain old trail horse could, with patience and encouragement, be made into a reining horse if you're able to teach him flying changes of lead, pivots, and rollbacks, though cutting or barrel racing may be beyond (or behind) him. Never assume that an old horse can't learn new tricks. Some friends of mine own a nineteen-year-old Quarter Horse who recently acquired a new lease on life by learning to jump low crossrails. They don't work him very hard, of course, but they swear that he acts like a seven-year-old every time he is headed in the direction of their jumping course.

Although lungeing a horse doesn't involve riding—since the lunger stands in the middle of an area while the lungee circles around him or her at the end of a longe, or lunge, line— this is a useful training technique that will benefit both horse and horseman. In addition to its value in initial training, lungeing is an excellent way to give an under-exercised or overexcited animal a chance to warm up or cool down as the case may be. You can use a plain halter or a special lungeing cavesson (a halter with one or three rings attached to a special noseband), attaching the swivel snap of the lunge line, a twenty-five-foot length of lightweight material (usually cotton or nylon) to the ring under the horse's jaw. You will also need a long whip to act in place of your legs as a cue, supplemented by your voice, to make the horse walk, trot, canter, and stop in both directions around you. Lunged horses usually wear a saddle with the stirrups tied down to the girth to prevent flapping and sometimes a bridle or a bitting rig instead of a halter.

Long-reining is a variation of lungeing in which two long lines are attached to the bridle, the line on the inside (near you) run through the stirrup and the outside rein brought through the outside stirrup and run around behind the horse's hocks. If you have never used a lunge line or long reins, the simplest way to learn is to watch an expert at work and then to try your hand under supervision. Long reins can also be used to train a horse to drive when the trainer walks directly

Lungeing a horse—for exercise or special schooling.

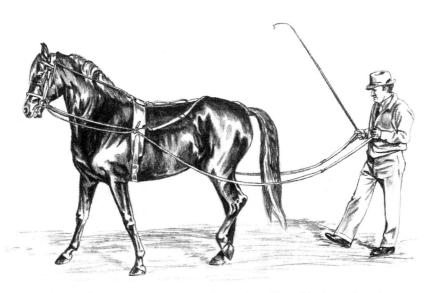

Teaching a horse to drive by using long reins. The whip is used to give cues (along with the voice) in place of the rider's legs and seat.

behind the horse (also called working the horse "in hand"). Driving is another useful technique for the horseless rider to know, and here again the best way to learn is to have someone teach you. (During a brief respite from horselessness, I owned a young Morgan gelding who had been trained only for driving; I had a lot of fun training him to carry me and learning to drive him, but the experience was most valuable in teaching me the virtues of long-reining. Rex was always straight and flexed at the poll.) Many harnesses are turning up in old barns and at tag sales these days, and with a little reconditioning (or a lot, depending on the previous owner), they are perfectly useful.

Speaking of old tack, you may, as I did once, come across an old forgotten sidesaddle. Don't just chuckle, but try it on a willing animal with broad shoulders. The first time I tried I was awkwardness personified until I got a feel for the proper seat at the walk, whereupon I felt elegant and nicely balanced. Until I started to trot, that is, which took a lot more practice to perfect; frankly I never did get very good because I didn't spend enough time at it, but I had fun trying. I have no idea what the pony I rode thought of it all, but I'd be glad to try it again (even if he wouldn't), though I know I'll only do so if no one else is going to be around to watch! (See page 195 for more on the sidesaddle.)

Reschooling a difficult or spoiled horse is a great art as well as a challenge, and one that any stable manager will appreciate. If you notice that one or two of the hack horses have picked up some bad habits, offer your services as a remedial teacher. This will work only if your methods are effective, and that will take study, patience, and skill, but if you are beyond the novice stage, you should be able to handle whatever comes along. (There are a lot of books on this subject.)

Most instructors I've talked with tell me that they rely on their advanced students to reschool problem horses, and it goes without saying that learning to do so is an important step toward becoming a horseman. It may also get you a few free rides, especially if your work results in savings for the horse's owner by making it unnecessary for him or her to get a new horse or by increasing the number of trustworthy animals in the stable. You won't be able to hang out a shingle announcing yourself as an equine psychiatrist or a full-fledged trainer until you get a couple of years of experience under your belt, but the satisfaction will be well worth the trouble.

If none of this is possible or interesting to you, you can try to talk the stable manager into getting a new, more advanced horse, not just for yourself but for other regular customers as well. Try to get other frustrated riders to help you do the convincing; suggest that the stable might attract more clients if their stock improved. You can even look around for a horse that's for sale—perhaps a neglected backyard horse whose owner is off in college—and offer to try it out for the stable. If you were a professional, you could get a percentage of the sale price, but perhaps you can negotiate a free ride for the service; in any event, you'd have a better horse available the next time you want one. Most public stables have a certain amount of turnover in horses; offer your services as a trial rider for the new ones. Not every ride will be a pleasure, but at least life won't be boring!

IMPROVING THE INSTRUCTOR

This can be a delicate business, especially if the teacher's schedule is a busy one or if he or she is limited in ability or interest, but I've found that most instructors who care about their profession are open to new ideas if presented intelligently and tactfully. As I've already said, being completely frank with your instructor is a very important aspect of the entire relationship, and the point when you are frustrated or not altogether satisfied with your lessons is no exception. Instead of complaining to your friends or family, tell your instructor your true feelings about the lesson program and ask for advice. If you have read a new book about a particular type of riding that interests you, lend the book to your instructor and ask for comments. Suggest that you try a new direction in your own lessons—such as jumping or dressage or even a specific type of activity, such as barrel racing or fox hunting. If your instructor thinks that you are making a mistake or getting in over your head by trying something new, he or she may be right and you should weigh the argument carefully. If the instructor isn't interested in helping you, ask for recommendations for different instructors to whom you might apply. If you're not the only student interested in something new, it might even be worth the instructor's while to get another expert to help out by giving a weekly group lesson or an occasional clinic at the stable.

You shouldn't feel embarrassed about leaving one teacher for another; be appreciative for what you have learned but remember that you are the one who's paying, and that you deserve to get something in return. The situation may be particularly touchy if you have decided to move from one instructor to another at the same stable, and this may take some political diplomacy as well as honesty, especially if your reasons for changing have more to do with personality than with riding. If the stable pays its teachers a commission or part of the fee rather than a straight salary, your move may have a financial as well as a personal effect on the relationship between the instructors. The only advice I can offer here is to be absolutely sure you want to make the change and to be certain that the reasons are sound enough for you to undergo whatever discomfort the change may provoke. If honesty with both instructors doesn't clear the air, you might ask the stable manager for advice or help in smoothing things out.

Another, virtually inevitable difficulty that will arise in changing instructors is that the transition will not be entirely smooth in terms of your own riding. You will be asked to unlearn some techniques or to do things that your previous teacher had trained you not to do. This will be especially true if you are attempting to learn an entirely different style of riding, but don't be tempted to argue or disobey. If you have questions or difficulty in adapting, ask the new instructor to explain what he or she is teaching and why it is different. If you understand the new technique intellectually, you should eventually be able to pass the information along to your body until your reactions become automatic.

The jumper rider and Olympic bronze medalist Norman dello Joio once told me that he had studied with several different trainers until he managed to arrive at what he felt was his own, most natural style. He feels that riding with a single teacher—like riding a single horse—can limit your experience, and though he was often confused at first by a new trainer, he was fortunate—or foresighted—enough early in the game to know what he wanted to learn from each one.

If your problem is simply that your instructor is too busy to give you special lessons or your schedule doesn't coincide with a different or more advanced class, you might consider the possibility of helping the teacher by giving a few beginner lessons yourself. If you show any ability in being able to help others with their riding problems, you could end up lightening your instructor's load to the extent that he or she could be free to give you the special attention you want. Learning how to teach is useful in any case, for the sake of your own riding. It is virtually impossible to spend an hour repeating "Heels down" or "Heads up" and to forget about your own heels and head the next time you find yourself in the saddle!

IMPROVING THE RIDE

If you are becoming frustrated by the kind of riding you've been doing simply because you're in the rut of the same old ring and same old trails, changing horses or instructors may not answer your needs. In the next chapter we'll look at some of the competitive and advanced activities open to the horseless rider, but on a less ambitious level, there are plenty of easy ways in which to make the most of the average hour hack. First of all, if you haven't been taking lessons for a while, you will find that one or a series of sessions with a more experienced rider or an instructor will give you a new lease on your equestrian life. If you've been riding alone, try teaming up with one or two other people when you go out on the trail—or even into the ring. Even watching someone else ride can teach you something, but the main difference will be in the interest that any social occasion will stimulate. Riding can be a wonderful way of meeting new people, and I for one can say that I've made more than a dozen close friends through a mutual interest in equines. If you meet someone who enjoys riding, ask them to join you one day for a hack through the countryside; it's not exactly as seductive as an evening looking over your etchings or as productive as a sewing bee, but it is fun and it will give your usual hour astride a new dimension. A friend of mine admits that he rides primarily for the social pleasure that it gives him; he is a fine rider who enjoys the sport for its own sake, but he is also a gregarious sort who gets an enormous amount of satisfaction out of the company of other, like-minded people. His degree of cordial hospitality to new riders to the stable or to visitors from out of town is invariably rewarded by similar hospitality when he visits other parts of the country. He finds, as I did, that his reception at a new stable—and the quality of his horse—is always better if he knows someone who is a regular rider there.

If you have tried all the new trails, all the horses, and all the company, and your hour hack is still not giving you as much pleasure as you'd like, you can always pretend that you are working rather than just riding for the fun of it. I often find in traveling to new places that I get much more out of the trip if I have something to do rather than just enjoy myself. Sightseeing is fine until you have seen all the sights, but being somewhere *for a reason* can make you feel like more of a participant than a passenger. And the same goes for riding. The next time you go out on the trail on old dobbin, set yourself a program or schedule, whether it is to improve yourself or the horse. Make a list of things that you or the animal need to work on and set up an hour's worth of exercises to work on them. If you need a goal, pretend that you're going to enter a horse show (even better, plan to enter a horse show—see the next chapter). Here are some suggestions.

RIDER IMPROVEMENT

To keep your heels down: Stand up in the stirrups in a two-point seat for five minutes at the walk and trot.

To develop a strong seat: Ride at the sitting trot for five minutes or ride without stirrups at the walk, trot, and canter.

To develop good hands: Ride for five minutes at the walk, alternately collecting and extending, but think *only* about your hands. Then try this at the trot.

To improve your balance: Have someone hold the horse still while you practice leaning forward and back in the saddle with your arms outstretched from the shoulder. Twist from the waist in both directions with your arms out. Ask someone to lunge the horse for you while you ride, and drop the reins, knotting them to keep them from flapping. Work at the walk, trot, and canter.

HORSE IMPROVEMENT

Head carriage: Work at the walk and then the trot and canter by alternately collecting the horse and extending the gaits in both directions around a ring. Change direction frequently and make your signals distinct and deliberate so that the horse is "listening" to you. Don't overdo this; three minutes at each gait should suffice.

Bending around corners: Concentrate on making specific cues at turns in the ring or trail. At the trot

*If simple hacking is not challenging enough, try schooling the horse—
teaching it to bend properly into a turn as this rider is doing.*

make increasingly smaller circles, using your signals deliberately until the horse responds by bending. Weave the horse around a slalom pattern of cones or poles to develop flexibility. Concentrate on the use of your legs rather than the reins.

Response to leg pressure: Work on leg yields by making the horse move ahead on a diagonal track. Practice turns on the forehand and haunches, first by a wall or fence and then in the open.

General conditioning: To strengthen muscles, balance, and surefootedness, walk and trot the horse up and down gradual slopes for a few minutes during each ride. Be sure to shift diagonals at the trot when you post, even on a straightaway.

Attitude: Make a change of scene when you can. If you are accustomed to ring riding, take the horse out on the trail to relax. If you are a trail rider, ride the horse for half an hour in the ring to work on cues for correct leads at the canter or lope simply to give him the idea that he is working. I once rode an overenthusiastic field hunter for an hour in the ring. At first he hated the sight of the ring and pretended that he was afraid of the jumps so that it took some doing to get him into a steady trot. But after he realized that he wasn't going to get his own way and that the painted walls and crossrails weren't going to bite him, he settled down and eventually jumped a course of small jumps that must have looked like sticks on the ground to him. His owner told me later that the following day in the field, he behaved like a gentleman for the first time in ages, taking his fences with care and not trying to race to the front of the pack.

If you have tried all that and still want more, how about forming a club? In Chapter 4, I mentioned certain types of clubs open to children and adults, but there's no reason why you couldn't put together an informal group right in your own stable. Talk to some of the other regulars and suggest monthly meetings to discuss stable activities over a drink, a potluck supper, or just coffee and doughnuts. By pooling your resources, you should easily be able to afford the services of one of the many experts that travel throughout the country giving lectures and clinics on various aspects of riding. A quick glance at one of the horse magazines will give you some ideas for people to invite or you can get your instructor or stable manager to help you by recommending local experts whom you may not know. Have the farrier and the veterinarian speak about their specialties; ask a local jumper rider or dressage coach to talk about their areas of expertise. Get one of the grooms to give a lecture on stable management or even a course covering various aspects of horse care. (The clever groom might even get some of the "students" to clean some tack or muck out a few stalls.) If one member of the group has been to a special equestrian resort or a horse show, get him or her to give a lecture about the experience. These sessions will be even more fun if you can get hold of some slides, films, or videotapes to accompany the discussion. Videos, if not available in your local tack shop, can be rented from various organizations (check the ads in the horse magazines or write to one of the breed associations, the American Horse Shows Association, or the Jockey Club for a list), or from local colleges and universities with agricultural programs. Other club activities could include day trips to nearby horse shows or rodeos, polo games or racetracks, dressage trials or breeding farms.

One informal club I know meets every Sunday morning at a nearby stable to take a cross-country ride on rented horses. The only prerequisite for membership is a good deal of expertise and courage, since the ride involves some tricky terrain and fences. There are no dues (beyond the rental fee), but if anyone falls off during the ride, that person is required to buy everyone else breakfast afterward.

The next chapter will give you ideas for competitive or advanced equestrian activities, but first how about taking a vacation? A vacation on horseback, that is. Two weeks at a dude ranch for an English-saddle aficionado can do wonders, and trekking through the hills of Hungary or the moors of England in an English saddle can be a great change of pace for a rider accustomed only to cactus and tumbleweed. As horseback riding becomes increasingly popular worldwide, resorts and tourist centers begin to add riding to their attractions. A friend of mine, born in Argentina, paid a dutiful filial visit to his parents and found, to his considerable pleasure, that his hometown of Buenos Aires had become a very horsy town since his childhood. He joined the local Hipoteca for the month he stayed in Argentina and rode every day on an extremely fine Thoroughbred stallion under the tutelage of the local instructor who was, it turned out, a former member of the Argentine Equestrian Team. That, plus the fact that he was able to buy custom-made boots and a saddle at very reasonable prices, caused his friends back home to turn pea-green with envy, but his renewed enthusiasm for the sport was enough to infect all of us as well.

IMPROVING YOUR MORALE

Sometimes all it takes to make horselessness bearable is a boost to the ego. One way to give yourself a lift, even if you're stuck on the same old hack every weekend, is to visit the local tack shop and invest in a new pair of riding pants or a jacket. The visit itself will be fun, even if you may walk out with only a new crop or a catalogue of things to put on your Christmas list. I have always felt a great deal better in the saddle if I'm wearing a well-fitting hacking jacket (which doubles as office wear during the week), but just sitting in a store entirely filled with horsy stuff is a nice way to spend time if not money. There is always someone there who's got time for talk, and for some reason tack-shop people seem to be far more patient than most store salespeople about explaining new products or letting you try on things. During these conversations I've met other customers interested in discussing local stables, and I get a kick out of reading the bulletin boards, too, since they are always covered with index cards describing horses in need of a new owner. I can be very selective about my horses then, shaking my head in mock dismay at those ads for outgrown ponies and horses that are the wrong color or height for my particular purposes.

If you come into a windfall and have some extra cash to get rid of, one of the most satisfying purchases can be a saddle of your own. Don't think that only horse owners need saddles. Most of the truly dedicated horseless riders have saddles of their own, and this is not simply because they make attractive conversation pieces in the living room. Although it is crucial that a saddle not cause a horse discomfort, saddles are not like shoes from the horse's point of view; in other words, most horses can wear many different saddles. Surprising as it may seem, it is important that the saddle fit the rider properly, and most instructors I've had were delighted to learn that I could bring my own. Although I can't truthfully say that owning a saddle is as good as owning a horse, it gave me peculiar satisfaction to install a saddle rack in my "tack room" (which most people mistakenly think is my study), and it gives me pleasure just to look at it from time to time as I sit at my desk. Soon after I got the saddle, a colleague of mine—a former cowboy and polo player from the West Coast—gave me a can of leather conditioner. "How often do you use it," I asked him, knowing that he still owned his old stock saddle, though it hadn't touched the back of a cowpony for some years. "Oh every night at saddle-appreciation time," he replied, not altogether in jest.

Another friend of mine went wild and bought an enormously expensive Hermès saddle that sits on its own rack in front of the fireplace in her living room. When I suggested that perhaps she could have spent the same amount of money for a horse of her own, she told me that in fact she didn't have nearly enough time to ride (she lived in New York City) or enough money to board the horse close to home. "In four months I'd have turned over more money to that stable than I invested in this saddle," she told me, "and I'll have this forever."

If you can't afford a saddle, don't buy a bridle instead but invest in a pair of stirrup leathers and irons as the more practical alternative for the English saddle. A pair of stirrups in which your feet feel comfortable and secure can be a reassuring presence even on an unfamiliar horse or saddle, and you'll have the added advantage of not having to change the length each time you ride. Bridles are usually more difficult to fit to a particular horse, especially if he has been trained in a particular way or needs a special bit. If you ride Western, a pair of stirrups isn't a good idea, of course, but you might consider getting your own saddle blanket if you can't swing the whole saddle. Used saddles are not as expensive as new ones, and if you find one that fits you, go ahead and splurge. I got my jumping saddle that way, though my other saddle came into my possession just as both of my dogs and two of my cats did—from someone (in this case my aunt) who wanted me to give her old one a good home.

But when you do get yourself some tack, don't assume that you can walk into any old stable and use it. Be sure that the stable management approves and that the saddle fits the horse you are going to ride. If those technicalities can be ironed out, I grant you that your enjoyment will be multiplied endlessly. Other riders will be complimentary (as well as envious), and your self-confidence will grow with every ride.

IMPROVING YOUR CHANCES TO RIDE

Another form of improving your morale is to expand your riding opportunities. In other words, learn to think like a horseless rider and don't be shy about it. I have mentioned elsewhere various methods of getting yourself a free ride or two—offering to exercise a friend's horse, mucking out a stable for a horse owner, and such. But there are other ways in which you can work horses into your life without revamping your lifestyle completely as you'd have to do if you owned a horse. This involves getting to know horse people, but not necessarily as a forlorn beggar in search of a horse.

The first step is to figure out what you know or are talented in that the horse owners around you are not. If you are interested in photography, for instance, get yourself and your camera around to local horse shows and take some pictures. Take notes on the names of your subjects (horses and riders), and if the pictures come out, send a print to the owner of the horse. Don't ask for money but offer your services as a photographer at the next show or inquire whether the owner might be interested in a portrait. Horse photography requires practice, and professionals are respected and plentiful in horsy areas, but if you have a gift and are willing to perfect it, you could find yourself combining your two interests to some advantage.

A good friend of mine (the illustrator for this book, incidentally) began his career as a commercial artist, drawing automobile tires and aerosol cans for anyone who needed an attractive advertisement, but he always drew horses in his spare time just for the fun of it. One day he realized that his horses weren't half bad, and on the basis of some photographs taken at a horse race, he started to make some paintings of various prominent animals. Before long, thanks to the fact that his talent was made obvious in a couple of ads well placed in horse magazines, to say nothing of a couple of magazine covers and a gallery show held at horse-show time, he soon found himself the recipient of portrait commissions and now has built up for himself a nice business doing what he used to do just for fun. Now he is president of the American Academy of Equine Art, a group of colleagues who have managed to combine their love of horses with a career.

As a book editor, I have found myself able at times to edit and publish books by experts in the horse field, as a result of which I have met some enormously interesting people who were willing to swap riding lessons for lessons in writing. Freelance writers with a special interest in horses can also turn their careers in an equestrian direction by covering horsy events for newspapers or magazines; by doing books of their own, often in collaboration with horse people who don't write; and by working as consultants to equestrian organizations that need assistance in writing newsletters, press releases, and other kinds of copy.

Accountants who ride can make themselves invaluable to stables that have erratic accounting or billing procedures or that need help at tax time. People who like to sew can help out horse people by lending (or trading for a ride) their expertise in making custom-made riding clothes. People in public relations can help stables to improve their image or enlarge their clientele or attract the public to their horse shows. Wizards in the insurance and banking fields can give financial advice, and lawyers can lend a legal hand, wearing two hats (hard and professional) to the local hacking stable in times of need. Computer nerds can make posters, prize lists, programs, and other desktop productions for a barn that puts on occasional horse shows.

While not an equine specialist, my late husband was a veterinarian and did treat the occasional horse. I, of course, trailed along behind him carrying his bag, preparing syringes, comforting patients, and otherwise making myself useful. Anyone with an equal love for animals and the medical profession has undoubtedly considered veterinary work, though it is a highly competitive field these days. A former assistant of my husband spent a year as a veterinary assistant in order to improve her chances of being accepted at a vet school. She found herself working for an equine practitioner who let her work in his "recovery" barn full of horses in need of rest and rehabilitation, which meant tender loving care and regular exercise. And that, of course, meant regular riding for her, occasionally on some very fine animals.

Those with an interest in both police work and riding should move to cities with mounted units to work either as full-time police officers or as auxiliaries. Police horses aren't show-ring specimens or anything you'd ride to the hounds, but they tend to be intelligent, savvy, and extremely reliable.

Obviously you can't turn every sort of career into something that will make your presence at a stable necessary or useful, but it's worth thinking about in your spare time. And speaking of spare time, use it well. In *Reflections on Riding and Jumping*, Olympic rider Bill Steinkraus urges weekend riders to make good use of their time not on horseback. He recalls his long career with the U. S. Equestrian Team, when he had to juggle his riding with a job that required several hours of commuting time each week. "I occupied a lot of this commuting time in thinking about my horses—on my way out there, planning what I was going to try to accomplish, and on the drive back, reviewing what had happened, and what I wanted to work on next time. In those days, I thought this was a considerable disadvantage and that I'd have been much more competitive if only I could have ridden every day. But in retrospect, I think it may even have been an advantage."

8

Hanging Around the Stable

One of the facets of horsemanship most ignored by horseless riders is that vast area known as stable or horse management, yet it is considered by all horsemen to be as important if not more so than the ability to win blue ribbons. As Canadian Equestrian Team jumper rider Ian Millar puts it, "You must know when something is bothering the horse so you can reassure him. It's a matter of feel and the only way you can get that feel is to be with the horse, clean out his stall, be with him when he's happy, be with him when he's tired, and know him inside out."

The only way to know a horse inside out, of course, is to know what he eats, when he eats it, when he sleeps, and what his habits are, whether he has any special medical problems and how they are prevented or treated, and how to care for and clean the horse, his tack, and his stall. All of that is what is meant by stable management, and all of that is what any horseless horseman must learn. If you like horses, learning won't be a drudge, though the work is sometimes hard and inconvenient. But it's also a way of earning free rides, so think of it as a carrot rather than a stick.

As I suggested earlier, the best way to learn about how a stable runs is to hang around before and after you ride. If your hour in the saddle starts at 10 A.M., arrive at the stable at 9 or 9:30 and watch the horses being groomed and tacked up. When your ride is over, your horse may be handed over to the next rider or he may need to be taken back to the stable and cooled off or untacked or both. Someone has to do these things, and if the stable management allows, offer to be that some-one. Learn by watching the grooms muck out the stalls or handle the horses, and ask questions so long as you don't run the risk of interfering with their work or otherwise making a pest of yourself.

Many public stables, camps, and clubs offer instruction in stable management as well as in riding, and I strongly recom-mend that you take a course or two to get yourself familiar with the terms and the techniques involved. Although it is much easier to learn how to braid a mane, lunge a horse, or clean a hoof by watching someone else than by reading the instructions in a book, there are several good basic books around that will give you a head start on subjects such as feeding, caring for tack, or veterinary care. Keep in mind, though, that each horseman has his or her own methods, brand-name products, and attitudes, so don't come on over-confident as a result of your book learning. Although there are many different books available, three especially good ones are M. A. Stoneridge's *A Horse of Your Own* (Doubleday), *The Whole Horse Catalog* (Simon & Schuster), and Mills and Carne's *A Basic Guide to Horse Care and Management* (Howell Book House). These books are addressed primarily to horse owners, but keep your mind open in any case. If you're feel-ing rich, you might invest in a reference copy of *Veterinary Encyclopedia for Horsemen* (Equine Research); if not, try one of the books listed on page 56.

If you should be given a chance to work in a stable—either for money or free rides—don't hesitate to jump at the chance, for this is the best of all possible ways to learn. As Norman dello Joio says, "Don't be afraid of work and don't be afraid to get your hands dirty." He worked in stables as a groom for some years waiting for the chance to be an exercise rider and eventually a competitor and feels that the experi-ence was invaluable in preparing him for his career as a Grand Prix jumper rider. If you feel that the person for whom you work is doing something wrong or something different from what you have read or learned elsewhere, don't argue or sim-ply do things your own way but ask questions in the most tactful way. You may learn something new and (if you hap-pen to be right) so may your boss. Until you know your way around, however, keep quiet as much as possible and do as you are instructed. These jobs are not easy to get, since many professionals feel that teaching someone the ropes takes more time and trouble than it's worth, and there are probably half a dozen people waiting right behind you for your job.

The following sections are not intended as a complete guide to the art of management but cover various areas in which the horseless rider can learn enough to become valuable in assisting an owner either as an employee or as a volunteer. If you become experienced and proficient at these tasks, you may even find yourself in demand for jobs or at the very least invaluable to those people whose horses you want to ride.

MUCKING OUT

We might as well start with the least attractive and dirtiest part of the job, for this is the chore that nearly any owner would be delighted to turn over to someone else. Horses that are confined to stalls for all or part of the day when they are not being worked invariably soil the bedding, which must be kept clean if the animal isn't to develop such ailments as thrush, infections, or respiratory disorders. A horse that is turned out in the pasture all day and kept in the stall only at night will not do as much damage as a continuously stabled animal, but there will always be something to clean up. (And the pasture, too, must be kept clean, since intestinal parasites breed in manure and can reinfest a horse if the droppings are not removed.) One horse I know spends a good deal of time outside but always, without fail, urinates in his stall the moment he is put in. He makes up for this by always making manure in the same part of his stall, leaving the area around his feed bin pristine, although his stablemate makes up for *that* by carefully depositing his droppings in every possible corner of the stall next door. My horse-loving aunt tells me that she once made a valiant effort to housebreak her mare by training her always to defecate in one part of the pasture on a pile of straw, but it never really worked, mainly because horses have little control over their bowel movements. (My young Morgan, incidentally, was trained to stop short the moment he produced manure when he was being driven, because it was his trainer's responsibility to keep the pathways clean on the property where they worked. This was all well and good until I started riding Rex, and I had to spend a good deal of time untraining him or risk deep embarrassment in the show ring.) Horses do control their urinating, however, since they are forced to take a special stance, and many horses will not urinate under saddle.

Individual toilet habits aside, the procedure is the same for every horse: mucking out. On a daily basis, droppings and wet bedding must be removed (usually with a pitchfork or manure fork) and carted away (usually in a wheelbarrow) to the muck heap, which is generally near the stable, though not so near that flies and other muck lovers will be attracted into the stable itself. (This pile will be made smaller periodically either by someone's trucking it away or by removal to a compost heap where it can season before it is ready to use on the garden.) Don't make the mistake of removing more bedding than you need to, since it is expensive and perfectly reusable if not soiled.

Once a week—or more if necessary—the stall should be given a thorough cleaning. Take the horse out of the stall first, then remove the obvious manure and wet bedding. Gradually work your way around the stall, picking up all the bedding, shaking it on the pitchfork to separate the soiled from the clean portion, and setting the clean stuff to one side. When you have dug down to the bottom all the way around, scrape it with a shovel and disinfect with lime, and then return the clean bedding to make a level layer, adding new bedding as necessary.

One thing to keep in mind as you muck is the condition of the horse's manure. If there are many visible grains of feed in it, the horse is obviously not digesting his food, which may indicate tooth problems that should be brought to the attention of the owner. If the droppings are loose, discolored, or otherwise different from the normal quality and consistency or if the urine is unusually colored, tell someone about it. Keep an eye on the salt block too. Most horses get mineral supplements and if the block is being used more rapidly than normal, there may be something the matter with the animal.

During this weekly session, it may also be necessary to wash the water and feed buckets or bins thoroughly with warm water and detergent (rinsing carefully) and to scrub down doors, windows, walls, or whatever else seems in need of cleaning.

Whether you are doing the daily or the weekly chores, remember always to leave the center aisle or the area outside the stall as clean as possible. Nothing is untidier than a stable with loose wisps of hay or straw lying about, and nothing is more dangerous than leaving a wheelbarrow or a pitchfork around on the floor for human or horse to knock over or step onto.

FEEDING AND WATERING

Most people who know their horses take great care in their choice of feed, method of feeding, and schedule, since nutrition is such an important part of general equine health and condition. If you are given specific instructions about feeding a horse, follow them to the letter; if you are given no instructions, ask before you make some bad guesses. Horses that get a great deal of fresh grass in the pasture may get less food in the stall than those who are confined; on the other hand, confined horses that are not worked hard may be fed less to keep them from getting more energy than they need, though they might have as much hay as they will eat to keep them occupied and contented. In other words, each horse has a different diet because nutritional requirements vary from one animal to the next. Some are worked harder than others; some are "easy keepers" that need little food to keep them fit; some have deficiencies or medical problems that may require supplements or special feeds. The same horse may get a different diet at different times of the year, depending on weather, work, and type of feed.

There are, however, a few useful generalizations about feeding horses that will help you get started. In preparing hay for a horse, don't simply throw a bale or part of one (called a "flake") into the stall. Outside the stall, preferably in an area where the hay is stored, pull off the amount you will need and break it apart with your hands. Then lift a bit with a pitchfork and shake it to remove dust and to separate the stalks. Dust can be damaging to a horse's eyes or respiratory tract, and bits of twigs and rough stalks that fall out in the winnowing process can be rough on a horse's throat. If the hay still seems dusty, sprinkle some water on it. When you have a nice, light pile, convey it by fork to the horse's stall—putting it on the floor near the bin (always in the same place—horses are creatures of habit, remember) unless there is an overhead hay rack.

In feeding grain, be sure that you measure properly using a special measuring can. (Horse owners often use coffee cans for measuring, but just as coffee companies use different sizes, so do horse owners; be sure you match the right can—and amount of grain—to the horse.) Even if the horse has a feed bin built into the stall, use a bucket to carry the grain to the bin and be sure to mix the grains together if you are using more than one type. Supplements or medications are often mixed into the grain, and you may be asked—if the horse tends to refuse "tampered" feed—to lace the mixture with a few tablespoons of molasses to mask the taste. If you are feeding treats into the grain such as carrots or apples, don't break them into too small of chunks that might be swallowed without chewing.

If you are given a regular schedule to follow, stick to it, and if you aren't, try to find out somehow at what times the horse is accustomed to eating. I have known perfectly placid animals to raise perfect hell when their meals weren't delivered on time, and some have even reached such a state that their digestion was upset. The digestive tract of a horse is one of the most delicate things there is, and it seems that anything can disturb it, even tension or anxiety. So when you feed a horse, notice whether he is really eating or simply picking at the food. A horse that goes off his feed is giving a signal that something is wrong, and the sooner you know that the better your chances will be to prevent serious trouble. One way of stopping trouble before it starts is to make sure that the food you give is of the highest possible quality; if the hay and grain seem moldy and the carrots and grass are less than fresh, complain to the owner, who is probably counting on you for that sort of information.

One substance that all horses get, regardless of individual diet, is water, and a normal horse will drink from five to fifteen gallons a day. Stables that don't have watering devices have to have people willing to haul water buckets, i.e., people like you. Horses should have access to water most of the time, but there are exceptions to that rule. When a horse is hot from exertion or has been deprived of water for some time, it should be offered in very small quantities if at all; preferably, the horse should be cooled down before being allowed free access to the water bucket. It is easy to lead a horse to water but impossible to keep him from drinking if the bucket contains more water than you want him to have. So wait for a while before watering or don't fill the bucket to the top. Don't let water sit in a bucket for so long that it gets soiled or murky-looking, and be sure to break the ice from the top of a bucket in cold weather.

GROOMING

Although show horses always seem to have been shined like well-polished silver, the point of grooming is not simply to keep a horse looking good. Horses that are stabled year-round need daily grooming in order to tone their muscles and to stimulate blood circulation and the glands that secrete the oils that keep the skin and coat soft and glossy. These horses may also be clipped during cold weather to keep their heavy winter coats under control, since the presence of a long hair-coat will cause profuse sweating if a horse is heavily worked, and this can lead to problems. Clipped horses must be blanketed if they are to be protected against the cold (blankets called coolers are also used in warm weather to keep a horse from cooling off too fast). Horses that are pastured for most of the year will need only occasional brushing to remove clumps of dirt, mats, burrs, lice, and so on to prevent skin trouble, but they should not be overgroomed, since they need a natural layer of oil and dust in the coat as a protective covering against the elements. (These horses should also not be overworked when their winter coats are heavy.)

Many horses enjoy a cooling bath after a day of work, and many horseless riders enjoy obliging them, only one of various chores that must be performed around a stable.

Most grooms develop their own techniques and methods of grooming their charges, and the best way to learn is to apprentice yourself to someone who knows what he or she is doing. I won't go into the various chores here, but I can recommend that you become familiar with the tools of the trade and their uses: the currycomb, the body brush, the dandy or mud brush, the finishing brush, the rub rag or stable rubber, the sponge and the sweat scraper (used to give a horse a bath), the hoof pick, the mane comb, and the clippers (usually electric or battery operated).

While you are watching your mentor at work on a horse, make yourself useful by keeping the tools clean (use the currycomb to clean the brushes, for instance) or by picking up clumps of dirt and hair that fall. Especially important to learn is the use of the hoof pick, since this is an object that you should carry with you on long rides in case the horse picks up a stone in his shoe. If you find yourself confronting a horse that you are about to ride but must groom and tack up yourself, keep in mind that you should:

1. Not go below the knees or onto any tender area with the currycomb, if you must use it at all (never use it on clipped or fine-skinned horses).

2. Always brush in the direction in which the hair lies.

3. Clean out the horse's feet.

4. Make sure that there is no dust or other foreign substance beneath the areas on which you put the tack.

That's not much of a grooming job, but it is the essential minimum that you must do before riding.

After your ride, there may be no one available to take your horse. Don't just put him away in a stall, but be prepared to untack him and give him a rubdown and perhaps even a bath once his halter has replaced the bridle. Don't do anything without asking first, but if you are given the go-ahead, take a few precautions. Always use a lead rope. Never put a horse away wet or overheated. If the animal is sweating from exertion, ride him at the walk until he feels dry just behind his elbows in the girth area, or walk him on a lead line until he is cool (see the section on exercising below). If the area under the saddle is marked with dried sweat, offer to give the horse a bath or brush the horse until the hair is smooth. Pick out each foot and brush each leg carefully and check thoroughly for any potential problems. In some areas, horses may be scratched by thorns along the trail or pick up ticks that can cause serious disease if not removed. Horses that have been worked hard, especially at jumping, may have been bruised about the legs or suffer muscle strain that could require hosing with cold water or the use of liniment. Ask the stable manager or owner for advice if you see anything out of the ordinary. When the horse is turned out or put back in his stall, be sure he has sufficient water and that latches are carefully fastened. Oh, and don't forget to put away the tack in the proper spot; a quick wipe of the bit with a damp cloth and an offer to clean the leather would probably convince the management that you are a customer worth cultivating.

Another reason to learn the grooming procedure properly is to become familiar with signs of ill health or injury that may require attention either from the owner or from the veterinarian. Eyes, nose, or ears that are runny or filled with mucus, teeth that are broken or malformed, sores or cuts on the skin, areas that are sensitive to the touch, or hot areas on the legs and feet may all indicate trouble—some more serious than others. Loss of hair or a particularly dry coat or rigid skin can indicate anything from nutritional deficiency to parasites (worms) or even serious disease, and it is always the groom that notices these things first. Read up on horse health, and be sure to be on hand when the vet turns up for his or her regular visit or in an emergency. Many vets got their start by taking an interest in equine health, and some of them are horsemen still.

Clipping and braiding are two jobs that are time consuming but demanding in terms of skill and are often up for grabs if there is someone around willing to undertake them. These procedures are usually reserved for horses that are shown, hunted, or raced regularly and are useful to know if you plan to go into competition yourself, but any horse that is stabled or used frequently during the cold weather will probably need clipping even if braids may never grace his neck. Not only is a clipped horse more attractive and easier to clean, he is also easier to cool down, since the sweat evaporates more quickly to keep the animal's internal temperature level. Most horses in temperate climates need clipping twice a year (late

October and January), but draft horses, Shetland ponies, and other animals with fast-growing haircoats will need to be clipped more often. Clipping should not be done toward the end of winter as the new haircoat is beginning to grow in; at this time of year, the shedding process will have begun and the groom will be plenty busy just grooming!

There are different types of clips, one of them involving the whole horse, one (the hunter clip) leaving the legs and saddle area unclipped, and one (the trace clip) leaving all but the lower part of the shoulder, belly, and hindquarters fully furred. But learning the pattern is only the first step. Next you must learn to wield the clippers in such a way that the hair is removed evenly and neatly from such hard-to-reach areas as around the ears, around the dock (tail area), and around the legs. Some horses don't care much for the sound though they will get used to it in time; one friend of mine owns a horse that objects so violently to the noise of large clippers that he must tranquilize the animal and then use a pair of small clippers, which take a long time to cover very little area. If the job begins to get you down, just keep in mind that your grooming chores will be a lot easier after clipping and be grateful that you weren't a groom in the good old days when clipping was done by hand with a razor or by using a candle to singe the long hairs.

Braiding is the ultimate procedure in mane care, used for show, hunting, and for training the mane to lie flat. There are many traditions, rules, and techniques for braiding, and here again, learning is best done by watching or by working under the eagle eye of an expert. Tails may also be braided, either for show or for practicality on muddy days. There are many other things to do with these parts of the horse in addition to keeping them combed and clean: pulling or plucking a tail involves pulling a few hairs at a time along the edge of the upper tail to keep it neat and pulling the long hairs from the mane to keep the length at four to six inches; banging involves cutting the long hair of the tail straight across the bottom even with the hock; hogging involves clipping the mane flat to the neck; and roaching is clipping the mane but leaving the center hairs slightly longer. Some horses, such as Arabs and Morgans, wear a bridle-path style mane, which means that the mane is roached for about a third of the way down the neck from behind the ears to show off the animal's neck and to make the bridle easier to put on. Some cuts are chosen because of tradition or breed, while others are selected because they show the horse to advantage, masking faults or highlighting strong points. If you are going to play hairdresser to someone else's horse, be sure that you clear the style selection with them, but if you show some talent, you may find yourself the Vidal Sassoon of the barn. You will also find yourself getting up well before the crack of dawn to prepare someone's pony for a show, which may be one of the reasons this job is frequently open.

TACK

Anyone who has gone beyond the beginner stage in riding should know how to put on a bridle and saddle and how to take them off, but it never ceases to amaze me how many horseless riders—even those with a good deal of skill in the saddle—seem to believe that horses were born with tack in place. Because their animals have been led out to them fully tacked and are led away tacked after the ride, they have never had the chance to learn either procedure. But what should happen if they find themselves confronted with a naked horse? Refuse to ride? Put things on backward? Horrible thoughts to contemplate. Any skier or fisherman worth his or her salt knows the equipment inside and out, and it serves to reason that anyone who plans to ride more than once should know not only how to work his or her equipment, but how it is made, cared for, and repaired.

As plastic takes over the world, I find that one of the aspects of riding that gives me special pleasure is the fact that there is so much lovely, smelly leather around. But leather requires good care if it is to stay in good condition, and care means work—often a lot of it. Saddles and bridles and martingales and halters and breastplates and stirrup leathers and girths and all those leather items need constant cleaning—brushing off of dust, dirt, or dried sweat or saliva after each use, frequent applications of saddle soap, and weekly (or more frequent) thorough cleanings, which involve taking the bridle and saddle apart, checking for signs of wear, and getting them sponged or scrubbed, wiped dry, and oiled. Leather that is not cared for carefully will dry out, rot, or break apart, and leather tack that is in poor condition will be uncomfortable and potentially dangerous for both rider and beast. The metal parts will also need an occasional thorough soaking and scrubbing with metal cleaner, and fabrics, as in the saddle

Even if you don't have your own horse, you should learn the proper way to put on a bridle (left) before a ride and to untack a horse after a ride, replacing the bridle with a halter (right).

pad or blanket and girth, will also need washing, drying, and brushing.

The first step is to learn how the various items are put together, and that means taking them apart, cleaning them, and putting them back in the proper way. Learning to put them on the horse is step two, usually done saddle first, martingale (if any) second, and bridle last. Although many horses consent to being tacked up in their stalls, some prefer to be tacked up (and groomed) on cross-ties outside the stall. Whatever you do, don't let the horse loose until you are sure that everything is in place and you are in control; nothing is more embarrassing than having a half-tacked animal wandering around without its bridle on. Some horses object to being tacked up and have picked up a number of tricks to put first-timers or novices off their stride. "Blowing up" or expanding the belly to make the girth difficult (or impossible) to tighten is one; if a sharp but not damaging blow to the belly doesn't convince the horse to breathe out, simply walk the animal around until he releases the air and tighten the girth then. Some horses cowkick when the girth is tightened—or flatten their ears in a threatening manner. Don't let yourself get into a vulnerable position relative to the legs, and keep up a constant chatter and a confident manner so that the horse will be reassured and know you mean business. I once knew a mare who was so head shy that the bridle had to be taken almost entirely apart before she would allow it to be put on; I assumed that she had ear problems, since she seemed so sensitive, but I found that she was perfectly content to let me remove the bridle no matter how firmly I pressed on her ears in the process. I didn't alert the vet but thought she could be worked out of this bad habit with some painstaking care. (It turned out that the groom had already taken such care, but the mare was unusually stubborn so we just continued to take the bridle apart each time.)

Removing tack is much easier than putting it on, but here you must take care to leave it in the proper way—clean and suitably stored to avoid damage to the structure or the materials. Most horses in large barns have their own tack, and the places for it should be carefully marked with the animals' names; if you are confused, ask. An error here can be a great deal of discomfort for the horse or confusion for the next rider.

You'll notice that I haven't described the proper procedures for tacking up and down and that's because it would take many pages to do so when one watching session will do. There are different methods, but the one that works is obviously the best, so if you find yourself having trouble dressing a particular horse, adapt what you know to what he seems willing to tolerate, so long as you don't let him take advantage of you. It should go without saying that most of your tacking-up procedures should be carried out on the near (left) side of the horse, the one from which most people mount and dismount; you will, of course, need to visit the other side occasionally to tighten the girth and pull the stirrups up and down.

EXERCISING AND HOT-WALKING

Obviously the horseless rider's chief aim in hanging around a stable is to be allowed to exercise the inhabitants, but riding isn't the only way this is done. For one thing, you must learn how to lead a horse properly, which, surprisingly enough, is not as simple as it seems. A bridled horse should be led only for short distances by the reins; for anything longer than that one must remove the bridle, replace it with a halter (or put a halter on over the bridle), and use a lead rope. If the horse you are leading by the reins is skittish or seems anxious to get away from you, do not bring the reins over his head (he could step on a rein if he gets away from you) but hold the reins rather closely beneath his jaw for firm control. If the horse is tired or placid or well-behaved, pull the reins over the head and, holding the horse just under the jaw with your right hand, place the rest of the reins in your left so that they don't get stepped on. Also, be sure that you pull the stirrups up on the saddle so that they don't flop around on the horse's sides. Even if you are using a halter and lead rope, don't get careless and allow the lead to get too slack; I've had more than one halter ring break on me because a grazing horse managed to step firmly on the lead and pull his head up suddenly.

I have discussed elsewhere the methods of lungeing and long-reining, two ways of giving a horse exercise without getting aboard, especially useful in schooling or when you haven't enough time to ride. Stables large and opulent enough to afford an automatic walker can take care of this task for you, but the horse will need constant supervision and you should know how it works, in case of emergency or misfire. These walkers are used for cooling down as well as for exercise, and this is a technique that any stablehand must learn to a "T" if only because overheating can cause so many problems. If a horse comes back from a ride sweating and hot, curse the rider who brought him back that way and plan to spend fifteen or twenty minutes cooling the horse off. Leading the horse around and allowing him to graze is the most natural way, but you may also have to put on a cooler (to avoid chilling) and keep the horse away from the watering trough. You may also have to give the animal a bath and scrape off the water and sweat, and then walk around until the horse is completely dry. Don't ever put any horse back in a stall when he is still hot, and don't let him drink much water until his temperature and respiration have returned to normal.

Hot-walking is a job unto itself around the racetrack, where the horses are delicate, young, and prone to high-spirits. Many young people get into the business of exercise riding and eventually jockeying or training that way, so it needn't be pointed out that this is a useful thing to know how to do.

If a horse is to be turned out to the paddock or pasture for exercise, relaxation, or for a period of time, be sure that you know exactly where to put the horse and what other animals are in there. Some horses will fight if pastured together, and more than several of them have gotten out by poorly fastened gates or fences that have fallen into disrepair. If you have any questions, don't guess but ask. And don't let the horse go until you are well within the paddock with the gate closed behind you. It's easier for you to reopen it to get out or crawl over the fence than it is to chase an animal who has the whole world to explore.

9

BROADENING YOUR HORIZONS

UP TO THIS POINT we've been doing a lot of learning, what with instructors, lesson programs, schooling sessions in the ring and on the trail, and experience on as many horses as possible. Although horsemen never stop learning, there comes a time in every rider's life when the basics become second nature and the real challenge lies in being able to prove to yourself and to others that you can ride and that you can do it well. For some people, it is enough simply to be able to enjoy a cross-country hack for its own sake or to be satisfied with that hard-earned ability to ride whatever horse comes along. But to many other people, the proving ground is a show ring, a racetrack, a polo field, or a piece of the countryside in which foxes abide. After all, riding is a sport and, as in other sports, the name of the game is competition. Whether you compete for prizes or fun, for the thrill of winning, or for the satisfaction of holding your own in the company of like-minded sportsmen, this is what it's all about. Some of the activities described in this chapter will mean a change of scene, apparel, or equipment, others only a change of attitude; many will demand special training of the horse as well as the rider. But none of them demands that you own a horse, and most of them take place year-round throughout the country.

HORSE SHOWS

If the stable at which you ride puts on a regular horse show or a series of them, your instructor or the stable manager will probably encourage you to enter one as you make progress with your riding. Even a fairly advanced show geared to top riders and horses will generally have one or more classes for less experienced riders and for the horseless variety who must rely on the stable's own animals. If the stable does not sponsor any shows, and if there are none in your area, suggest that the management put one on or offer to do so for them. There is a lot of work involved in managing a horse show, even a small, informal one, but there is a great deal of satisfaction as well, especially if the atmosphere is properly competitive—not dog-eat-dog but active and spirited. All you really need is a head for organization, a set of ribbons (available through tack shops), and, of course, some interested people to enter the various classes. If your stable's manager hasn't had any experience, join the American Horse Shows Association in order to get a copy of the rule book (220 East 42nd Street, New York, NY 10017-5806). The main point is to get everyone into the act—braiding manes, grooming horses within an inch of their dapples (or closer, if you want them to shine), setting up jumps or musical stalls or barrels, as well as the less horsy chores, such as announcing, selling refreshments, collecting entry fees, handing out numbers, and presenting ribbons to the winners. The function of a stable or schooling show is for everyone to get experience and to have fun, not just to win prizes. Judges should be expert horsemen (not the stable's own instructors, but perhaps instructors from other stables), and they should be encouraged to help out all entrants, winners and losers, by giving constructive criticism when asked and by awarding as many ribbons as there are colors in the rainbow.

First prize—blue
Second prize—red
Third prize—yellow
Fourth prize—white
Fifth prize—pink
Sixth prize—green
Seventh prize—purple
Eighth prize—brown
Ninth prize—gray
Tenth prize—light blue

Grand champion—blue, red, yellow, and white
Reserve to grand champion—red, yellow, white, and pink
Champion—blue, red, and yellow
Reserve champion—red, yellow, and white

With a good basic seat and experience on many different horses, a young rider may look forward to a successful future in the show ring.

Large horse shows have several different divisions, but small events often feature only the classes that will be of interest to local riders and horse owners. Regardless of a show's specialty, however, there are two types of classes: those in which the rider is judged and those in which the horse is. Equitation classes are for the rider, and most of these are restricted to riders eighteen or under, though many shows also offer adult equitation classes. (Most of my ribbons, in fact, were earned many years after I passed the age of eighteen, on the backs of horses that spent their lives giving lessons to novices.)

Divisions in which the horse is judged vary considerably in type and level of competition, but except for breed and conformation classes, the emphasis is usually on performance rather than appearance, and this is where the rider's skill is as important as the horse's natural ability or degree of schooling. Western riders can enter stock-horse events for reining or cutting horses; pleasure-horse classes in which the horse is judged at the walk, jog, lope, and backing; or trail-horse classes in which horses are judged at different gaits and on their obedience and willingness to undertake special tasks. The obstacles that a trail horse may face in the ring are often as much a test of the show officials' imagination as of the horse: ramps to be climbed, boxes resembling trailers to be entered, gates to be opened and closed, automobile tires to be stepped into and out of, seesaws to be walked across, mazes to be backed through, and so on.

Under English saddle, horses may be entered in the saddle-horse division to show their stuff as five-gaited or three-gaited performers. Pleasure-horse classes—sometimes limited to specific breeds and sometimes not—are judged on the horse's performance at the walk, trot, and canter. In hunter classes, the horses are judged as much on manners and way of going as ability to jump, while in the jumper division, speed and jumping skill are essential and style matters not at all. The harness division features high-stepping horses or ponies, while driving classes may vary from pleasure driving to time classes or those in which various difficult maneuvers must be executed. There is even a three-day event for driving horses, involving a dressage phase, a cross-country run, and an obstacle test in which time is a crucial factor. One lovely old-fashioned type of competition is the sidesaddle class, usually made part of the hunter division.

Entering a horse show is a simple matter. A few days before the show, study the prize list to determine which classes will be suitable for your level of expertise and then fill out an entry blank for each class as soon as you know what horse will be available to ride. If other riders will be using the same horse, make absolutely sure ahead of time that there will be no conflicts and that the poor creature won't be expected to enter every class in the show. Sharing a horse may not be an ideal situation, but if the animal must be shipped to the show grounds, you will be able to share expenses instead of bearing the cost alone. There will probably be a fee for each class, and if your instructor is going to be there coaching you, you'll have to pay him or her something too. Other than that—plus whatever rental you may pay for the horse—your only worry will be to get yourself properly outfitted. On the day of the show, make sure that the horse is groomed and tacked up (and his mane braided, if necessary) and that you are registered, which involves paying the entry fees and getting your number. And be ready at the ingate several minutes before your class starts, boots polished, number in place, and nerves at ease. There may be some time for you to school the horse a bit, not to do any last-minute cramming as for an exam but to do a bit of trotting about to relax yourself and the horse, perhaps including a fence or two if you are about to enter a jumping class. When your class is called, walk serenely into the ring and do your stuff—but don't forget to smile. In some classes, the horses and riders perform individually and you must wait your turn; don't use those few minutes to sit there and fret but watch the competition if you can or think pleasant thoughts.

There is no avoiding the fact that you will need a good horse to do well at the better shows against strong competition from people with their own mounts, but even here the horseless rider has a chance. Ask someone who owns a horse but isn't interested in showing whether you might borrow the animal for a particular event (and preferably for a period before the show so that you may practice). If you should do well, the owner will be as pleased as you are and may encourage you to ride the horse at other shows. Several famous riders got their start doing just this kind of thing—called "catch riding"—for fun and ribbons at first and eventually for money or for the chance to go on the horse-show circuit or even onto the Equestrian Team. Just as dog shows have their professional handlers, so horse shows have their professional riders. The next time you go to a show, notice in the program how many horses don't belong to the people who are riding them. Neither Margie Goldstein-Engle, one of the most renowned riders in the jumper field, nor race rider Julie Krone reached the top of their professions riding their own animals! (In the next chapter we will look further into the world of the professional rider.)

Because many excellent riders do not have the time or money to support their own stables full of competition horses, they tend to rely on the generosity of sponsors or employers—well-to-do individuals with a great interest in horses and with trophy rooms waiting for ribbons but without the children or ability to ride the horses they own. If you are fortunate and talented enough to attract the attention of one of these people, count your blessings.

But even if you are not, you can work at a somewhat less glamorous level by making your presence known to horse owners as someone who could do well by their horses simply for the privilege of keeping the ribbons rather than for any money or other support. Catch riders have some responsibilities as well as pleasures, however, which include undertaking the risk of injury (unless there is a written agreement, though most horse owners will usually cover the cost of medical bills), the purchase and maintenance of an appropriate and impeccable wardrobe, the keeping of accurate records, and the responsibility for being on time for each class—to say nothing of riding each horse as if it were one's own.

Devoting a great deal of time to the horse-show circuit can be a big commitment, and as the business of showing becomes more popular and the horses become more expensive, the costs can be considerable as well. But Ian Millar, the brilliant Canadian rider, has some reassuring words for the horseless:

> There is an old hang-up about this sport. In certain levels of horse showing, rich people get involved and buy their kids nice horses and they win. But in show jumping, all the money in the world won't help you. You've got to know how to ride a horse. And so my advice to young people is not to get discouraged if they don't have money. All the industry, owners, trainers, and the like are always looking for a young rider with talent. I can't think of a rider or trainer who won't bend over backward to help that talented person. The horse shows are full of young people who are working as grooms now. If they show their aptitude, they'll be allowed to ride and to jump a little bit. So it is possible to ride and get to the Grand Prix level without having a million dollars.

GYMKHANAS

Games on horseback come in all shapes, sizes, and degrees of seriousness. A Hindu word for "field day," the gymkhana was invented by British cavalrymen stationed in India, but the event has now become popular throughout the United States, mostly as a sport for youngsters. There is no special tack required—it *may* be English or Western, so long as it is comfortable for the horse—and riding apparel for the rider will depend on the rules of the show, which may be part of a large horse show, a spontaneous, informal backyard event, or a more formal occasion recognized and regulated by the American Horse Shows Association.

Informal gymkhanas can be as simple or as complex as the imagination of the participants and instigators of the show, but they usually include races against the clock, competitive games, and non-competitive games. Speed races can be

One of the features of a gymkhana, pole bending, like slalom on skis, is a sport demanding skill, practice, and teamwork on the part of horse and rider.

anything from ring spearing (as in jousting matches of old), racing from a starting point around a pole and back, Coke or beer races (in which riders must ride to a barrel, drink a full can of liquid, turn it upside down without spilling any, and ride back across the finish line), and Gambler's Choice (in which riders try to jump a series of jumps each worth a number of points according to difficulty and accumulate the largest number of points in the shortest time). Competitive games include musical stalls or tires (run like musical chairs), egg-and-spoon races, relay races, backing races, and the dollar-bill marathon (a bareback class in which a dollar bill is placed under each rider's seat—the winner being the rider who keeps the dollar bill the longest through the walk, trot, and canter). Non-competitive games, such as tag, Simon says, and follow the leader, are particularly good for very young children, since the rules are the same as those played on foot.

Of the gymkhana classes recognized by the AHSA, barrel racing is undoubtedly the best known, since it has become a popular attraction in Western shows and rodeos. Defying gravity at each turn, horse and rider careen against the clock in a cloverleaf course around three barrels, and though it sounds easy, the practice involved in perfecting the flying changes of lead, spurts of speed, and sharp turns is no simple matter. Pole bending—a variation of the slalom on skis—and the keyhole race, in which the rider crosses the timing line, races into a keyhole shape, turns in the circle, and races back across the line, are two other events in which the utmost skill and precision are demanded. At high levels of competition, these are not for the occasional rider, since they require horses that are trained and riders who can make them do their best. But the informal games, where fun is more important than winning, can be wonderful sport for riders at any stage and horses of any type. My particular favorite is one whose outcome is invariably up to the horse: bobbing for apples, in which horses and riders race to one end of a ring where riders dismount and try to get their animals to bob for apples in buckets of water. Not until a horse has picked up an apple can the rider remount and race back across the finish line. Everyone knows that you can lead a horse to water and not make him drink, but the sight of ten youngsters trying to defy the old adage is worth its weight in Polaroids.

For some ideas about the kinds of games that may be included in a gymkhana, look at the book *Gymkhanas and Rally Games* from the British Horse Society and Pony Club and the three *United States Pony Club Manuals of Horsemanship.*

RODEOS

This is probably the most truly American of all equestrian events, deriving from the informal competitions that cowboys would hold after the roundup to show who was better than whom at roping and riding. Nowadays, rodeos are a bit more formal, but no less popular, since there are more than two thousand of them held every year, and not just in the West. Schools, colleges, and even prisons put on rodeos, and the Professional Rodeo Cowboys Association sanctions more than five hundred rodeos a year. The most traditional events are bronc riding (bareback and saddle), bull riding, steer wrestling, and calf roping, but most rodeos also offer barrel racing for women, trick-riding, roping exhibitions, and grand parades, in which horses and riders wear their very finest apparel.

Although the competitions are judged on the rider's ability, the horses are usually well trained since their cooperation is of the utmost importance. It may take months of training to get a reining horse or a barrel racer up to winning peak, but even the broncs—used by the horseless riders, of course, since they are generally owned by stock dealers rather than individual cowboys—have their own particular talents to show off. Most cowboys do own their own reining horses, and cowgirls their barrel racers, but plenty of riders carry only their saddles with them and count on picking up rides as they go. Many of them work for ranches or competitive groups, while others simply hang around waiting for a riderless horse. For more information about dates and locations of rodeos, write the Professional Rodeo Cowboys Association (101 Pro Rodeo Drive, Colorado Springs, CO 80919-9989).

Cutting horse competitions, in which horse and rider (primarily horse) have three minutes to "cut" a cow from the herd and keep it separated, have become increasingly popular over the years. A cutting horse is a valuable animal, and if you are offered the chance to ride one, take it. The National Cutting Horse Association is located at 4704 Highway 377 South, Fort Worth, TX 76116-8805.

DRESSAGE TESTS

We have already considered dressage in the chapter on instruction as a style of riding and a method of training, but it is becoming increasingly popular here as a competitive sport in itself as well as a famous spectacle performed by the "high school" horses of the Spanish Riding School in Vienna, the Cadre Noir of Saumur, in France, and the Andalusian Riding School in Spain. Andalusian, Arab, and American Lipizzaners perform exhibitions of "airs above the ground," but competitive dressage, like the system itself, begins with elementary levels and progresses to increasingly higher levels, culminating with the Olympics.

A dressage test is held in a special arena, marked with letters at the corners and along the sides, and each horse and rider perform a prescribed series or pattern of movements one at a time while one or more judges comment and keep score. There are usually two or three tests for each level, starting with the Training Level, Test 1, and working up through First, Second, Third, and Fourth levels to Prix St.-Georges, Intermédiaire, and the Grand Prix de Dressage, which is an Olympic test. The tests are increasingly difficult, of course, and the standards by which the horses are judged become higher as the level rises. In other words, less will be expected of a trot at the Training Level than at a higher level.

Before you decide that dressage is out of your league because you don't have a horse you can work with on a daily basis, ask your teacher for some dressage instruction or apply to a special dressage instructor and work, even on an intermittent basis, with a horse to which you do have access. Keep in mind that the first test of the Training Level involves only being able to walk, trot, and canter on correct leads going both ways around the ring, making smooth transitions from one gait to the next (halt and walk, walk and trot, trot and canter), and making smooth circles while changing direction. Of course, those gaits must be sufficiently balanced and rhythmic to win points, but this is what every rider wants from every horse he or she rides. More advanced tests include collection and extension, complicated patterns, and various lateral or two-track movements (such as the shoulder-in), as well as turns on the haunches and ten-meter cantered circles.

For information about dressage tests and clubs in your area and special events, such as clinics and demonstrations given by experts, write to the U.S. Dressage Federation, P.O. Box 6669, Lincoln, NE 68506, and subscribe to its official magazine *Dressage Today* (656 Quince Orchard Road, Gaithersburg, MD 10878).

DISTANCE RIDING

Trail riding is often simply a pleasant way to see the countryside from horseback, but it is also an activity in which riders may compete at various levels. Trail-horse classes in horse shows, as mentioned earlier, are designed to test a horse's ability to face all manner of obstacles or types of footing, but distance riding as a sport involves a great deal more than that. There are two types of distance riding: competitive trail rides in which the entrants must cover a specified stretch of country in a specified time, neither too fast nor too slow; and endurance rides, in which the first sound horse to cover the distance is the winner. Competitive rides vary in length from twenty-five miles in one day to a hundred miles over three days, while endurance rides vary from fifty to a hundred miles in a single day. There are often different levels (Novice and Open, for example) or weight classes, and the terrain to be covered can be relatively flat (as in the southern competitive rides), or terrifically rough (as in the Tevis Cup 100-mile endurance ride in Squaw Valley, California). Although these distance rides vary considerably, they all have in common the fact that the horse's condition is given primary importance. In the old days, organized trail rides were literally killers, often as long as several hundred miles and several days. Today, however, the rides are strictly managed and horses are checked by lay judges and veterinarians before, during, and after the rides. In competitive trail rides, the judging is done first on the basis of the horse's condition, with points deducted for time penalties; in endurance rides the winner is the horse that comes in first, but points are deducted for animals in poor condition.

Preparing for a distance ride can involve months of conditioning as well as training in specifics such as backing, dealing with steep hills and difficult footing, and working on extended gaits, particularly the trot. Although most competitors ride their own horses—and some enthusiasts are even trying to breed the best possible animals for distance riding, many riders have done well on other people's horses, rented or borrowed, so long as those horses were fit and properly prepared. It will cost money to compete on the circuits in the East and West, but distance riding does not involve nearly the investment that the horse-show circuit does. For one thing, there are few frills—no special apparel or tack, though what one wears or puts on one's horse must be perfectly fitted for the sake of comfort. And for another it is not necessary to have any particular type of horse except one that is physically capable of doing the job. Arabs seem to do best in competition, but Morgans, Standardbreds (whose long-strided trot is a great ground coverer), Quarter Horses, and Appaloosas, as well as any number of grades, have been highly successful as well.

Probably the best way to break into the field is to get to know some people who participate in the sport and to offer to help them condition their horses, which consists of many long rides that are both demanding and time consuming. Or you can join one of the many available non-competitive pleasure rides with a borrowed horse and, if you like the activity, work up to a competitive level on your own. Ann Hyland's book *Riding Long Distance* (J. A. Allen) encourages riders to combine trail riding for pleasure as well as competition, and Karen Paulo's *America's Long-Distance Challenge* (Dutton) is a complete guide to both endurance and competitive riding. There are trail-ride associations in most states, each one with its own rules, point systems, and series of rides, and there are independent rides as well, in which riders from all over the country enter every year. For information, write to the North American Trail Riding Conference (P.O. Box 2136, Ranchos de Taos, NM 87557-2136) or to the American Endurance Ride Conference (701 High Street, Auburn, CA 95603-4727).

CROSS-COUNTRY JUMPING

If this activity is your idea of the best way to spend a couple of hours on horseback, you have a wide variety of competitive ways to indulge yourself or to show off what you can do. Fox hunting, which will be discussed later in this chapter, is not competitive (or shouldn't be) but hunter-pace trials are. These are generally sponsored by a hunt or by stables that specialize in training hunters and entered by teams of riders who are required to complete a course in a predetermined time, no more and no less. In addition to maintaining the optimum pace, the contestants are also judged on the general handiness, condition, and manners of their horses—the standard being the ideal field hunter. Rules of dress and decorum for the ride vary according to the sponsor of the event, but in most cases they are not as rigid as for a formal hunt.

Although a good working relationship between horse and rider is desirable, I have known many people to do well on rented horses, relying on their own common sense and on the horse's familiarity with the terrain. A good friend of mine, in fact, entered a hunter pace for the first time, using a horse that was borrowed from the stable that sponsored the event, and she ended up winning first prize—a nice silver plate and a great deal of personal satisfaction. Needless to say, it behooves a newcomer on an unfamiliar horse to team up with a rider who already knows the ropes, as my friend did on her

Cross-country jumping is a demanding but exhilarating way for the experienced horse and rider to enjoy working together.

first time out. There may be no foxes, hounds, or hunt breakfast in sight, but the exhilaration of fox hunting is very much
present, not to mention the added excitement of a competitive atmosphere. If you do not know of any local hunts or
hunter stables in your area that sponsor hunter paces, write
to *The Chronicle of the Horse* for dates and locations (P.O.
Box 46, Middleburg, VA 22117).

Another kind of cross-country jumping against a clock is
the second phase of the three-phase sport of combined training or three-day eventing. Speed is what counts most here,
although points are deducted for falls, refusals, and running
out at jumps (no points are deducted for knocking jumps down
only because they are so solid that they *can't* be knocked
down!). Designing cross-country courses for events is an art
requiring imagination and general fiendishness, for the obstacles are not only imposing looking at high-level competitions but demanding in other ways, such as appearance (stacks
of tires, for instance, or a picnic table) and pure difficulty
(complicated in-and-outs, two jumps separated by a steep hill,
jumps in the middle of streams or ditches, and so on for five
miles or more at high speed). A horse that is able to cope with
such a course must be a talented jumper in top condition, but
more than that he must be unusually brave and trusting in
his rider. For more information about combined training as a
whole, see the following section.

Steeplechasing, or race riding over fences, may seem similar to the cross-country phase of combined training, since speed
is the deciding factor, but actually the two are distinct, if only
because steeplechasing or point-to-point racing involves competition against other horses and three-day riders compete
only with the clock. Also, with a couple of notable exceptions
such as the Grand National at Aintree in England and the
Maryland Hunt Cup, the obstacles in a steeplechase are far
less demanding than those in a cross-country course. But
steeplechasing nonetheless is probably one of the most demanding and dangerous sports from the rider's point of view
because the fences—some of them as high as five and a half
feet or as wide as six feet—must be negotiated at racing speed.
This means that each jump must be approached perfectly in
stride to avoid bad takeoffs, and this necessitates perfect timing and control on the part of the rider as well as a certain
amount of savvy on the part of the animal. This is a sport to
be avoided by all but the most experienced or foolhardy, but

one can still learn a good deal by watching a steeplechase in action. Note how the riders often sit back while taking a jump, rather than forward in the classic jumping position. This is not to help the horse (who needs very little enforced impulsion since he's going at full speed) but to help the rider stay in place. This is known as the safety seat and, not surprisingly, it resembles the position taken by all those fox hunters in all those famous old prints and paintings. (You'll also see it over drop fences in cross-country events.) It's not very pretty, and it's not particularly good for the horse, but it is much safer than landing on a horse's neck (or worse, ahead of the horse on the other side of the jump).

COMBINED TRAINING

I have already discussed briefly the three phases of combined training—dressage, cross-country jumping, and stadium jumping (as part of horse shows)—but when they are all put together in one sport, you have perhaps the utmost in all-around competitive events for horse and rider. Whether the trial takes place in one day or in three, when it is called three-day eventing and is *one* of the three equestrian sports in the Olympic Games, it is a demanding activity but a popular one in spite of its dangers (Christopher Reeve's tragic accident occurred during the cross-country phase of this activity). An event horse must be brave, willing, athletic, obedient, and perfectly conditioned; so must the rider. There are several different levels of competition, beginning with the Pre-Training Level, which involves a simple dressage test, a one- or two-mile cross-country phase at relatively slow speed over obstacles no higher than three feet, three inches, and even lower fences in the stadium-jumping phase. Some trials have only dressage and one of the two other phases. All of the competitions in combined training are regulated by the U.S. Combined Training Association (525 Old Waterford Road, NW, Leesburg, VA 20176), which publishes a list of events, gives year-end awards, and governs the rating system for event horses. Dates for events are also published in *The Chronicle of the Horse*.

Needless to say, because of the nature of each phase, combined training involves a great deal of work with a single horse, and if you don't own one, you must be able to have regular access to a prospect. Although many Equestrian Team members have done extremely well on borrowed horses (those lent to the Team), they have had to work together for weeks if not months to arrive at performance condition. If you don't have such access, you can, of course, work at dressage, cross-country jumping, and stadium jumping on different horses, perfecting your own skills so that when a horse does come along, you'll be ready for him. In the meantime, go out and watch some trials: You'll learn a great deal just seeing the experts at work and you may find yourself in company with some like-minded enthusiasts who just might be willing to coach you or let you ride one of their animals or form a group with you under the instruction of a three-day expert. And, of course, you can read books on the subject. Princess Anne of England no longer rides competitively in events, but her former husband, Captain Mark Phillips, was the Chef d'Equipe for the U.S. Three-Day team in 1996 and is the author of *Horse and Hound Book of Eventing* (Howell Book House). The most comprehensive in training techniques are A. L. d'Endrody's *Give Your Horse a Chance* (J.A. Allen) and Heinz von Opel's *Eventing Technique* (J. A. Allen). Articles about eventing appear regularly in *Practical Horseman* magazine (Box 589, Unionville, PA 19375).

FOX HUNTING

For many people the whole point of learning to ride is to become skilled enough to spend Saturday mornings during the fall and winter chasing a fox over hill and dale and fence and wall, together with a pack of hounds and a full array of beautifully dressed riders to whom traditional etiquette and proper behavior seem as important as equestrian skill. Actually, in spite of the various enemies that fox hunters have gained over the years (angry farmers with trampled fields, humane souls who worry for the foxes and overused horses, and earthy folks who think all the fuss is absurd), this activity can be one of the most exciting ways to spend time on horseback. In many areas where foxes are no longer abundant, vulpine scents are "dragged" to give the hounds something to chase, and the bloody aspect of the sport has diminished considerably. And hunters nowadays are far more conscientious about crossing private property without permission (it's not that easy to gallop through a housing development); they are also far more sensible in their use of horses. No longer will you see streams of thrill-crazy gents and sidesaddled ladies landing with a thump on their horses' kidneys as they race headlong through the fields and over the walls leaning as far back as possible.

The forward or hunter seat has become pretty universal, and the pace is more reasonable these days, though the atmosphere is no less spirited. In fact, even if you haven't had much (or any) jumping experience, you can still join a hunt, since most obstacles have walk-arounds and some of them—the stone walls in particular—get lower as the hunt progresses, turning into veritable kitty litter by the time the last riders reach them.

Nevertheless, hunting is still quite a sport and not one for the poor or timid. Formal hunting has very specific rules of conduct and dress, so if you are asked to join a pack for a Saturday's hunt, be sure to bone up on the rules and get yourself some appropriate riding apparel, which you can usually borrow or rent if this is going to be a one-time outing on your part. Read William Wadsworth's *Riding to Hounds in America* (published by *The Chronicle of the Horse)* or John Williams's *Riding to Hounds* (J. A. Allen).

And prepare yourself for a good workout as well: If you are accustomed to a few laps around the ring at a canter, you'll find that a ten-minute cross-country gallop will take your breath away. A friend of mine went hunting for the first time with the Blue Ridge Hunt in Virginia aboard a chipmunk-colored pony named Alvin. He had hoped for a few minutes to get to know the pony, but the hounds "found" at the first covert, whereupon the field was off and running. The run lasted for a good half hour, after which our friend sought in vain for an oxygen mask in his sandwich case; he could have pulled up to catch his breath somewhere but that would have left him and his horse deserted in unfamiliar country. Although he found his second wind somewhere and continued on (that was to be the only real run of the day), my friend suggests that first-time riders get themselves into condition before they put on their boots and breeches.

According to Susan Goode, an instructor who lives in Virginia, a rider is ready to hunt when he or she can jump a three-foot fence in the ring, is comfortable on the cross-country gallop, can jump uphill and downhill fences as well as ditches, and has had experience in large group trail rides. Alexander Mackay-Smith, formerly Master of Fox Hounds of the Blue Ridge Hunt and the sport's leading authority, suggests that one rides an experienced horse alongside a "pilot," an escort who knows the countryside and can keep an eye on you. Chris Howells, former Huntsman of the Blue Ridge, advises that the first-time hunter start off during the cubbing season, before the formal hunt season, when the young foxes are being encouraged to run cross-country. (The rules of dress are less formal then and the pace somewhat slower.) He also believes that novices should be warned not to interfere with the hunt staff or the hounds by chatting unnecessarily (or "coffeehousing") nor to interfere with the hounds by deviating from the path. If you have had enough and must go home, ask for the Master's permission and follow his directions. Stop if you hear hounds coming your way, and if you do "head" a fox (cause it to change direction), admit it. Don't hide behind a tree, even though you are embarrassed; point out the direction the fox took and you'll be able to show your face at the hunt breakfast later in the day.

The jumps that one usually encounters on a fox hunt are not easily knocked-down crossrails but solid fences, walls, and banks (only the stone walls may diminish in size during the hunt), but don't worry too much that your horse will run out or stop, for most animals enjoy the chase as much as the riders and are eager to take whatever lies in their path. If anything, you should worry about your horse getting overexcited and racing ahead, since it is absolutely forbidden for anyone, member or guest, to overtake the Master of Fox Hounds, who leads the hunt.

Although hunting has traditionally been a fairly exclusive activity, many packs throughout the country do allow the public to join (write to *The Chronicle of the Horse* for names and addresses), and most can provide rental horses for the occasion. Capping (or entrance) fees can be high, though, so plan to spend thirty to seventy-five dollars for a day's outing, plus horse rental and transportation. Although the horse may be unfamiliar to you, he will probably be familiar with the countryside, a great advantage to the first-timer. As Mr. Mackay-Smith suggests, the best way to be introduced to the sport is to have someone along to show you the ropes— preferably a member of the hunt. Those who are cautious or wish to be especially well prepared might ask (or pay) someone in the hunt to take you out in the field a few days beforehand just to get the feel of the terrain.

If you don't feel that you are up to hunting on horseback, you can always watch the proceedings by "hilltopping" or following the hunt on foot or in a car. There are always others who will join you in this horseless activity, and it can be fun, although I'll vow that you will be itching to ride before you

reach the top of the first hill. Because fox hunting traditionally takes place in the fall and hunt members love to ride
year-round, many hunts sponsor hunter-pace competitions at
various times of the year or non-competitive trail rides over
hunt country. These events are usually geared to varying
levels of expertise or courage, with different groups taking
different routes at different times and traveling over more-or-
less difficult terrain at varying speeds.

> Sarah Churchill, daughter of Sir Winston and a talented
> photographer, painter, actress, and writer, learned to fox hunt
> on her instructor's horses. He would put her on an "easy" horse
> going out and then on her own mount coming home, a fine
> animal who by that time was tired enough not to cause young
> Sarah any problems but who was talented enough to give her
> a real feel for the sport.

POLO

This is another sport that was not designed for the timid or
insecure rider. It has everything that football, ice hockey, and
soccer boast, and more—because it's all played on horseback.
(Even the referee or official rides a horse.) And for the horsy
set, polo is special because it demands the utmost in teamwork from its players, horses and humans alike. For years
polo was a sport for the very rich. Players had their own strings
of ponies because the game is demanding enough to require
as many as three or four mounts for each match. But horseless
riders have always been a part of polo, too, especially in the
West where playing polo is an occasional byline of cowboys
who double as players for their polo-enthusiastic employers.
Although riding herd on cattle seems worlds apart from riding
herd on a small white ball, the two activities do require much
the same kind of skill. Polo ponies (which as often as not are
Thoroughbreds or Quarter Horses) are quick starters and short
stoppers, able to turn on a dime and change leads at the drop
of a heel. They must be alert to the action, just as the cutting
horse is, and from what I've seen, the ponies are often quicker
than their riders to spot the ball and chase after it. This kind
of riding demands superb balance and instant reflexes from
the rider, and the game itself demands teamwork from the
players (as herding does from cowboys). Most important, however, is the teamwork between horse and rider, both of whom
must share a love and understanding of the game and a fan-
tastic disregard for personal safety.

These days, polo is a game for everyone—rich and poor, men and women. Although aggressiveness is an important characteristic of a good player, the ability to anticipate the play and a sense of timing are far more important than physical strength or even equestrian talent. In fact, the riding style is pretty unorthodox, since the rider is often well out of the saddle, the legs having little or no contact with the horse and the reins being held loosely in the left hand. But balance is essential, as well as a complete understanding between horse and rider of the signals for stopping, turning, and speeding up. Most experienced polo players will admit that at least 75 percent of the game depends on the horse, and well-schooled polo ponies are very valuable for that reason. But you needn't own a string or even one pony to play. There are polo clubs throughout the country, and many colleges and universities sponsor polo teams (some of them offering teams for women as well as men). Ponies, together with the money to support them, are often donated to the schools by older players so that the costs aren't high for students, and polo clubs may be joined by the horseless, depending on local regulations, of course. For information, write to the U.S. Polo Association, 4059 Iron Works Pike, Lexington, KY 40511; you may also want to subscribe to *Polo Magazine* (656 Quince Orchard Road, Gaithersburg, MD 20878). Peter Grace's book *Polo* (Howell Book House) contains just about all you will need (short of a polo pony and a fair amount of experience) regarding rules and tactics.

The four activities that follow are not so widespread nor as highly organized as those we have been exploring. In fact, about all they have in common is that the saddles and hence the riding styles are different from those that the average horseless rider is likely to confront. But because the motto of the horseless rider is adaptability and because our *modus operandi* is to be ready to ride whatever is offered whenever, I thought it might be worth considering them as part of the broader horizon.

VAULTING

This sport appeals to many youngsters—whether because of the horses involved or because the idea of gymnastics on horseback is so attractive, I really couldn't say. There is something of the circus-horse charm about vaulting as well, since the riders do all sorts of athletic tricks as their animals revolve around the ring. Actually, this activity is far more demanding for rider than horse, although one needs a well-schooled, obedient animal willing to canter around in circles (often at the end of a lunge line) while someone performs movements on his back. One needn't be a superb rider to excel at the sport, but a good sense of balance and a certain amount of flexibility and skill are required. And the horse will need a special vaulting surcingle, a leather-padded girthlike affair with two handles to hold on to while doing vaults on and off, handstands, and the various other moves on and around the horse. Vaulting is an ancient branch of horsemanship going back to Roman times, and it is a highly competitive sport in Europe today. But it has caught on in some parts of the country, too, especially in California, and vaulting competitions are held in many different areas. For further information, read Ann Sagar's book *Vaulting: Develop Your Riding and Gymnastic Skills* (Tralfalgar).

MILITARY OR POLICE RIDING

The cavalry is long gone in most countries except as a parade activity, and police horses are generally reserved for police officers in big cities where parks must be patrolled, theater districts and crowded areas viewed from on high, and holidays celebrated with equestrian panache. Nevertheless, mounted-police units occasionally make use of amateur auxiliary riders, and one may occasionally meet up with a horse wearing a McClellan saddle and wonder whether one should ride it like an English or a Western saddle. Actually, it is neither but an adaptation of a Hungarian cavalry saddle to an American army saddle tree that Captain George B. McClellan (later a general in the Union Army) devised during the 1850s after a tour of European duty. Captain McClellan retained the open slit between pommel and cantle that he found in Hungary, but he added a high pommel, a deep seat, and the squared skirts and cinches of the stock saddle. Add to this contraption a breastplate complete with American bald eagle in brass, four brass rings to hold a saber, canteen, crupper, and martingale, a blue wool blanket with orange border and an orange U.S. in the center, and you have a most impressive military sight. The traditional McClellan has been somewhat modified in the interest of comfort for long hours in ceremonial parades and on the streets of cities with mounted-police units, but it is probably the least comfortable of saddles in use today.

The military seat has also gone by the boards for the most part, but if you find yourself on a McClellan and want to know how to ride it like a cavalry officer, I can recommend the style suggested to me by Bill Brayton, a former officer who continues to school his young horses in the old way. Bill rides with his legs rather far forward, cueing the horse to turn or to take a faster gait by touching the animal on one or both shoulders. His weight remains back in the saddle and his left hand holds four reins of the double bridle (or bit and bradoon), leaving the right free. The rein hand is held relatively high, since the horse's head is high and tucked in, and the animal responds to neck reining rather than a direct rein. The McClellan isn't comfortable enough to make cantering or sitting at the trot a truly delightful experience, so the gaits are fairly slow and collected. Dennis Byrnes, formerly an officer with New York City's Mounted Unit and now an equine dentist, told me that he usually rode in a forward seat but had to adapt his style somewhat to cope with the department's version of the McClellan, which is closer to an English saddle than the original but still possesses a good deal of leather between human leg and equine side, and thus calls for the use of spurs.

SIDESADDLE RIDING

If the McClellan saddle is a thing of the past, the sidesaddle is even more so—at least until relatively recently, which has seen something of a revival of this elegant, traditional, and downright strange-looking method of riding a horse. Reserved for ladies for whom riding astride was considered most unladylike, this form of riding came into fashion during the eighteenth century in England and remained *de rigeur* in many parts of the world—including the United States—through the first quarter of the twentieth century. The sidesaddle made it possible for ladies to ride in full skirts without compromising their modesty, although it made riding a perilous business—especially in the hunt field—until the development in the mid-nineteenth century of the third pommel, which helped to give the rider some measure of security. Horses had to be specially selected and trained to carry their sidesaddles and riders, for it was impossible to post, to ride a two-point position at the gallop and over jumps, and to control both sides of the horse with leg pressure. Horses thus had to have steady, slow trots, strong shoulders to manage gallops and jumps without much help from the rider, and sensitive responses to the use of the leg on the near side (the left) and to the whip on the off, or right, side.

Thanks primarily to the efforts of the International Side-Saddle Organization (R.D. 2, Box 2055, Mount Holly, NJ 08060) and its publication *Side-Saddle News*, this form of riding has become popular again. It is no longer surprising to see sidesaddle classes at horse shows or to see ladies riding to hounds unastride. Although poor sidesaddle horsemanship is hardly a joy to watch (or perform), seeing a fine horsewoman decked out in a special habit and sitting elegantly to the trot can be a real pleasure.

If you are ever offered the chance to ride sidesaddle, don't giggle and refuse but give it a try. The most important thing to remember is to keep your balance as centered as possible, without leaning at all (either forward, backward, or sideways), sitting as straight as you can and remaining as relaxed as you can manage. If you have learned to ride a jog or sitting trot, you shouldn't have too much trouble maintaining both your position and your cool; the walk and the canter (providing you can get the horse to respond to the appropriate cue for the appropriate lead), should be a cinch. As in the balanced seat, the idea is not to grip and clutch but to move in rhythm with the motion of the horse rather than against it. Although I can't recommend jumping until you have attained some degree of confidence and security, chances are that you won't fall off if you remember that the horse is the one doing the work, not yourself. Don't interfere with the horse (which means keeping your hands light), and don't panic. Relax and enjoy yourself, and pretend you're Queen Victoria. It's a great feeling.

RACE RIDING

Although the idea of mounting a son of Seattle Slew for a spin down the track is about as far from your own sense of reality as riding a hunter sidesaddle across the downs of Southern England, don't bet on it. The open-minded opportunistic horseless rider is capable of almost anything. Take my friend Steve Price, a writer by profession, a rider by avocation, and a horseless person by necessity. He was once given a chance to help a famous jockey write his autobiography and off he went (boots and breeches in his suitcase, as always). It turns out that the book never materialized, but Steve did manage to ride an outrider's pony (a retired racer past his prime) for

Once considered a thing of the past, sidesaddle equitation is enjoying a new surge of popularity.

some exercise at Santa Anita. A slow gallop was all that the horse needed ("Sure," says Steve, "like a Maserati full throttle!"), and once around the track was all that Steve needed to know that this form of transportation had to be as fast as anything he'd ever known, jet age or no. I, too, have had my experiences in the backstretch, the most exciting of which was a spin around a training track aboard a three-year-old colt under the watchful eye of his trainer and an exercise rider who poised himself on a pony at the edge of the track just in case I got into trouble. The colt was an enormous, powerful animal, full of oats and eagerness to run, and I was apprehensive, to say the least, since I felt as though I were sitting on a coiled spring with only my sense of balance to keep me in place. After a few moments of walking to the track, however, I realized that this was, after all, a horse like any other, responsive to legs, hands, and voice, and that my previous riding experience was perfectly applicable. The stirrups were shorter than I expected, and the reins had to be held differently (race-horses do not have sensitive mouths but need a strong pair of hands supported by body weight), but the basic principles were the same. Although my facial expression for those few minutes around the track revealed (I was told later) more fear than delight, my confidence did not elude me entirely and the experience was exhilarating. Though I don't have the time or the inclination to become a professional exercise rider, I can enthusiastically recommend the backstretch for those who do. (See page 207 for information about the professional side of this world.)

Everyone who has ever seen a horse race knows that the stirrups have to be as short as humanly possible and that one's position must be as far into the horse's mane as one can manage. But actually, the exercise jockeys aren't as extreme in position as the real jockeys in a race. After all, a horse being galloped in its daily routine doesn't need to go like the wind, only like a freight train, and the jockeys don't need to weigh as little as children to make them move. The idea of the jockey's position is to create as little wind resistance as possible and to stay forward in order to free the hindquarters to do their stuff and to keep the horse's balance on its forelegs. But there are some other techniques worth knowing by the occasional rider—not for real racehorses but for the occasional former racer who has somehow found his way into private or public life as a saddle horse. The tighter you hold the reins, the faster the horse is likely to go. This isn't just a matter of training, since any unschooled or poorly schooled horse given a certain amount of resistance will try to fight it. This natural inclination is what trainers exploit in working with their animals: Resist with the hands and you're off to the races. Another racing technique is to keep your weight in the stirrups rather than in your upper thighs and seat. This means that the rider has precious little security and control, but that's what makes horse races so exciting. Actually, racing jockeys must have some control over their mounts in order to rate them (get them to run faster or slower) and to push them into strategic positions for the stretch run. In addition to the whip, the jockey uses voice, reins (to change leads or direction), and hands, which can urge a horse forward when they are moved up on the horse's neck. Beyond that, jockeys must use their eyes to avoid running into other horses and to gauge position on the track (by recognizing the track poles as they ride by), and their wits, which must be as sharp as tacks. An up-and-coming jockey once told me that your reactions must be instantaneous in making decisions; if you have to think about what you're going to do, it will already be too late!

Although race riding is particularly demanding in these ways, the methods that jockeys use are both natural and universal, which is what makes it possible for them to ride horses they have never seen before.

RIDING FOR THE HANDICAPPED

Riding programs for handicapped adults and children have become widespread since the first edition of this book was published, and like most horse-related activities, it involves plenty for the horseless rider to consider. Many disabled riders are themselves horseless, like many of their instructors, and while the programs are not always easy to run and require a certain amount of money and personnel, the benefits can be many. The therapeutic benefits of animals for humans are widely recognized, and it is evident that riding programs for people who are physically or emotionally disadvantaged can be very rewarding for riders and teachers alike.

Although it doesn't take much training to help a teacher (and two or three people are often required for each student rider), one must be patient and alert, as well as knowledgeable about horses. Some riders require special equipment, such as a mounting ramp, handholds, special belts, and stirrups, but many do not need more than standard English or Western tack and a hard hat (a must for all riding students). Mounting, dismounting, and exercises are easier in an English saddle, but a stock saddle offers greater security and support. The most important requirement is a safe, gentle horse, as in any good riding school.

There are a number of good books on the subject, including Vanessa Britton's *Riding for the Disabled* (B. T. Batsford), and a list of these and of programs in your area is available from the North American Riding for the Handicapped Association (P.O. Box 33150, Denver, CO 80233).

10

THIS CHAPTER IS devoted to those horseless riders who have allowed horse fever to get completely out of hand. They are the dedicated, the obsessed, the incurable. Prevention is no cure at this point. What you need is treatment, pure and simple, and that treatment has to take the form of full-time horsemanship. There are two courses open to you—becoming a professional if you must remain horseless or becoming a horse owner.

PROFESSIONAL HORSEMANSHIP

We have talked about part-time jobs as a way of getting more rides, free rides, or simply learning the basics of stable management and horse care. Becoming a professional, however, involves a full-time commitment, whether this is a formal position paying a salary or a freelance sort of activity repaid in the form of commissions or occasional windfalls. Whatever your situation, you can't expect to start at the top—or even halfway up the ladder—until you have paid your dues by working and getting experience from the ground up.

STARTING OUT

No matter what your ultimate goal—trainer, instructor, stable manager, or rider—starting out usually means work as a groom or at some other chore that takes place on foot, such as teaching other people how to ride. Trail guides and exercise riders work in the saddle, of course, but their experience is limited unless the job also includes other aspects of horse care. All of these jobs mean hard work and long hours, and most of them are found around large stables, whether they be hacking stables or private barns at racetracks, equestrian centers, ranches, or the estates of wealthy horse owners. The people who run these establishments come in all shapes and personalities, so don't count on getting a wise old horseman as your first employer (count yourself lucky, though, if you do get one). And don't count on exactly the type of job you want; be willing to do anything at first until you have learned your way around. The salary won't be lavish, since there are many other young people eager for these jobs, some of them willing to work for nothing but experience. You can, however, be somewhat choosy about the kind of stable. Although you'll learn a lot at a poor stable with horrible-looking horses, you are more likely to learn better management methods and ways of handling horses at a good place under good supervision. If you find yourself at a bad stable, you can try to improve the situation yourself or you can use the experience to get another position, but learning things the right way will give you a much better background for your future career.

Finding a stable in need of an eager, loyal employee like yourself isn't always easy, but it isn't impossible either. Look for advertisements in newspapers, horse magazines, and on stable bulletin boards (to say nothing of the electronic type, as horsy chat lines are increasing in number over the Internet). Go around to local barns and offer to work, for nothing at first, if necessary, just to show that you are worth your weight in silver if not gold. Ask the veterinarian and the farrier in your neighborhood about available positions, since they often are tuned into the stable grapevines. Get to know people who work at stables so that you can be made part of the grapevine yourself if a job should open up. Learn what you can about working conditions at various places and pull whatever strings you have.

A woman who now runs a boarding stable in California wrote me about her own experience as a horseless child growing up in London and her first job:

I had one of those splendid British mums, and she seemed to understand the passion and the frustration that I felt and took it upon herself to write to the Queen's race horse trainer. In her letter she asked him if her horse-crazed daughter could please come and

spend summer holiday.
exercising racehorses, m.
Rochford duly wrote my mothe.
told her that he didn't employ girls .
in the days before women's lib) but he a.
try another trainer, Gerry Wilson, who was .
steeplechase jockey in his day (rode Golden Mih.
two victories in the Grand National) and was now
trainer. So my lovely mum wrote Mr. Wilson and I was
invited to spend my summer vacation at his home. The
fact that I didn't ride particularly well didn't appear to
bother Mr. Wilson too much and he kindly pretended
not to notice that for the most part on the morning
gallops I was totally unable to stop. I would just pretend
to ride like the exercise lads, short stirrups and
crouched over the horse's neck but I couldn't have
stopped when I wanted if my life had depended on it.
So you might warn your readers to assess their own
capabilities as a rider very honestly before they climb
aboard. The life they save might be their own!

If you find yourself a willing employer, be as honest as
possible about yourself, your experience, and your intentions
about working. If you plan to work only temporarily, for the
summer or for only a month, be sure to say so; it's unfair
otherwise. Dishonesty with your first employer will reflect
badly on your future record, and because the horse world is
really a small one, your reputation will always precede you to
the next stable. Of course, you should work as hard as possible, do what you are asked (*always*—never disobey, unless
there is something very much wrong), and learn everything
you are capable of absorbing. If you show aptitude around
horses, it will be noticed, and not just by the horses. Horse
owners who care about their animals care about who works
for them. Don't be too content, however, with mucking out
and grooming your charges. Keep your eyes open to everything else around the stable, ask a lot of questions, and if
you are particularly eager to try your hand (and seat and
legs) at riding or at some other aspect of stable work, pipe up
at the first opportunity. The owner may not think you are
ready yet, but when the time comes, he or she will be unlikely
to forget your interest if you have proven your worth doing
your job.

Be serious, be on time, and if for some reason you can't show up for work, let your employer know as soon as possible. There is no excuse for allowing a horse to go unfed and uncared for, and such negligence can be a good excuse for a quick dismissal. If something confuses you or if you don't understand a particular instruction, don't guess but ask questions until you are sure that you know exactly what is required. If you do something wrong, admit it instantly rather than trying to cover it up. A broken bridle or a loose horse is very difficult to hide, and it's not worth trying.

Now let's take a look at some of the job opportunities available once you have completed a term of service as an apprentice around the stable.

STABLE MANAGEMENT

There are a number of jobs to be done around a stable that don't necessarily involve riding, though that could be considered a fringe benefit. Most small stables are run by the owner, but any sizeable operation generally employs someone to act on the owner's behalf to take care of the myriad details: ordering food, bedding, and equipment; seeing that the proper goods are delivered on time; hiring, supervising, and firing stable help; setting up and managing a lesson program; billing customers; arranging for trailers to ship incoming and outgoing horses; dealing with veterinarians and farriers; and running special events, such as clinics, shows, lectures, videos, films, and other programs. If the stable is primarily interested in hacking or instruction, the manager may be responsible for finding and purchasing suitable horses and making the decision about which horses are to be offered to which renting riders. It is the manager's responsibility to see that the horses are cared for properly, that customers are satisfied (the owners of boarding horses as well as riders), and that the money comes in and goes out in a businesslike way.

The job is not a simple one and requires a good head for organization and administration, as well as the ability to get along with people. More important, it requires a great deal of knowledge about horses and what is involved in good care. A background in stable work is essential, since a good manager must know how a stable works from the bottom up, but direct experience in riding is also important as well as a working knowledge of health care, food quality, horseshoeing, and first aid. It is also useful to have good contacts beyond the

Walking "hots," or cooling off young racehorses in training, is one of the various jobs available at the racetrack and at large stables.

stable itself with dealers, feed suppliers, instructors, and other professionals in the field.

Some stable managers double as instructors or head the lesson program; others concentrate on breeding and must be familiar not only with the management of stallions, brood-mares, and foals but also with the roles of matchmaker, midwife, nurse, trainer, and salesperson. Often a stable manager will be the trainer with individual animals to care for in addition to the operation of the stable itself.

Stable employees who are not interested in the administrative responsibility that goes with a manager's job can, of course, work as assistant managers, instructors, or grooms—or in a special capacity as show manager, scout for new horses, and such. In many stables, the job of groom is an end in itself not a stepping stone to something bigger, and good grooms are probably the most valuable members of the staff in a well-run stable. In very large stables, there are often head grooms, who supervise the work of those who attend to a certain number of animals—from one to ten apiece—but it is the individual groom on whom the veterinarian relies for essential information about a horse's symptoms and unusual changes in behavior, on whom the farrier relies for assistance, on whom riders count for tips about temperament and habits, and on whom the trainers and owners depend for general equine well-being.

For it is the groom who knows the horse inside and out. He or she is constantly alert to the animal's condition and is the first to note any situation that may require a change in feed or a call to the vet or farrier. The groom must be skilled also in the fine art of bandaging legs, applying medications, removing or readjusting horseshoes—in short, doing a great deal more than simply grooming.

Hot-walking is another job around a large stable, usually one where the horses are in training and are exercised on a regular and demanding basis. This job, like grooming, involves more than the name of the occupation implies. One must, of course, lead an animal around until it is cooled off, but there are other skills needed—knowing an animal's temperament and condition well enough to know when the cooling-off process is complete, being able to operate a mechanical hot-walker, and being willing to pitch in at other tasks around the barn. It isn't a particularly demanding job in itself, if you like to walk, that is, and a novice can easily learn the ropes, but in at least one famous case, the hot-walker was a very special person indeed. In fact, people in Seattle Slew's barn admitted willingly that Donald Carroll, the hot-walker, was probably Slew's "best friend."

Two very important aspects of stable management require special training—veterinary work and horseshoeing. Licensed veterinarians must study for four years in graduate school, and the field is an extremely competitive one because there are so few veterinary schools. Not all veterinarians go into equine work; many limit their practices to dogs and cats, to exotic and wild animals, or to cattle and other farm animals. Equine practitioners are specialists within the field, and a summer spent working as an assistant to a horse doctor can be a marvelous experience. It will also give anyone interested in horses a first-rate opportunity to learn about the fine art of maintaining horse health. Veterinary work is, of course, a branch of the medical profession, and becoming a vet is as demanding as becoming a physician (even more so if you consider that the patients are unable to explain what ails them and are often unwilling to be handled). If you don't have the time or inclination to invest in the extensive program, you may choose veterinary technology instead, which requires two to four years of undergraduate work that emphasizes science and mathematics as well as animal work. For information about veterinary education and opportunities, write to the American Veterinary Medical Association (1931 North Meacham Road, #100, Schaumburg, IL 60173-4360) and subscribe to *Equus* magazine (published by Fleetstreet Publishing at 656 Quince Orchard Road, Gaithersburg, MD 10878, the same outfit that publishes *Polo* and *Dressage Today*). *Equus* is one of the most informative journals in the horse world, featuring valuable veterinary and horse-care articles every month.

Blacksmiths who work with horses prefer to be called farriers (to distinguish themselves from those who make iron grillwork and gates and such). They, too, must learn their trade by specialized study, though this needn't be in a formal school but can be as an apprentice under an expert. Many schools offer courses in horseshoeing (check the horse magazines or write to the Veterans Administration or your County Extension office for information), and there are several good books on the subject, but it will take practice before you become expert yourself. In addition to learning about the craft of working with metal and using a forge, you will have to learn an enormous amount about horse conformation and movement, since shoeing involves a great deal more than making shoes fit. Corrective shoeing has helped turn many poor performers into stars and many useless animals into valuable ones.

PROFESSIONAL RIDING

Although most horseless riders pay for the privilege, riders who are talented or opportunistic enough can have their cake and eat it too—spending their careers in the saddle and getting paid for it besides. Some years ago, when American competitors in the Olympic Games were limited to those of amateur status, riders could not accept money for showing other people's horses, either as a salary or in the form of prizes, and amateurs over the age of eighteen had to have a special amateur card (issued by the American Horse Shows Association). Now that the amateur code for the Olympics is a thing of the past and amateurism is usually a factor only for horse owners in certain horse-show classes, it is theoretically (if not actually) a good deal easier to earn money as you work your way toward the top in the riding ranks.

Racetrack trainers employ exercise riders to get their horses into condition and keep them that way. Both men and women can get these jobs, so long as their weight is within reason (one hundred to one hundred twenty-five pounds, depending on the horse and the trainer) and they are capable of following instructions as well as handling lively, strong, young animals. Having a good time sense or being experienced in using timeclocks is an important part of the job, too, as is the ability to adapt one's style to many different kinds and temperaments of horses. Exercise for flat racers may vary from easy gallops to breezes (which are faster) to real workouts that are timed by the clockers and published in the racing sheets read by bettors. Exercise for steeplechasers can be anything from long, steady gallops across country (up and down hills, along beaches, and so on) to concentrated work over fences. Many exercise riders work on salary, although freelancers will work for a certain sum per horse exercised (more for problem horses). The salaried rider may not make as much money but often prefers the steady employment and the chance to ride the same horses every day. Some riders are young and looking forward to the time when they can become licensed jockeys, but many riders have no such ambitions or have already been through the jockey stage, having gained too much weight or lost too many races.

Another racetrack job is that of the pony-rider or out-rider, who fulfills an important service to both trainers and jockeys before and after races and during training sessions. These riders are mounted on relatively undistinguished animals that may wear anything from stock saddles and hackamores to jumping saddles and snaffles, but their presence on the backstretch is invaluable. Their mounts are not usually ponies in the technical sense (under fourteen and a half hands in height) but are full-grown horses that are used to "pony" or lead young racehorses out to the post before races or around training tracks during the morning gallops. Horses are, of course, herd animals by nature, and it is not surprising that nervous adolescent equines are reassured when escorted by older, wiser horses with steady temperaments. Perhaps more important, however, is the fact that these ponies are capable of quick bursts of speed necessary to catch runaways or eager beavers who continue to run their races long past the finish line. Horses bred to run often don't know enough to stop—nor can they be controlled when straps break or riders lack the strength or weight to pull them in. The out-rider stationed along the edge of the track can therefore play a crucial role in stopping a valuable animal before it runs itself literally into the ground. A trainer friend of mine owned a very old pony, one that many other trainers would have given up on years earlier and sold off to a hacking stable or relegated to some other obscure occupation. Old Billygoat, however, saved the life of more than one talented racer and was assured of a comfortable life around the racetrack as long as he lived.

Pony-rider or outrider jobs are usually paid on a freelance basis, in that trainers will pay a fee to them for their services, but some of these positions are salaried, either by trainers or by the racetracks. Although the idea of being mounted on an old grade gelding isn't so glamorous when everyone around you is riding an elegant young speedster, the responsibility involved is a very important one and many lives, both horse and human, have been saved by the quick action taken on the part of the outrider.

Off the racetrack, riders may be employed by trainers who need help schooling a stableful of horses, by stable managers who are paid by owners to keep their horses fit as well as fed, and by dealers who want someone to show off a saleable beast to best advantage. Advanced students may work for their in-structors; grooms can double as exercise riders; trusted cus-tomers may work for their rides by helping out around the hack stable. In short, if you have the talent, the time, and the energy, you can probably find yourself gainful employment by riding for more than simple pleasure. If an owner is pleased with a rider's performance on the horse (or, more likely, the horse's performance under the rider), the next step may mean going into horse shows or other forms of competition for which the rider is paid. "Catch-riding," as I have mentioned earlier, is an excellent way for a rider to build up a reputation and to get backing or support for a career in the show ring. The bet-ter the reputation, the better the horses one is likely to be offered, and this requires, of course, a great deal of adaptabil-ity as well as pure talent. Rodney Jenkins, who earned a great deal of money as a professional rider on the hunter-jumper circuit, often found himself mounting a horse for the first time moments before entering the show ring, and he frequently rode several horses in each class. I once asked him how he could possibly keep the different, unfamiliar animals straight in his mind, to say nothing of straight on the course. He explained that since childhood he was always given the "left-over" horses in his father's barn to ride and that he rode so many horses in his career that he developed a sixth sense about them. He can tell in a few hundred feet of trotting what a horse's potential may be and he knows what he will be like over fences by taking only a couple of schooling jumps. Jenkins relies almost entirely on balance (rather than strong hands, different kinds of bits, and so on) and says that keeping his balance on a horse is the best way to get the most out of him.

Cowboys are also riders for hire, of course, though their work involves a great deal more than simply being able to sit a horse effectively. They must know as much about cattle as about horses and be familiar with the whole range of the range, so to speak. Some cowboys work for a single employer; others are freelancers, working their way through the West hiring themselves out for special jobs (breaking horses, working the roundup, and so on). Many cowboys do no ranch work at all but compete on the rodeo circuit, while some double as polo players and catch-riders for reining or cutting-horse competitions and rodeos, or simply hang around drugstores a lot.

On dude ranches, cowboys may never see a cow but assume the job of wrangler, keeping the horses in shape and setting them up for novice riders. This sort of job requires a combination of groom, trainer, teacher, and trail guide, and good wranglers can make the difference between a successful operation and a dismal failure.

Trail guides can be found not only in the West, of course, but along highways in the East and on back roads in the South. Any public stable that rents horses to beginners for trail rides must employ one or more guides to see that everyone makes it back in one piece, and the trail guide's responsibility is a serious one. The guide must be able to handle his or her own horse properly because there are many other things that must be watched and also because the novice riders will be watching the guide in order to learn something. The guide must see that each rider in the group is handling the horse correctly (which usually involves an instant on-the-spot lesson), that all riders stay in suitable formation, that traffic laws are obeyed and public roads safely crossed, and that emergencies are dealt with promptly and efficiently. A trail guide must always be prepared to handle one or more horses at a time, either to lead a fractious beast for a complete novice or to ride the beast and put the novice on his or her own animal. In other words, the guide must be teacher, disciplinarian, object lesson, traffic cop, paramedic, and above all horseman. Many stables I've visited have had indifferent guides who are inexperienced with both people and horses, and nothing is more frustrating than taking orders from someone who doesn't know the difference between a hip and a hock. But I've always been glad to have a guide along, if only because it shows that the stable cares to some extent about the safety of their customers, and of course one can always pick up information from the guide about trails and individual horses so that the next ride out alone will not result in getting lost or run away with.

Anyone who knows how to ride could probably get a job as a guide, but one must be prepared to do more than just ride, and being able to tell a prospective employer that one has a solid grounding in first aid, instruction, and/or stable management will give you a definite advantage over other prospective candidates for employment.

Someone with experience as a trail guide who also has a passion for dogs (or hounds) and enjoys the tradition of fox hunting can work as a member of the hunt staff, as a whipper-in, or as a huntsman, which in many areas are professional occupations. One must, of course, know horses, the territory, and the rules and traditions of the sport, but one must also get involved in breeding and training fox hounds, which, for some, is a refreshing supplement to full-time horsemanship.

Mounted police officers are police officers first and horsemen second, but anyone who wants to combine careers can have the best of both worlds in this line of work. (See page 194.)

TEACHING

Like stable work, riding instruction runs the gamut from friendly advice given out gratis to highly paid coaching jobs, and the background required for employment varies considerably. Sometimes a talented rider will turn to instruction because people are willing to pay for the chance to learn his or her techniques. Bertalan de Nemethy, former jumping coach for the United States Equestrian Team, started out in Hungary as a veterinarian; when he arrived in this country, knowing little English and unable to get a veterinary license, he started to teach riding and eventually ended up with one of the most coveted jobs in the profession. His job involved not only coaching team members and supervising the schooling of team horses but required him to be constantly on the lookout for potential team members and to work with young riders to develop their skills to Olympic level.

If you know that you want to teach, you must, of course, have a certain amount of talent and experience in riding yourself. But you will also need that special aptitude required of teachers: the ability to convey to another rider what is wrong and what can be done to make it right. A teacher must be observant, articulate, patient, and knowledgeable about both horses and people. Teaching riding at summer camp is an excellent short-term way for a potential instructor to test his or her capabilities and interest, though I know many teachers who began as assistants to their own instructors who were delighted to pass along their own theories to their talented protégés. Courses in riding instruction are given at various schools and colleges that offer horsemanship. Meredith Manor in West Virginia offers several full courses on the subject, from basic teaching skills to the history of equitation theory to an apprenticeship program. You might want to contact the American Riding Instructor Certification Program (ARICP) for information as well: P.O. Box 282, Alton Bay, NH 03810-0282. Some stables hire their instructors on the basis of certificates from such schools and organizations, while others simply require experience.

The rewards in teaching are varied; some instructors are satisfied only if their students win blue ribbons, while others are delighted just to know that a frightened beginner has achieved some self-confidence and the ability to master a posting trot. Some instructors are paid a salary, while others receive a commission on the basis of the number of students they teach; most teachers do their job more for love than for money, though a few top coaches can make up to a thousand dollars a month for each student.

Instructors may work every day from dawn to dusk teaching "up-down" lessons to beginners (which means posting, of course), or they may work once a month giving special clinics at other stables to a handful of riders. Any instructor should have the ability to work with beginners who have never been on a horse, but the job will be more interesting if those classes can be alternated with intermediate and advanced instruction. In a busy stable one must be flexible enough to conduct a group lesson of twelve students as well as private lessons with one or two riders. Whether one devises a "lesson plan" at the beginning of each class or simply plays the lesson by ear will depend on the riders as well as the instructors, as will the type and level of riding that is taught. In addition to knowing the capabilities and limitations of the student, the instructor must also know his or her school horses intimately in order to assign them to individual students. Reschooling sour horses, schooling green ones, and dealing with difficult situations during a class will involve riding for the instructor who may turn the occasion into a "show not tell" lesson. A few instructors I know call out commands and corrections from the center of the ring; some will give mini-lectures before or after the students ride; some yell at mistakes, while others speak softly and reassuringly; many instructors concentrate on one thing at a time (hands, legs, seat, head), while others work on the total picture; some aim for an attractive appearance and self-confidence in their riders, while others work toward developing flexibility and courage on more demanding and varied animals.

In addition to knowing students, horses, and the theories and methods of instruction, an instructor must also be capable of dealing with the demands of the show ring or the competitive aspects of the sport. This means that one should know when a student is ready to compete and be prepared to coach the rider through the great event—selecting the appropriate classes and the horse, giving last-minute instructions and advice, and following up with praise, constructive criticism, and encouragement for the next time out. At one's first few shows, the psychological influence of the instructor can be far more important than any specific instruction. I recall one equitation class in which I was riding a new horse and concentrating very hard on my diagonals and leads and so on; when I looked over at my instructor to see how I was doing, he simply said "Smile!" Suddenly I relaxed and began enjoying myself, presenting a far more confident appearance to the judge than I had been doing (I got a third). In the same show, however, jumping the same unfamiliar horse over a newly set-up course of fences I had never seen, my instructor was called away at the last minute by another contestant just as I entered the ring, so I had to memorize the course fast and jump it with no real idea of what I was doing. Needless to say, my nervousness transmitted itself to the horse and we didn't do very well at all.

In other words, the instructor is more than simply a human riding manual. He or she must assume a certain amount of psychological responsibility for students—building up self-confidence, developing a sense of reality and a respect for hard work, and emphasizing attitude as well as ability. The relationship between teacher and student (and even the student's family) can be the making or breaking of the student's future as a horseman. Many talented beginners have been turned off riding by an insensitive or indifferent teacher, while other less apt pupils have developed into fine horsemen just because they had the encouragement and information given them at a crucial stage in their development.

If you don't happen to be affiliated with a stable that has the facilities for a lesson program and you don't own a school horse or two that would enable you to start your own academy, take heart. Plenty of people own horses but don't have the time or energy to trailer them to a local riding stable for lessons. A friend of mine caters to these poor folks who are hampered by owning horses; she drives from barn to barn and gives them lessons at home. She travels to horse shows, where she coaches her students, and to sale barns, where she seeks out suitable mounts for her clients, and though her car takes a beating, her overhead costs are minimal at best.

TRAINING

The ancient art of training horses goes hand in hand with instructing riders, but the emphasis here is on the horse, and the opportunities to a fine trainer are far greater than those for one who concentrates on riding alone. One must be a horseman through and through—understanding all aspects of horse selection, horse care, and horse psychology—as well as being capable of administering a staff, dealing with owners, and knowing every detail of the particular business, whether it be racing, showing, or preparing horses for pleasure riding. In competition, a trainer must know the opposition as well as his or her own animals and must be able to carry out his or her own theories in practice effectively. The trainer should know what he or she wants at the outset and be willing to do whatever is necessary to reach that goal, whether it means

schooling one horse (or a dozen) every day for an hour or
relying on capable assistants to follow instructions.

Obviously, the background for an aspiring trainer should
be in as many different aspects of the horse business as
possible—from stable management to horse dealing—but a
definite prerequisite is that of working with animals and
being able to bring out the best in them. This means that one
must know what a horse is capable of doing and the most
effective ways of teaching it to do those things. Understanding a horse's physical and psychological limitations is a very
complicated business, and while it comes naturally to some
people who are born with what can only be described as horse
sense, it can be developed through years of experience. Some
trainers are riders, while others never get on the back of a
horse; some have an "eye" for a potentially good animal, while
others make do with what they get; still others get into breeding in order to create what they want.

A trainer should, of course, understand what it is that the
owner of a horse wants but be knowledgeable, strong-minded,
and persuasive enough to convince the owner that the trainer
knows best. The most satisfactory owners are those who will
rely on the judgment of their trainers, and there are many
unhappy stories about misunderstandings or struggles for
authority that have resulted in lost jobs or poor performances
by the animals caught in the middle. The trainer must accept
the responsibility when the horse in his or her charge does
poorly but is the one who can take most of the credit when the
horse does well. Although the monetary rewards can be
great for a few, money is not usually the ultimate goal for a
trainer, whose long hours and constant worries couldn't be
reckoned in dollars and cents, regardless of the talent of the
accountant.

Horse Dealing

Buying and selling horses is a profession that has been around
as long as there have been horses to buy and sell, and of all
the horse-related occupations, it is probably the most controversial. Horse traders have been subject to more bad jokes
and wonderful stories than any other kind of horseman.
Through the ages, horse traders have been despised and hung,
trusted and respected, accused of stealing or misrepresenting
their animals, and praised for their perceptions. Yet horse
owners and riders couldn't possibly exist without them. One

can, of course, come across an advertisement describing a horse for sale and simply buy it without using a dealer, but people in the market for special kinds of horses can't rely on local newspapers or backyards as sources for what they need. It is the job of the dealer to find animals and to get them into the hands of the people who will pay for them, and for performing this service the dealer receives a commission of the selling price from the seller or the buyer; he or she may also make money by buying horses and reselling them at higher prices, or simply get a slice of another dealer's commission by having referred a buyer or a seller. Anyone involved in the purchase of a horse can be a dealer. Sometimes stable managers and trainers are dealers themselves, although some dealers may not be horsemen at all. All one needs is a sense of what a horse is worth, a source for animals, and a list of potential clients. Most hacking stables in the eastern states, for example, get their horses from dealers who drive huge vans out west, fill them up with grades, and transport them back east. Many dealers go to a great deal of trouble having an animal schooled for a particular purpose or a particular buyer, buying a few yearlings each year from breeders or at auctions and putting a sizeable investment into getting them ready for sale a year or more later.

Although stories are legion about gypsy horse traders who paint white horses black and who feed tranquilizers to high-strung rogues, most dealers must be honest if they are to stay in business. There are laws governing the sale of horses, and anyone who routinely disobeys those laws—selling unsuitable animals under false claims—will be in trouble legally as well as professionally.

In addition to knowing about horses, dealers must know a great deal about people in order to analyze what a potential owner really wants (often not what the buyer says) and how to present the animal in a convincing way. Many dealers will go to a lot of trouble grooming a horse, getting a good rider to show it off, and sometimes even having the animal reschooled. Newcomers to the profession often find themselves severely out of pocket because they have misread the requirements of a buyer; I have even known dealers taken in by people who make a hobby of getting free rides by "trying out" one horse after another with no intention of making a purchase. Other dealers will spend months looking for the perfect horse when the buyer really needs to be convinced that a less-than-perfect animal would be quite satisfactory. Indecisive and unknowledgeable buyers, the bane of a dealer's existence, are unfortunately far more common than unscrupulous dealers.

A dealer must, naturally, be completely aware of what certain types of horses are worth in order to set prices that are in line with the market. Since the name of the game is making money, one can't be too sentimental about animals or make the mistake of falling in love with a particular horse unless one is prepared to keep it. One must also be prepared to accept "returns"—horses that haven't worked out for one reason or another. One must be ready to make a decision to have an unsaleable horse put to death or sold for meat, or to watch another dealer make a bundle reselling a horse on which one may have only made a few dollars. It's not an easy business, but the rewards are perhaps more easily banked than they are in other professions.

OWNING A HORSE

Up to this point, every word in the book you've been reading has been directed to the horseless rider, and you should by now be convinced that horselessness has as many advantages as it does challenges to offer. Nevertheless, I suspect that deep down inside each reader still remains that residual, repressed desire to own one of the infernal creatures in spite of all the problems involved. (I admit that I've always had a saddle and bridle on hand just in case.) When I was a kid, I used to enter contests that offered horses as prizes, though all I ever won was a pretty silver crayon for a Lone Ranger coloring competition. I used to write delightful, if thankfully forgotten, lyrics to celebrate things like the birth of the Black Stallion's daughter for whom I did not, however, select the winning name, and the ballot barrel for the Courvoisier Arabian that used to be given away at the National Horse Show every year in Madison Square Garden would have been considerably lighter were it not for my annual contribution of several dozen entries. I guess I always hoped that if a free horse should happen to turn up in the front yard with reporters and photographers in tow, my parents would be somehow embarrassed into keeping the animal just to keep the family reputation intact.

Although we all know by now that the purchase price of a horse is the least of the investment (unless you are prepared to spend a hundred thousand dollars or more for a fine show horse or for the front half of a yearling at the Saratoga sales), and that any horse regardless of price will cost far more to keep over the long run than on the day of purchase, it has always been my philosophy that it is folly not to enter some contest—any contest—that will make one a horse owner, even if only briefly.

However, there are other inexpensive ways to come by a perfectly respectable animal, even if it isn't a purebred Arab or a daughter of the Black Stallion. Mounted-police departments in many cities retire their animals to farms where they will be given a good home, and school or hack horses that can no longer work the necessary four or five hours a day can often be picked up for very little indeed. It may take a good deal of reschooling, resting, and reassuring to turn these well-used beasts into good pleasure horses, but it's been done. The parents of children who have gone off to school or gone off horses can be approached with a "let me take that burden off your hands" attitude, and professionals with show horses past their prime may be more willing to let their animals go to a conscientious individual than to a public stable or out to pasture. These horses may be spoiled in some way—by injury, overuse, neglect, or overindulgence—but the determined and experienced amateur can often remake them into very satisfactory mounts, given time and patience.

If you find yourself with a gift horse on your hands, do look in its mouth (and everywhere else you and the vet can think of) to make sure you are not also getting a future filled with worries and vet bills (or doctor bills for yourself). But if the horse is potentially a good one and you are willing to do what it takes (or not do anything but let it get a good rest until it's back in shape), there are a number of ways to keep your maintenance expenses to a minimum and still guarantee the horse good care.

LEASING

How about renting a horse for a year rather than just an hour? Many owners who do not have the opportunity to ride are willing to let a trusted individual have complete use of the horse without selling it. The renter in this case will agree to pay all maintenance expenses—boarding, feed, vet bills, horseshoes, and so on—and the horse is effectively theirs without any initial investment in its ownership. This arrangement may sound ideal, but it can be fraught with danger if the agreement is not made in writing to cover contingencies such as accident or loss of the horse. The renter must be sure that he or she will not be held liable if the animal should suddenly take ill and die or be severely injured or killed in an accident. The renter should also try to get the owner to agree to a certain amount of notice should the horse be sold. It would be a very disheartening situation to have "your" horse win a blue ribbon and be sold out from under you to someone who noticed him at the show. All of your schooling and work might have doubled the value of the horse and you'd have nothing to show for it, not even the horse.

Co-leasing, or sharing the expenses with a second renter, is even more complicated, for although the cost to you is halved, the amount of time you can use the horse is halved as well. In addition to an agreement with the owner, you should have one with the other leaser so that there won't be arguments about which days one has access to the animal and who caused what saddle sores. Many friendships have been broken because these details weren't worked out ahead of time. I was once offered half a horse for a third of the cost, but it turned out that the horse needed more than the usual amount of veterinary care and my veterinarian husband made me a pretty attractive leaser. My husband would have had to spend more time with the animal than I would have, so I said no.

CO-OWNING

Like leasing, owning a horse with someone else can be an attractive economic arrangement but a complicated one if nothing is put in writing. Again, it should be made clear at the outset exactly what is to be expected by way of responsibility, expense, and accessibility. In addition, it should be understood that both riders won't try to expect too much from the horse; it would be silly and impractical for one rider to school an animal in dressage while the other rider spends alternate days trying to *make* a cutting horse out of him. Specific schedules as to the care of the horse should be worked out in detail so that nothing gets overlooked, and someone should be responsible for regular appointments with the vet and the farrier and for ordering feed and bedding. Another part of the agreement should cover the contingency of accident or illness, and last but not least, the mechanics of withdrawing from the arrangement in the event that one owner moves away or loses interest should also be considered. Whether the horse is sold and the profit split or whether one owner will buy out the other seems a simple decision until the situation actually arises without that decision having been made.

Some co-ownership arrangements involve a "silent partner," who foots the bills and a rider who enters the horse in competitions to further the animal's career and boost its value. Here, too, agreements must be in writing—even down to tiny details such as who keeps the ribbons, trophies, and prize money, who decides about which shows to enter, and who gets what share of the profits if the horse is sold.

OWNING

In some "silent partner" arrangements, the one who pays the bills actually owns the horse while the rider simply gets a share of the winnings and profits rather than a salary or even expenses. In other cases, the rider is simply a hired employee who earns a salary and/or expenses without making any investment except that of skill and time. But what about owning a horse and wanting to ride it while saving some money by letting other people ride? Many people keep their horses at boarding stables and allow the managers or instructors use of the animals in return for discounts on boarding fees. The decision to do this is not to be made without serious consideration. What if the animal is soured by constant jabs in the mouth delivered by beginners? What if the horse is injured or, worse, what if a rider is injured and sues the owner of the horse, now you, for damages? This kind of arrangement may work beautifully if you trust the stable operator or instructor and are insured to cover any contingencies, but the owner has to be aware of these possibilities before entering into any such agreement.

I have always disapproved of absentee owners who selfishly keep animals to themselves but not *for* themselves. I have often ridden private horses in lessons with their trainers and have been delighted by the experience; I've also been told that such an experience can be good for a horse who would otherwise get only an occasional lungeing or a brief schooling session, since that's all the trainer has time to give. But I can understand the owner's point of view as well. Because of the risks involved, it is a good idea to be able to have some control over the use of your animal—whether it is through a trusted trainer or by direct means.

What this boils down to, of course, is that if you are going to own a horse, you should take the time and trouble to keep it well and fit. But if you want a trophy room full of ribbons and silver cups and you can't ride well enough yourself, you will have to let someone else do the riding for you. And if you want to keep the horse in peak condition and can't afford the daily hour or more to exercise it yourself, you will have to hire or persuade someone else to spend the time for you. In other words, if you own a riderless horse, get a horseless rider for it. Like my friend with the boarding stable in California, remember your horseless days and do unto others as others once did unto you.

EPILOGUE

SHORTLY AFTER I finished the manuscript for the first edition of this book, I had the great good fortune to be offered a gift horse. I thought to myself that accepting this animal would not be a denial of my enthusiasm for horselessness but a legitimate experience and perhaps even the subject for an upbeat, inspiring ending to my book. The horse was a four-year-old chestnut Thoroughbred gelding, as unschooled as he was gorgeous, and completely unsuited to his owner, who felt that I could provide him with a good home and an education at the same time. I read all the training manuals and made out that shopping list I had dreamed of making for years (the kind that begins "one halter, one currycomb . . . "). I located an empty stall in a nearby stable, hired a van to truck the horse there, and made the mistake of trying him out before putting him in the van. The inside of his mouth looked fine to me (I wasn't dumb enough to obey *that* old gift-horse maxim) but his outward behavior was erratic enough to convince me that there might be a reason he was completely untrained at the age of four. He was—to put it mildly—disrespectful of humans and in need of a strong professional trainer rather than an enthusiastic amateur. He was, in other words, as unsuitable for me as he was for his owner. So, heavy in heart, I ripped up my list and rejoined the ranks of the horseless, happy only in the fact that I had come to my senses before he came into my possession.

Needless to say, my happy ending for the book was suddenly as empty as that stall, until I realized the following weekend that everything wasn't as bleak as it seemed. Saturday morning I helped someone reschool a talented but sour jumper; Sunday morning found me riding a three-year-old colt at Belmont track under the supervision of a trainer friend; and Sunday afternoon I spent two hours working with a former racehorse that had enlisted in the local mounted police unit. By Sunday evening, it dawned on me that the horseless life had its moments, that none of this would have been possible if I had made the commitment to a horse of my own. Perhaps my good luck that weekend was a kind of coincidental compensation for my bad luck with the gift horse, but I prefer to believe that my commitment to horselessness was what had opened up those opportunities in the first place. In fact, the month that followed included a "lunch" date exercising a vacationing friend's Thoroughbred at the local city stable and a day in the country fox hunting with one of the oldest packs in America.

And that's the way it went for a few years, until the bug bit me again—twice—and I succumbed. When I asked my husband if we might not think about having a child, he (already the father of two) said "Let's get that horse you wanted," hoping to distract me. And so I ended up with a very green Quarter Horse I named Editor in Chief, appropriately so for a lowly editor, as it turned out, because he quickly found out who was boss—himself. So I gave up Chief and had a baby (whom I named Philip, of course, which means horse lover) and rejoined the ranks of the horseless.

After Philip became old enough to stay out of trouble while hanging around a stable, I bought my other horse, a black Morgan named Rex, who came to us through my husband's job as the veterinarian at the Bronx Zoo. Rex and a stablemate had been purchased as weanlings by the zoo administration to be trained as carriage horses to drive important visitors around the park. When the zoo decided it could no longer afford this luxury, I was persuaded to give him a good home for an "insider's" price. Although Rex had hardly been ridden at all, I was most fortunate in that his trainer, who doubled as the elephant trainer, was exceptionally skilled, making it easy for a neophyte like myself to train Rex for trail riding, stadium jumping, hunter paces, and even dressage. I excelled at none of these, but Rex was always willing and able to try something new. In short, I had found myself the perfect horseless rider's horse—one who could do anything.

Unfortunately, my husband became seriously ill and Rex was given to some friends with a farm. During the difficult period that followed, I regretted at times not having Rex close by, where I could ride or drive him on a moment's notice, but I soon found myself reverting to my original idea about horselessness. When the weather is bad or my schedule is full of meetings at work or my son's school or the local civic association, Rex is happy in a field filled with other horses and not waiting in a stall for me to find the time to give him attention. To satisfy the urge for riding, I found a public stable in the Bronx that offers good lessons in dressage, a discipline much more suitable to my age and ability than cross-country jumping. And I have learned to fit riding into vacation trips—through the American Southwest, to England, Ireland, and even India, as well as to my friends' farm, where Rex still recognizes me as the carrot lady.

When Madelyn Larsen asked me to revise this book for a new generation of the horseless, I was happy to accept the invitation, not just because it would give a new lease on life to this old gray mare, but because I would have a chance to say again what I believed in long ago: that *not* owning a horse is as valuable an experience as owning one, perhaps even more so.

INDEX